REGNUM EDINBURGH CENTENARY SERIES
Volume 24

Theology, Mission and Child:
Global Perspectives

The centenary of the World Missionary Conference of 1910, held in Edinburgh, was a suggestive moment for many people seeking direction for Christian mission in the 21st century. Several different constituencies within world Christianity held significant events around 2010. From 2005, an international group worked collaboratively to develop an intercontinental and multi-denominational project, known as Edinburgh 2010, based at New College, University of Edinburgh. This initiative brought together representatives of twenty different global Christian bodies, representing all major Christian denominations and confessions, and many different strands of mission and church life, to mark the centenary.

Essential to the work of the Edinburgh 1910 Conference, and of abiding value, were the findings of the eight think-tanks or 'commissions'. These inspired the idea of a new round of collaborative reflection on Christian mission – but now focused on nine themes identified as being key to mission in the 21st century. The study process was polycentric, open-ended, and as inclusive as possible of the different genders, regions of the world, and theological and confessional perspectives in today's church. It was overseen by the Study Process Monitoring Group: Miss Maria Aranzazu Aguado (Spain, The Vatican), Dr Daryl Balia (South Africa, Edinburgh 2010), Mrs Rosemary Dowsett (UK, World Evangelical Alliance), Dr Knud Jørgensen (Norway, Areopagos), Rev John Kafwanka (Zambia, Anglican Communion), Rev Dr Jooseop Keum (Korea, World Council of Churches), Dr Wonsuk Ma (Korea, Oxford Centre for Mission Studies), Rev Dr Kenneth R. Ross (UK, Church of Scotland), Dr Petros Vassiliadis (Greece, Aristotle University of Thessalonikki), and co-ordinated by Dr Kirsteen Kim (UK, Edinburgh 2010).

These publications reflect the ethos of Edinburgh 2010 and will make a significant contribution to ongoing studies in mission. It should be clear that material published in this series will inevitably reflect a diverse range of views and positions. These will not necessarily represent those of the series' editors or of the Edinburgh 2010 General Council, but in publishing them the leadership of Edinburgh 2010 hopes to encourage conversation between Christians and collaboration in mission. All the series' volumes are commended for study and reflection in both church and academy.

Series Editors

Knud Jørgensen	Areopagos, Norway, MF Norwegian School of Theology & the Lutheran School of Theology, Hong Kong. Former Chair of Edinburgh 2010 Study Process Monitoring Group
Kirsteen Kim	Leeds Trinity University and former Edinburgh 2010 Research Co-ordinator, UK
Wonsuk Ma	Oxford Centre for Mission Studies, Oxford, UK
Tony Gray	Words by Design, Bicester, UK

REGNUM EDINBURGH CENTENARY SERIES
Volume 24

Theology, Mission and Child: Global Perspectives

Edited by
Bill Prevette, Keith J. White,
C. Rosalee Velloso Ewell and D.J. Konz

First published 2014 by Regnum Books International
Regnum is an imprint of the Oxford Centre for Mission Studies
St Philip and St James Church
Woodstock Road
Oxford OX2 6HR, UK
www.ocms.ac.uk/regnum

09 08 07 06 05 04 03 7 6 5 4 3 2 1

British Library Cataloguing in Publication Data
A catalogue record for this book is available from the British Library

ISBN: 978-1-908355-62-1

Typeset by Words by Design
Printed and bound in Great Britain for Regnum Books International
by TJ International Ltd, Padstow, Cornwall

Front cover photo © 'The girl child with Elder' was taken in the Central
Highlands of Vietnam – courtesy of David Dobson Photography.
Back cover photo shows a scene from the Edinburgh 2010 conference.

The publication of this title is made possible through the generous financial
assistance of the Crowell Trust, Hope Trust, Drummond Trust and the BGMC
Fund of the Assembly of God World Missions USA through the Europe
Office.

CONTENTS

PREFACE

The Edinburgh 2010 Common Call emerged from the Edinburgh 2010 study process and conference marking the centenary of the World Missionary Conference, Edinburgh 1910. The Common Call, cited below, was affirmed in the Church of Scotland Assembly Hall in Edinburgh on 6 June 2010, by representatives of world Christianity, including Catholic, Orthodox, Evangelical, Pentecostal, and other major Protestant churches.

As we gather for the centenary of the World Missionary Conference of Edinburgh 1910, we believe the church, as a sign and symbol of the reign of God, is called to witness to Christ today by sharing in God's mission of love through the transforming power of the Holy Spirit.

1. Trusting in the Triune God and with a renewed sense of urgency, we are called to incarnate and proclaim the good news of salvation, of forgiveness of sin, of life in abundance, and of liberation for all poor and oppressed. We are challenged to witness and evangelism in such a way that we are a living demonstration of the love, righteousness and justice that God intends for the whole world.

2. Remembering Christ's sacrifice on the Cross and his resurrection for the world's salvation, and empowered by the Holy Spirit, we are called to authentic dialogue, respectful engagement and humble witness among people of other faiths – and no faith – to the uniqueness of Christ. Our approach is marked with bold confidence in the gospel message; it builds friendship, seeks reconciliation and practises hospitality.

3. Knowing the Holy Spirit who blows over the world at will, reconnecting creation and bringing authentic life, we are called to become communities of compassion and healing, where young people are actively participating in mission, and women and men share power and responsibilities fairly, where there is a new zeal for justice, peace and the protection of the environment, and renewed liturgy reflecting the beauties of the Creator and creation.

4. Disturbed by the asymmetries and imbalances of power that divide and trouble us in church and world, we are called to repentance, to critical reflection on systems of power, and to accountable use of power structures. We are called to find practical ways to live as members of One Body in full awareness that God resists the proud, Christ welcomes and empowers the poor and afflicted, and the power of the Holy Spirit is manifested in our vulnerability.

5. Affirming the importance of the biblical foundations of our missional engagement and valuing the witness of the Apostles and martyrs, we are called to rejoice in the expressions of the gospel in many nations all over the world. We celebrate the renewal experienced through movements of migration and mission in all directions, the way all are equipped for mission by the gifts of the Holy Spirit, and God's continual calling of children and young people to further the gospel.

6. Recognising the need to shape a new generation of leaders with authenticity for mission in a world of diversities in the twenty-first century, we are called to work together in new forms of theological education. Because we are all made in the image of God, these will draw on one another's unique charisms, challenge each other to grow in faith and understanding, share resources equitably worldwide, involve the entire human being and the whole family of God, and respect the wisdom of our elders while also fostering the participation of children.

7. Hearing the call of Jesus to make disciples of all people – poor, wealthy, marginalised, ignored, powerful, living with disability, young, and old – we are called as communities of faith to mission from everywhere to everywhere. In joy we hear the call to receive from one another in our witness by word and action, in streets, fields, offices, homes, and schools, offering reconciliation, showing love, demonstrating grace and speaking out truth.

8. Recalling Christ, the host at the banquet, and committed to that unity for which he lived and prayed, we are called to ongoing co-operation, to deal with controversial issues and to work towards a common vision. We are challenged to welcome one another in our diversity, affirm our membership through baptism in the One Body of Christ, and recognise our need for mutuality, partnership, collaboration and networking in mission, so that the world might believe.

9. Remembering Jesus' way of witness and service, we believe we are called by God to follow this way joyfully, inspired, anointed, sent and empowered by the Holy Spirit, and nurtured by Christian disciplines in community. As we look to Christ's coming in glory and judgment, we experience his presence with us in the Holy Spirit, and we invite all to join with us as we participate in God's transforming and reconciling mission of love to the whole creation.

Themes Explored

The 2010 conference was shaped around the following nine study themes:
1. Foundations for mission
2. Christian mission among other faiths
3. Mission and post-modernities
4. Mission and power
5. Forms of missionary engagement
6. Theological education and formation
7. Christian communities in contemporary contexts
8. Mission and unity – ecclesiology and mission
9. Mission spirituality and authentic discipleship

The Regnum Edinburgh Centenary Series to Date

Against this background a series of books was commissioned, with the intention of making a significant contribution to ongoing studies of mission. This series currently includes: [1]

Edinburgh 2010: Mission Then and Now, David A. Kerr and Kenneth R. Ross (eds).

Edinburgh 2010 Volume II: Witnessing to Christ Today, Daryl Balia and Kirsteen Kim (eds).

Mission Continues: Global Impulses for the 21ˢᵗ Century, Claudia Wahrisch-Oblau and Fidon Mwombeki (eds).

Holistic Mission: God's Plan for God's People, Brian Woolnough and Wonsuk Ma (eds).

Mission Today and Tomorrow, Kirsteen Kim and Andrew Anderson (eds).

The Church Going Local: Mission and Globalization, Tormod Engelsviken, Erling Lundeby and Dagfinn Solheim (eds).

Evangelical and Frontier Mission: Perspectives on the Global Progress of the Gospel, A. Scott Moreau and Beth Snodderly (eds).

Interfaith Relations after One Hundred Years: Christian Mission among Other Faiths, Marina Ngursangzeli Behera (ed).

Witnessing to Christ in a Pluralistic Age: Christian Mission among Other Faiths, Lalsangkima Pachuau and Knud Jørgensen (eds).

Mission and Post Modernities, Rolv Olsen (ed).

A Learning Missional Church: Reflections from Young Missiologists, Beate Fagerli, Knud Jørgensen, Rolv Olsen, Kari Storstein Haug and Knut Tveitereid (eds).

Life-Widening Mission: Global Anglican Perspectives, Cathy Ross (ed).

Foundations for Mission, Emma Wild-Wood and Peniel Rajkumar (eds).

Mission Spirituality and Authentic Discipleship, Wonsuk Ma and Kenneth R. Ross (eds).

A Century of Catholic Missions, Stephen Bevans (ed).

Mission as Ministry of Reconciliation, Robert Schreiter and Knud Jørgensen (eds).

Orthodox Perspectives on Mission, Petros Vassiliadis (ed).

Bible in Mission, Pauline Hoggarth, Fergus Macdonald, Knud Jørgensen and Bill Mitchell (eds).

Pentecostal Mission and Global Christianity, Wonsuk Ma, Veli-Matti Karkkainen and J. Kwabena Asamoah-Gyadu (eds).

Engaging the World: Christian Communities in Contemporary Global Society, Afe Adogame, Janice McLean and Anderson Jeremiah (eds).

Mission At and From the Margins: Patterns, Protagonists and Perspectives, Peniel Rajkumar, Joseph Dayam, I.P. Asheervadham (eds).

The Lausanne Movement: A Range of Perspectives, Margunn Serigstad Dahle, Lars Dahle and Knud Jørgensen (eds).

---

[1] For an up-to-date list and full publication details, see www.ocms.ac.uk/regnum/

This Volume

What is notable – and encouraging – in _The Common Call_ are the numerous references to 'children', the 'young', and 'young people', alongside references to other groups. This conscious inclusion of children in particular has not frequently been the case in statements on mission, or the outputs of mission colloquia. Among missiological publications, including the volumes in this series to date, there remains an equally notable absence of material addressing questions of _child and children_ in relation to mission, theology of mission, and theology more generally.

We have therefore been tasked by the series editors with producing a volume which does address the important question of children and young people in relation to theology and mission. It should be stressed that this is not simply a book about missiological _praxis_ and children. The inseparable themes of theology and mission remain vital concerns of this book; from the outset we have sought in process and content to produce a cohesive collection of papers in which matters of theology, mission theory _and_ practice are _informed by_ as well as _inform_ considerations of 'child'. Indeed, it is our belief, implicit in this volume, that considering 'child' together with theology and mission raises new questions and possibilities for understanding God, his mission and call to mission, that may not be seen, at least as clearly, in other volumes on the three topics in isolation. We hope, therefore, that in addressing Theology, Mission and Child as equal and integrated concerns, this book will indeed bring fresh, global perspectives on the constructive possibilities of considering three of these important themes together.

ACKNOWLEDGEMENTS

This book, like most good theology, mission, and walking with children, has been a long-term project, and its eventual completion is testimony to the unwavering support, determination and efforts of the following people.

Wonsuk Ma, the Series Editors, and Regnum International for believing in the worth of the project, and having the patience to let it grow at its own pace, perhaps rather like a child.

The contributors, for working with the guiding notion of The Triangle, and on that basis bringing something to the table as an open-handed offering in hope that the results would feed and nourish, and provide fresh perspectives on these important topics.

The Oxford Centre for Mission Studies for hosting the initial gathering of contributors, and for ongoing logistical support, as well as for releasing Bill Prevette for the time needed to herd the project towards completion. Bill, for corralling each of us along towards the sometimes distant end of publication. Ky Prevette also for her ever-warm welcome and hospitality.

DJ Konz for going beyond the call of duty and finding himself in a different role than he had anticipated, providing along the way the additional impetus and drive towards completion.

Rosalee Ewell, for astute comments and invaluable contributions amid a punishing schedule and mixed series of life events.

Mill Grove for hosting fruitful conversations at early stages in the life of the volume, as well as being a living representation of The Triangle. Also for freeing Keith up to be a co-editor, and Keith himself for endless encouragements and gracious emails to his editorial colleagues and contributors.

The Child Theology Movement (CTM) and its directors for willingness to network around the world in the search for contributors; for the community of Child Theology (CT) and other scholars that are discussing theology, mission and child in many ways and places.

Haddon Willmer, for offering vital and constructive feedback on a number of papers, some of which bear no reference to his input, but which certainly bear its stamp.

The long-suffering spouses of the editorial team – Ky, Ruth, Sam and Louise – who have endured absences and preoccupied partners, all the while offering gracious support; and to the children (and grandchildren) of their families, who bring joy and new insights just by being.

To those who generously financially supported this project: The Crowell Trust supported our initial consultation and the publication, The Hope Trust and The Diamond Trust contributed to the publication and BGMC of the Assemblies of God which enabled the printing and distribution of the volume.

Finally, to all who labour at theology, mission and life with children in determination not to let go of any point of The Triangle in the process.

ABBREVIATIONS

CD	*Church Dogmatics*, Karl Barth. 4 vols. Edinburgh: T&T Clark, 1936-77
CT	Child Theology
CTM	Child Theology Movement
CWME	Commission on World Mission and Evangelism (WCC)
CWMS	*The Complete Works of Menno Simons*: c. 1496-1561. Menno Simons. Scottdale, PA: Herald Press, 1956
ET	English Translation
FBO	Faith-Based Organisation
IBMR	*International Bulletin of Missionary Research*
IMC	International Missionary Council
JSNT	*Journal for the Study of the New Testament*
LW	*Luther's Works*, Martin Luther. 55 vols. Philadelphia, PA: Fortress Press, 1955-86
NGO	Non-Governmental Organisation
ST	*Summa Theologica*, Thomas Aquinas. Three parts, 60 vols (ET). London: Blackfriars, 1964-81.
UNAIDS	Joint United Nations Programme on HIV/AIDS
UNICEF	United Nations Children's Fund
WCC	World Council of Churches

PART ONE

INTRODUCTION AND THE TRIANGLE

INTRODUCTION

Keith J. White

Any book addressing the subject of children in the context of theology or mission has attendant risks. The Child Theology Movement has found since its inception in 2002, for example, that when the two words 'child' and 'theology' are placed side-by-side, there is a pronounced tendency for the word 'child' to eclipse the word 'theology'. It seemed quite possible therefore that any volume with a focus on child might render mission and theology as junior partners, or even background figures. There is also the tendency for theologians to pay little or no attention to any volume or work that has the words 'child' or 'youth' in the title. This is based on the presumption that serious or 'robust' theology is no place for a discussion about or with children.

In our view there are *three primary* and equally constituent parts to the volume we have been commissioned to edit and collate, and these are therefore indicated in the title. They are neatly summed up by the following question:

> What is the gospel of Jesus Christ for a girl-child in a Muslim country and context, who is still living with her family, unable legally go to church, or become a Christian without upsetting her parents, her extended family, and her community? What, if anything, does the gospel mean, in essence and in practice, for this child?

The three elements implicit in the question are:
1. a child in context;
2. a theologically informed understanding of the nature of the gospel;
3. a missiological dynamic that cannot abandon the commission of God in Christ, and is therefore determined to discover what Church and Gospel mean to a real child in a specific situation.

This led us in time to conceive of a triangle with its three corners named theology, mission and child. To be true to the nature of Edinburgh 1910 and 2010, we realised that we had been called to work in a relatively unexplored area denoted by the limits of this triangle. Christians have long been engaged alongside children in the name of Christ, whether as parents, teachers, carers, doctors and nurses, or other vocations. Christian schools, Sunday Schools, children's homes and hospices have been integral to the history of Christian mission around the world. But, on reflection, it is clear that these initiatives have often not been accompanied by rigorous biblical and theological reflection. Sometimes the theology has been unspoken and intuitive to the point of invisibility. Sometimes it has been articulated by pastors and Christian leaders who have sought to communicate the gospel to children. But there is evidence that understandings of the particular context of childhood and children in relation to the gospel have at times been embarrassingly rudimentary. And many engaged in Christian action with children have been so aware of the urgency and crying need of the situations in which they have found themselves that they have not had time for or seen the point of pausing to consider either theology or mission. This, however, has risks: doing good things badly can be nearly as damaging as doing bad things well.

Our task was to be tenacious in holding the three points of the triangle together in our minds, always resisting the temptation to let go of any one. The first chapter beyond this introduction sets out to explain in more detail what we herein call 'The Triangle'. A preliminary form of this chapter was sent to all contributors as a way of encouraging each one to work within The Triangle, without being overly confining or prescriptive.

The Range of Issues and Contexts

In the process of refining the content and shape of this volume, which is part of a series and context that is global in scope, we realised that we should attempt to give due attention to gender, ethnicity, geographical regions, as well as a variety of theological, missiological and ecclesiological contexts. It would not be possible within the space of a single volume to deal adequately with them all, but the contributors were aware of the variety and extent of contexts. What is more, we have sought to gather contributors who represent as wide a spread of experience and knowledge as possible. There would inevitably be overlaps with other volumes in the series, but our focus has always drawn us back to The Triangle of theology, mission and child.

Issues particular to children that informed our thinking

Among the issues specific to theology and mission with children as a focus are the following:
1. Changing perspectives worldwide on childhood and children's rights;
2. Children as social actors and subjects who are fully human;
3. *Oikos* (household) as a primary locus of children's lives and experience;
4. Child Theology;
5. Managerial Missiology with the risk of instrumentalising children;
6. The three cultures of childhood: local, religious and global.

At a gathering of the editors and potential contributors in Oxford in November 2012, these and other themes were considered in relation to the focus, extent and shape of this volume. One suggested framework was to take the nine Edinburgh themes[1] and explore them with The Triangle in mind. We wondered how this Triangle might throw light on these themes, as well as help to identify others.

Some of these themes and possible indicative questions were:

1. The theology of mission with a child in the midst. What are the contributions of the discipline known as Child Theology to this question?

2. Christian mission among other faiths. What are the particular theological and practical issues that arise when children and young people are seen as the focus of Christian mission in these, or strictly secular, contexts? (Proselytisation is an obvious negative issue, but are there positive issues as well?)

3. Mission, identity, and social networks. What implications for church, and the way we see mission are there arising from the development of the 'network society'? How far should new forms of social networking be embraced, or resisted, in the cause of the gospel?

4. Mission and power. How are children to be welcomed in the name of Jesus without an abuse of power? How are young people to be encouraged as agents of mission without instrumentalising them?

5. Forms of missionary engagement. Particular reference to the history of Christian mission with children at the centre: education; evangelism; rescue and social action in its various forms. How appropriate are these models, theologically and practically, in 21st-century societies?

6. Theological education and formation. Re-assessing Sunday schools, youth work and para-church programmes with theological awareness. What responsible working models are there? What critique does Christian theology offer contemporary secular education of children? Also, the Bible for children – what forms and expressions of the Bible are suitable for children and young people? Who decides?

7. Christian communities in contemporary contexts. In an age characterised by obsessive attention to individualism, what models of life together might be the best contexts for the growth and nurture of children? Gathered church and 'little church'[2] as partners or rivals? How do we understand the family and parenting in these contexts?

8. Mission and unity – ecclesiology, ecumenism, and mission. Can children act as a focus for Christian unity? What new understandings into the life of the church does Child Theology offer?

9. Children's spirituality. How do theology and globalisation shed new light on or critique understandings of such spirituality?

The list was deliberately left open-ended.

---

[1] For a list of the nine themes, see the Preface in this volume.

[2] The church father John Chrysostom and, in the nineteenth century, Christian educator Horace Bushnell spoke of the family as a 'little church'.

Outline of the Book

These questions informed the constructive, lively discussion and prayer that ensued in the formation of the final framework used in the book. It is in four parts or sections. Following this brief introduction in *Part One: Introduction and The Triangle* there is an accompanying overview of our methodology, relating to what we have called The Triangle of theology, mission and child, lucidly outlined by Haddon Willmer. This is followed in *Part Two: Child in Theological and Missiological Context*, first by an outline of some trajectories in the history of theological thought and mission as they have related to children. This chapter by D.J. Konz concludes by noting the significance of this history of diverse understandings of the child for how we understand the child in relation to theology and mission, today. This is followed by extended reflections from Mark Oxbrow on contemporary Christian approaches to mission, with some thoughts on how these may relate to children.

What becomes apparent from these papers is that there is much work to be done when children are taken seriously as signs of the Kingdom of Heaven, and entry into it; when there is an uncanny, and perhaps uncomfortable, coming together of welcoming a child and welcoming Jesus and the One who sent him. This is not a case of special pleading on the part of the contributors or editors: it is Jesus who insisted on this proximity.[3] The reason for any surprise is perhaps more to do with the rather puzzling fact that, with some exceptions, it has taken two millennia for the significance of the words and actions of Jesus to be noted enough to merit serious and sustained theological reflection.

Part Three: Threats and Challenges brings together and places side-by-side some examples of the kind of contexts children find themselves in today, and what has been going on (or not going on) there in the name of Christ and his church. It allows the scene-setting of the first section to be disturbed, and the reader to be confronted by rugged encounters with real children and their challenging situations. It places in the foreground of attention, addressing both our hearts and minds, girl children in Botswana (in a chapter by Rosinah Gabaitse), the testimony of a young Christian in South Africa (related by Stephan de Beer with Genevieve James), and the competing and not always constructive purposes in evidence in Christian mission among orphans in Romania (in Bill Prevette's chapter).

In terms of The Triangle, these children represent one of the three corners. Taking their situations, suffering and plight seriously leads the writers to re-examine the theology and mission of the churches and Christian (or Faith-Based) organisations that have been actively involved in their contexts. Here theology and mission, singly and combined in the form of church, are challenged to the roots: the very foundations are shaken. Conventional readings of the Bible, and assumptions and accepted forms of

---

[3] Matthew 18:1-5; Mark 9:36-37; Luke 9:47-48.

church or mission, along with patriarchally-determined and controlled ideologies and modes of relating, are exposed and tested and called under the disturbance, or judgement, of God. Fundamental repentance and penitence, personal and corporate, are called for. There is no place, in light of these chapters, for triumphalism or pride.

At the centre of the book, in *Part Four: The Hinge*, is a chapter that Haddon Willmer and I were asked to write, which serves as a reminder of a theological understanding of mission with children which takes the Cross and Resurrection of Christ as its fundamental and irreducible core. It is often forgotten that one of the offshoots of the 1910 Edinburgh Missionary Conference was the International Missionary Council; its 1952 gathering in Willingen, Germany, in the aftermath of World War Two, was entitled *Missions Under the Cross*. This chapter, like that conference, reminds us that the Cross represents the symbol of our Lord's victory, that He still reigns in the world as the Crucified Lord, and he still gathers his church under his Cross. There are alternative approaches to the story of Christian mission which are underpinned by a sense of triumphalism, as the gospel spreads unstoppably (so the narrative goes) from Jerusalem, to Judea, Samaria and the uttermost parts of the earth. Christian churches and organisations engaged in mission often resort to numbers and geographical reach to indicate the 'success' of what is going on. This chapter brings every Christian, and every Christian initiative, back to the foot of the Cross of Christ, where theology, mission and child-focused activity in the name of Jesus Christ must come together. In an era when the historical abuse of children in churches and by clergy has become seen to be extensive, this alone is surely cause for humility and contrition; even without revelations of such abhorrent abuse, the history of Christianity is far from being a story glowing with institutions representing Jesus in grace and truth to children in all settings. At the Cross is forgiveness in God's mercy and grace, but it is not cheap grace. And the Resurrection is that of the Crucified Lord who still bears his wounds and scars. All mission must therefore constantly kneel at the feet of the Crucified and Risen Christ, confessing its inadequacy, and seeking his forgiveness and gentle leading and help.

Following this central theological reflection, *Part Five: Signs of Life and Hope* explores some of the positive, life-giving insights which are encountered when children are in the midst. There is growth, hope, and a looking up and forward. This section does not leave the raw realism of Parts Three and Four behind, as if it has been dealt with, or can be quietly forgotten in light of more positive signs. The light still shines, but it at best flickering in what seems to be a menacing and heavy darkness.

Rather, in this section Paul Joshua Bhakiaraj notes that the household of faith is no longer simply a metaphor for churches and denominations, but refers also to specific households in which children and families live, eat, laugh, cry, play and pray together. Against this household backdrop, welcome and hospitality – the essence of the teaching of Jesus in Matthew

18:1-14, but also at the heart of the gospel of the welcoming God – are further examined in a chapter by Corneliu Constantineanu. The arrival of every child into the world demands a response, a reception, a welcome: how, we might ask, did this obvious link ever become obscured? John Baxter-Brown next revisits the upside-downness of the Kingdom of God with the formation of the identity of the child in mind, before Sam and Rosalee Ewell take this question of identity formation further, drawing on the work of Ivan Illich to confront the institutionalisation of society and church alike, pointing towards the alternative, hopefully formative, context of the community of the risen Lord.

The final section, *Part Six: Broader Horizons and Continuing Challenges*, builds on this trajectory, drawing from lived examples, and theological and biblical reflections from around the world, serving as a reminder that children will always demand responses from us as individuals, families and churches by the very nature of their being. David Chronic's moving reflection on incarnation in the context of ministry to the profoundly marginalised Roma children of Eastern Europe is in equal measures jolting, instructive and hopeful, calling us to hear afresh the call to being neighbours and participants in God's incarnational presence. The challenges of ethnicity and otherness, of poverty and alienation, and of living in a world where the claims of the Christian faith rarely exist without competing calls for allegiance and attention, are faced by children every day worldwide, seen further in Stuart Christine's chapter on the encounters with three children amid ministry in a Brazilian *favela*. His consideration of Luke 9:46-48 again highlights that to receive a child can be an epiphaneous receiving of God in Jesus Christ, and a sign or doorway to understanding the operation of the Kingdom of God in our world, and the nature of Jesus' call of his disciples to mission. Marcia Bunge then offers four perceptive proposals which together can contribute to a purposeful, rigorous and integral approach to seeing Christian identity and faith formed in our children, in the complex multi-faith and even non-faith environments in which they find themselves in the 21st-century world.

In this section we see again that responding to the challenges confronting children, and the challenge of being confronted by children, is not simply a matter of increasing our education and understanding of child development, or improving mission management or evangelistic techniques. Returning to the title and framework of the book, we are reminded in the final chapter by Beth Barnett that among the great 'calls' and vocations of Bible and history, Christ called also a child, and that this often overshadowed language of 'call', informed by the call to the child, may have great pertinence in how we conceive of and participate in God's mission in Christ and Spirit. For indeed this is the same God who in Christ and through the Holy Spirit calls us ourselves to change and become humble like little children, if we are to enter into the reign of Heaven.

In attempting a volume in a series on mission, with a focus on children, we have thus discovered ourselves coming back to the Author of our faith and mission, our Crucified and Risen Lord, Jesus Christ. He is the true and proper subject of this volume, and as we receive children in his name theology, mission and child find their proper expression and foundation.

THE TRIANGLE: THEOLOGY, MISSION AND CHILD

Haddon Willmer

How to Make a Book that is More than a Jumble

How is a mixed bunch of writers to make a coherent and useful book about theology, mission and child? One way would to be make sure some know theology, others practise mission and some care for children. Get each to write out of their experience and expertise and then give clever editors the hard work of making a stunning mosaic out of the disparate essays. It might work but it rarely does.

A better way, at least the way adopted in this book, is for all the writers to work with and within The Triangle. That is not a mystical location but a simple method. Readers may find it helpful to understand the method, not so much with a view to judging the success of the authors but so that readers can get the spirit of the book and, seeing its direction of travel, go further in their own thinking.

So What is The Triangle?

A triangle has three points, but three points do not necessarily make a triangle. If they stand in a row, there can be no triangle.

A row is often a useful way to organise discourse, but it has limitations. The points can be numbered. Numbering suggests relative weight. Points 2 and 3 may flow like subordinates from 1; or 1 and 2 may be preparatory to the authoritative or revelatory conclusion, 3; or 2 may be the substantial centrepiece, between introduction 1 and conclusion 3. The Triangle gives another more open way of relating three points.

Our three points are theology, mission and child. By themselves, these three topics do not make a visible triangle with each other. Each of them has numerous linkages with other practices, topics, disciplines and people. The child obviously links with education, psychology, questions of the good life, and the mystery of human being. Mission makes triangles with international politics, economics and social ethics, theology with religion, philosophy and church. The practice and study of theology does not necessarily involve the child; working with children is often done without theology; and strange as it may seem, even theology is often pursued without concern for mission, and mission without theology. To work with The Triangle of theology, mission and child is a choice of discernment, imagination, intention.

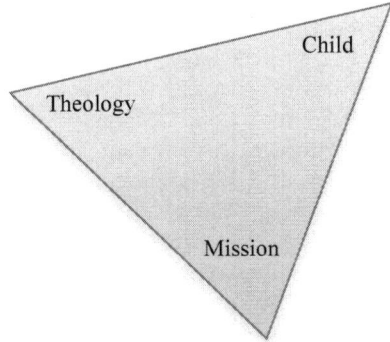

A triangle comes to light when three points are connected to each other by single straight lines. These lines can be drawn on paper, but in making this book, as in life, The Triangle involved people making intellectual and spiritual journeys from one point to another, learning and enlarging their vision as they went. Start from mission, for example, and walk to theology; meet different people to be challenged, puzzled, enriched. Having picked up some new companions there, go on towards the child point. Before you get there, you will meet Child and Child-people coming towards you. Let them take you back to their place, and then set out on the whole triangular pilgrimage as a richly mixed group. Do it more than once, and make sure you do it on foot: we meet people more deeply and learn more when we walk with the Three-Mile-an-Hour God.[1]

Thus The Triangle becomes something more than lines drawn on a page.[2] We live the linking of the points by practical engagement, walking and meeting. Theology, mission and child stimulate and fertilise each other. The Triangle is a creative process. But there is more to do than walk the perimeter of The Triangle. The Triangle delineates a space for living together, praying for the city we have been sent to; marrying and having children, planting and reaping.[3] How does the metaphor of The Triangle as a place to live together illumine the writing and reading of this book?

---

[1] Kosuke Koyama, *Three Mile an Hour God* (Maryknoll, NY: Orbis Books, 1980).

[2] You will notice also that while a triangle can appear hierarchical, with one point at the top and two beneath it, like a top-down organisational chart with the CEO at the top and the minimum wage-earners at the bottom, in our diagram we have set it at an angle to try to break such an effect, for in our Triangle and this volume no one point has priority over the others.

[3] Jeremiah 29:4-8.

In The Triangle we are all the time under the challenge and pressure of the three points. We can of course look to one point, and turn our backs on the other two, but if we are in The Triangle, we are still subject to each point's field of force. We may turn from the sun to shield our eyes, but it still warms our backs and casts shadows before us. When I am outside The Triangle, I may still be touched, say, by theology, but it will not be theology as it interacts with mission and child. But wherever I am in The Triangle, the message-laden rays from all three points not only touch me but intersect in me. I may be nearer to one than the others, so that its signal is stronger, but I am always at some meeting-point of child, theology and mission. Indeed, I am a meeting-point of all three. I can never think about one without thinking about the others at the same time. I no longer say, 'My speciality is mission; I will leave it to the theologian to add his bit and to the child specialist to adapt the result for use with children.'

The Triangle is a demanding brief for writers and for readers. It is an invitation to adventurous hard work. But it does not prescribe what anyone is to think in any detail. It is a large space of freedom and so of responsibility and invention. So there will be variety, maybe serious disagreement, amongst writers and readers. But at least they will be disagreeing within the same project, working with and within The Triangle. That shared commitment is what enables constructive discussion among them. They will not be talking past each other and getting at cross-purposes.

Exploring The Triangle

Thinking in The Triangle has three distinct modes. First, each point has its own substance and integrity. Theology, mission and child demand and inspire specialist concentration. Secondly, interdisciplinarity grows as we walk from point to point round The Triangle. Thirdly, it moves about in the territory defined by The Triangle.

Each point stands for a discourse or body of thinking, or an activity or a kind of personal human being. Each differs from the others and generates distinct identity in thought, action, imagination and project. The lines bring these identities into conversation, maybe as enriching conversation, maybe as mushy confusion and compromise, maybe as conflict and aversion. Conversation rescues identity from sterile narcissism, but if it goes wrong, people may be driven back into the fortress of their starting-point. In the space of The Triangle, life shaped by attention to child, theology and mission may become a common life in the freedom of the Spirit.

The Road Between Theology and Mission (Starting from Theology)

The connection between theology and mission is for some so short, it is more like two sides of the same coin than a road between two cities. It took few words and hardly any time to move Isaiah from seeing the holy Lord of hosts on his throne to being sent to go to the people.[4] Jesus lived as the Son of the Father, acknowledged by the Spirit, and shared his theology of the Kingdom of God coming near to those far off, including them in fellowship, and calling disciples to be sent out to serve in his Name. Jesus' being was fully open to God in and through its being given unreservedly for the world.[5] Paul was the first major Christian theologian, whose vision, spirit and thinking still shapes and stirs Christian theology controversially. He was at the same time a great missionary, travelling adventurously, suffering all kinds of trouble, inwardly acquiring a missionary spirit and personality, becoming 'all things to all men' rather than putting his energies into making the most of his own self with its distinctive treasured identity.[6] Paul's conversion on the road to Damascus was his being claimed by the Lord for a mission; he did not first become a Christian and then opt to be a missionary.[7]

Not everyone can be a missionary-theologian. Specialisation within the Body of Christ tends to imprison people in their specialisms, which may grow into empires to be defended against others. It has become possible to be some sort of theologian without interest or engagement in mission.

Theology is speaking and thinking (*logos*) of God (*theos*). By concentrating thought on God, it confronts us with the total claim of God, calling us to seek God, the One true God, with all our heart, leaving nothing for any competitor. The Creator, the Lord of glory, is the surpassing treasure and delight; so it is a good bargain to sell everything one has to gain God. God is the final Judge whose judgement is the only one that counts. God is the saving orientation of all existence; we ignore and despise God at eternal peril. 'Thou hast made us for thyself and our hearts are restless till they rest in Thee.'[8] 'Now this is eternal life: that they know you, the only true God, and Jesus Christ, whom you have sent.' [9]

Insisting on the oneness and the transcendent difference of God can be dangerous. By itself, it breeds and justifies fanaticism. Then, the proof of giving a wholehearted, unreserved Yes to God is taken to be saying No to all the world.[10] A religiosity which divides people into the godly and

---

[4] Isaiah 6:1-13.

[5] Matthew 3:13-17; 4:12-22; 9:35–10:42.

[6] 2 Corinthians 4:1-15; 5:11-6.13; 11:21-33; 1 Corinthians 9:15-23.

[7] Acts 9:5-6, 15-16; 22:8-10, 14-16 (commissioning comes before baptism!); 26:15-19.

[8] Augustine, *The Confessions*, Chapter 1 (London: Darton, Longman & Todd, 2013).

[9] John 17:3. NIV.

[10] This extreme runs through the much-loved hymn, *When I Survey the Wondrous Cross*. It is unmistakeably stark in the verse most hymnals omit:
His dying crimson, like a robe
Spreads o'er his body on the tree;

ungodly may develop. The Pharisee goes to the temple to pray, to brag before God and despise others, 'even this publican'.[11] Out of supposed faithfulness to God, godly people make humanism into a bad word and surrender it to atheists and secularists. God's simple response to this disastrous misanthropism is to become human.[12]

Spiritual concentration on God is not the only source of theology's separation from mission. Theology is intellectual activity. A religion of the Word and the Book generates a range of interlocking studies in various disciplines – linguistic, textual, hermeneutic. Thinking about God in transcendence and incarnation stirs metaphysical enquiry, poetic exploration, historical enquiry. The story of God invites endless telling, so it inspires artistic creativity; and it provokes serious questions about its truth and about the nature of reality and the meaning of being human. Thinking is hard and exciting play; it fascinates, seizes and shapes people, so that they build academic communities which can easily become ends in themselves.

Neither piety nor study lead inevitably to the atrophy of missionary vision and activity. But they do suggest ways in which theology can acquire theoretical and institutional identities distinct from mission. People can, with good reason, make a life in the city of Theology and never travel. For them, Theology is a settlement standing in its own territory, not a point in a triangle busy with traffic.

A Settlement Theology will never be at peace with itself. The ferment of the seed of the gospel breaks up the concrete. Jesus comes saying, 'Let us go on to the next towns, that I may preach there also, for that is why I came out.'[13] Faced with hungry crowds, Jesus said to his disciples, '*You* give them something to eat.'[14] When disciples stopped children coming to Jesus, he rebuked them: they and the Kingdom of God go together. Jesus breathes the Holy Spirit, saying, 'As the Father has sent me, so send I you.'[15] The love of Christ constrains. It is impossible to say we love God whom we do not see, if we do not love our brother whom we do see. 'Be perfect as your Father in Heaven is perfect: love your enemies.'[16] Theology ceases to be theology whenever it stays at home. It needs mission in order to be true about and to God and humanity.

Then am I dead to all the globe,
And all the globe is dead to me.
Isaac Watts develops Paul's witness, in Galatians 2.20 and 6.14.

[11] Luke 18:9-14; Matthew 6:1-21.

[12] The Bible and Christian tradition bear witness on this point; I specially value Karl Barth, *The Humanity of God* (Atlanta, GA: John Knox Press, 1960).

[13] Mark 1:38.

[14] Mark 6:37; 10:13-16.

[15] John 20:21.

[16] 2 Corinthians 5.14; 1 John 4:7-21; Matthew 5:43-48.

The Road Between Mission and Theology

So mission is inspired, called for and shaped by what theology points to, the living God in Jesus Christ, even though theologians in seminaries and universities, or even in the pulpit, may want to build booths on the mountain.[17] Theologians are a subsection of mission people and share in the ambiguity of all mission as a human practice. It can serve and transmit the gospel or it can obscure and get in its way.[18]

Mission is action, moving human bodies, individual and corporate, across geographical and cultural and spiritual distances. It is busyness for God. Typically, it is worked out through some form of church – planting churches, gathering new Christian communities engaging in Christian living. Christianity has become a global religion through missions of many different kinds. In mission, Christian faith engages with the world, looking for change so that the whole world becomes transparent to the glory of God. How to engage with the world without being compromised, corrupted and tamed by it, is an issue which besets mission at every step. Theology is not to be used merely to affirm mission as practised; it tests mission's faithfulness to the gospel.

Vincent Donovan described the Roman Catholic missionary work in East Africa as he found it in the mid-twentieth century.[19] For a hundred years slaves had been bought and brought into communities managed by the church, large mission compounds were built with schools, hospitals and their necessary infrastructure, and in time, they offered services to newly independent nations. Many people had been superficially Christianised, but not much more. As a new missionary, Donovan found, after a year, that he was busy in the mission station, driving the mission car to bring patients to hospital, but like his fellow priests, he had never talked with the Masai, who lived all around, about God. He had not begun to learn how to do that and was told by other priests that the people would not listen, so it was not to be attempted. He wrote to his bishop:

> I suddenly feel the urgent need to cast aside all theories and discussions, all efforts at strategy – and simply go to these people and do the work among them for which I came to Africa. I would propose cutting myself off from the schools and the hospital, as far as these people are concerned – as well as

---

[17] Mark 9:5.

[18] Fr Mychal Judge was chaplain to the New York Fire Department (Church Times, 7 Sept 2007, 16). He was killed on 11 September 2001 when ministering to those dying around the twin towers. He wrote and lived with this prayer:
Lord, take me where you want me to go;
Let me meet who you want me to meet;
Tell me what you want me to say;
And keep me out of your way.

[19] Vincent J. Donovan, *Christianity Rediscovered: An Epistle from the Masai*, 2nd edn (London: SCM Press, 1982).

socializing with them – and just go and talk to them about God and the Christian message.[20]

Donovan describes what came out of this 'cutting off' and 'going to talk about God'. The Christian message was freed from the entanglements of inherited 'mission'. Conversely, through facing the Masai openly on their home ground and trying to talk from the simple centre of the gospel, he 'rediscovered Christianity'. On the line between theology and mission, traffic is two-way.

Child Makes The Triangle

Singly or together, theology and mission cannot be complete by themselves, or masters of a coherent enterprise. They are called into being by something or Someone beyond themselves. They are servants and steps on the way.

Theology confesses this truth by talking about God from God, not about itself from itself. It is always prone to making idols, which is more easy and accessible than being true to the God who clothes himself in darkness, in the high and lofty place.[21] But the prophetic whisper of God exposes the futility of idol-making. Better to admit Nothingness than to worship the work of one's own hands, mind and imagination. Better to cry out in the darkness, waiting for God to show (reveal) himself than to invent a surrogate.

Mission confesses this radical dependence on God, by going to meet, talk with, and serve the Other, who in one way or another calls in the night: 'Come over and help us.'[22] Mission, called to give self to and for Others, is nevertheless beset by the danger of imposing its own culture, values, models for living, forms of Christian faith, prejudices and sins. Thus the Other is colonised, enslaved, disrespected, rather than being given good news of freedom.[23] Otherness is abolished in homogenisation and subordination.

The Triangle is implied in the essence of both theology and mission because they are not complete in themselves, but exist in dependence on and respect for Others. There is no real healthy saving triangle for them if it is made out of their own imagination, concerns, drives and activity, for then the Other is merely the creature and expression of themselves. Theology can venture a total explanation of all things; mission can set out to master

---

[20] Donovan, *Christianity Rediscovered*, 15.
[21] Exodus 32:1ff; Habakkuk 2:18-20; Jeremiah 10:1-16; Isaiah 44:1ff; 57:15. Christians need to hear these texts not as criticisms of other religions, but of our own theological heart and mind: Isaiah 44:19, 20. Beware the beam in our own eye.
[22] Acts 16:9.
[23] Galatians 5:1ff; Dorothee Sölle, *Christ the Representative* (London: SCM Press, 1967), distinguishes representation which holds the place open for the Other, and substitution which takes the place of the Other, excluding them.

and save the world, as the imperial agent of God who is above all kings. It is in their power to expand themselves out of their own energy and self-esteem, but when they make too much of themselves, and do not give space and respect to the Other,[24] they can never receive the blessing that comes from real meeting in humility and love. They miss the way into the Kingdom of God because they do not go as disciples of Jesus, defenceless as lambs, who take the risk of depending on being welcomed by Others.[25]

Triangular existence and practice is given to mission and theology by God, the free Lord, the Prime and Ultimate Other. God creates the world and, within it, humanity in all its diversity.[26] The world in God is not raw material for theology and mission to manage as they please. It rather has to be respected in its own being, as God's. Theology and mission cannot absorb this Other into themselves. They have to accept that they are confronted, transcended, challenged, by Others.

The distinctive third point that makes mission and theology a triangle comes into view, and its force is discovered when we let God be God, and follow God where his love takes him in creation, incarnation and redemption. God the Word became flesh, became human, a revealing gift of reality which is before and beyond all our theologising.[27] We respond and correspond to God in the world, we do not propose and initiate. God so loved the world … God despises nothing he has made …[28] 'In all life Thou livest the true life of all …'

Theology witnesses to God, the Lord of all. Mission is being sent by God into all the world. In such a triangle, our littleness is constantly challenged. God and the world call us beyond our convenience and

---

[24] The world is not an extension of God's being but is Other. The gift of creation is that God gives being, identity, finite power and freedom, integral yet reflective glory to others. Thus God creates secularity; invites and commands us to live in some real sense, 'before God without God in the world' (Dietrich Bonhoeffer).

[25] Matthew 10:1ff, especially v. 16. See Haddon Willmer and Keith J. White: *Entry Point: Towards Child Theology with Matthew 18* (London: WTL Publications, 2013), 165ff.

[26] Gerard Manley Hopkins' poem 'Pied Beauty' calls us to praise God for all 'dappled things', all the unmasterable othernesses in the world, 'fathered-forth' by God, and not to be assimilated to one another by translation.

All things counter, original, spare, strange;

Whatever is fickle, freckled (who knows how?)

With swift, slow, sweet, sour, adazzel, dim;

He fathers-forth whose beauty is past change:

Praise Him.

[27] Edwin Muir protested in his poem, 'The Incarnate One' against the Calvinist Church where 'The Word made flesh here is made word again'. Compare Willmer and White, *Entry Point*, 8.

[28] John 3:16; '*For thou lovest all things that are, and hatest none of the things which thou hast made: for thou didst not appoint, or make any thing hating it.*' Cf. Wisdom 11:25.

ourselves. 'Expect great things from God: attempt great things for God.'[29] It is no wonder those who are thus called try to escape, like Moses and Jonah. There is not only laziness and cowardice in this hesitation; there may be wisdom: is it not better to do a little well than to have grandiose ambitions and make a mess of things? Do human beings not need a triangle which is tailored to their capacity and which does not call for supermen or women because its third point is not too high or far away or heroic?[30]

Christian theology offers us neither a transcendent God insisting uncompromisingly and impatiently on perfection, nor a tailored God fitted to our interests and capacities. Rather, it is given to faith to live with a God who converses, with steady intention, patiently, inventively, with wayward, confused, stumbling human beings, lifting up the weak, chastening the mighty. God's engagement is manifold – wherever human beings go, God goes after them to be with them and for them; whatever tangles they get into, God works to sort them out. God encourages, chides, models, leads, inspires. God never stops giving us a third point for The Triangle, calling us out, not to fulfil merely human ambition but to thirst for the living God. God makes this the third point of our working triangle, not by handing it over to our designing, but by coming to us again and again, and finally in person and in presence.[31] Accommodating the third point of The Triangle to the realities of human capacity and incapacity (to what we can do, what we cannot do, and what we fail to do), is what God does in Jesus Christ and in the Spirit. God glorifies and fulfils his purpose not in being great and crushingly remote from creatures but in freely making creatures his care and – more – his partners.

The third point that sets theology and mission in a triangle must always be God in God's authentic being and freedom. We could say simply that God is the Third Point that makes The Triangle. But theology cannot speak directly of God in his transcendent being; abstract concepts and negative expressions do not bring us to the living God.[32] Theology cannot get far if the Word did not become flesh; if God did not choose to speak in our own vernaculars.[33] God the Word spoke and speaks in particular local words. Theology can only speak of God because God chooses and makes signs out of the material, events and persons of the created world.

---

[29] William Carey, urging the beginning of British Particular Baptist missionary action in 1792, originally spoke these now famous words. It is likely that he omitted 'from God' and 'for God', probably as it seemed to go without saying.

[30] Psalm 131.

[31] Hebrews 1:1-2.

[32] Compare the enigmatic challenge of Blaise Pascal's *Memorial*, 1654: 'God of Abraham, God of Isaac, God of Jacob, not of philosophers and scholars …'

[33] John 1:1, 14; Acts 2:7. No human language is the language of Heaven, though some champion their own tongue in that way. That we all hear God's good news in our own tongue is because God comes down and is poured out as Spirit on all people.

On one occasion, it is recorded, Jesus placed a child in the midst of a theological argument. The disciples were making serious mistakes in talking about the Kingdom of God. They were misled by their ambition for greatness; they were resistant to the 'Way of the Cross' Jesus had already been telling them about and was leading them into. They needed to be helped, for that teaching was too frightening and puzzling. The same Message had to be put to them in a different way, in the hope that the penny would sometime drop. The child might be a helpful sign, charming with new life rather than dark with death. Since the little child could not succeed in any competition for greatness, she was a sign of the Kingdom of God, in its openness to those who, like the poor, outcasts and sinners, are responsive to God's welcoming grace, because without it, they are marginalised outsiders. The only hope left is to become as children, in this sense. If the disciples don't, they won't enter the Kingdom of God. Even though they go preaching and doing powerful works, it will not be the Good News of God in Jesus that they share.[34]

The Child, thus seen in the gospel, is one of many ways in which the Impossible Demands of God and the World are translated into Possible Service to be given by Ordinary People. Child is the kind of focus, which mission, as an earthly practice, needs. Because mission is a limited human activity, which is never in control of the whole situation, and because it must walk a step at a time, not knowing what a day may bring forth, it must be shaped by practicable goals and feasible, ever revisable, projects. Idealism must be partnered by pragmatism in mission. Visionary ambition can damage mission; talk of global transformation (for example) is mostly overblown and corrupting rhetoric. Mission is not to be done on platforms or in grandiose conferences, but on the ground, where the Samaritan comes across the mugged man, a cup of cold water is given, a child is received. Genuinely receiving a child involves sustained daily personal involvement. It teaches realism. Parenting and caring is a visible activity; it is rightly analysed, monitored and celebrated. This public dimension must not obliterate or distort the special sort of secrecy which is necessary to the relation of child and anyone who receives her.[35]

Idealism is chastened and sobered by pragmatism, but merely to curb idealism is dangerous. Pragmatism needs to be called and stretched by idealism.[36] God is forever calling us away from the habit of home, to

---

[34] This paragraph gives the gist of Keith White and my recent *Entry Point*; cf. 1 Corinthians 13.1ff.

[35] Matthew 6:1-4; I Kings 3:23-28.

[36] Reinhold Niebuhr still gives significant help on this theme, as does John Howard Yoder. Living with and caring for a child is to be forever in the tension between idealism and the pragmatic. To be a child is to have one's being in finding and growing one's self within this tension, and each day experimenting with some new transient balance or truce between them. See also James E. Loder, *The Logic of the Spirit: Human Development in Theological Perspective* (San Francisco, CA:

wander with Abram; out of slavery into freedom; out of protective self-possession into risking our lives in following Jesus and loving universally, even our enemies.[37] Some missions are more obviously adventurous and sacrificial than others, but no Christian mission can be executed without breaking through pragmatic caution. In some cases, mission demands the sacrifice of physical life; all mission involves us in denying self, breaking through the barrier of self to be for Others, with the Man for Others.[38]

So child as placed by Jesus makes a triangle with mission and theology. In child as sign, God in his Kingdom is seen; thinking about child does not drive away thinking about God. Or child. The need of children generates massive humanitarian and mission activity. The usefulness of the child as future workforce generates education; and the usefulness of the child as the next generation of church and mission generates evangelism and Christian nurture. The manifold promise of the child requires holistic response, so that the whole child as called by God is opened up and encouraged on her way, and we with her.

Jossey-Bass, 1998).

[37] Genesis 12:1; Exodus 2:7ff; Galatians 5:1, 13-14; Matthew 16:24-28; 19:16-22; 5:43-48; Luke 14:12-14; 9:57-62.

[38] The key theme of the story of Jonah is not the successful mission to save the people of Nineveh from their sins, but God's possibly unavailing struggle to set Jonah free at heart to love the people. The inner struggle for Paul's conversion was nothing less than the end of one self and coming into the freedom of Christ, where his self became an indefinite quantity because it was intertwined with Christ and was totally *on the way* to what was not yet attained: Philippians 3:4-14; Galatians 2:20, 21. See also Dietrich Bonhoeffer, 'Outline for a Book', *Letters and Papers from Prison*. New greatly enlarged edition (NY: Touchstone, 1997), 380ff. Also, see 'Letter to Eberhard Bethge, 14 August 1944'. *Ibid.,* 386-387.

PART TWO

CHILD IN THEOLOGICAL AND MISSIOLOGICAL CONTEXT

THE MANY AND THE ONE: THEOLOGY, MISSION AND CHILD IN HISTORICAL PERSPECTIVE

D.J. Konz

The child is not a static or unitary being. Like Heraclitus' proverbial river which, he argued, the same person can never step into twice, as both stream and person will have changed, so both the child and those who engage with it are dynamic beings, continually changing through time. This is so, not only with the individual child over time, but also the *idea* of 'child' as it has been conceived by society through history.[1]

This is evident specifically in the Christian tradition. Throughout Christian history the child has been conceived by the church in many different, even conflicting ways. The historical and theological currents of the past two thousand years (and beyond) have given birth to such divergent understandings of 'child' that it seems more appropriate to speak not of *the child* of the Christian tradition – as if there were a singular concept – but rather the *many childs* of Christian history.[2] As this chapter will show, this alerts us to our adult tendency, well recognised (if perhaps overstated) in sociological disciplines, to 'construct' what we understand a child to be. At any one time our understanding of what 'the child' is, is shaped by a variety of presuppositions of which we are often unaware: for example, prevailing social and cultural attitudes and ideas, and (importantly for this book), also embedded theological beliefs. These received and

---

[1] In the highly influential *Centuries of Childhood*, Philippe Ariès proposed that 'childhood' is a relatively modern concept, developing as child mortality decreased (and thus as affective bonds between adults and children grew), as widespread child labour was replaced by extended education, and as 'childhood' became a period of life increasingly differentiated from adulthood. While his central claim is now widely dismissed by historians who have shown childhood to be understood as distinct from adulthood in many, if not all, historical periods, nevertheless, Ariès helped highlight the manner in which understandings of childhood have changed remarkably through time. Philippe Ariès, *Centuries of Childhood: A Social History of Family Life*, trans. Robert Baldick (London: Jonathan Cape, 1962).

[2] 'Childs' is an awkward expression, but it is used here to distinguish the multiple ways 'child' has been conceived in Christian history from more familiar understandings of the term 'children'. At the simplest level, there have been significant differences in understandings of boy and girl 'childs' through history and today, as well as understandings of the child at different stages in its growth from unborn, newborn, 'toddler', to adolescent and so forth.

contextual influences themselves also shift and develop through time, creating a fluid idea of the child.

Picking up the theme of The Triangle,[3] this chapter will provide a brief historical survey of some of these many 'childs', highlighting five of the more recurrent if evolving ways 'child' has been theologically imagined and missionally engaged by the church.[4] These five images of child – *inherently innocent; inherently sinful; situated in family; vulnerable and suffering;* and *Christian-adult-in-the-making* – will be examined alongside a similar number of ways the church has sought to pass on faith to successive generations: what could be called the 'mission postures' of church toward child.[5] These mission postures – *idealise; save; admonish parents; rescue and protect;* and *educate toward faith and virtue* – sometimes correlate relatively directly to particular images of the child, though more commonly the two sets of interacting themes represent a mix

---

[3] The concept of The Triangle as it is applied in this book is expounded by Haddon Willmer in Part One.

[4] There are many possible typologies of child in the Christian tradition; I am indebted particularly to Marcia Bunge who proposes three binary sets of understandings in Marcia J. Bunge, 'The Child, Religion and the Academy: Developing Robust Theological and Religious Understandings of Children and Childhood', in *Journal of Religion*, 86 (2006), 549-79. For alternative typologies – from a practical theology and an anthropological perspective respectively – see also Bonnie J. Miller-McLemore, *Let the Children Come: Re-Imagining Childhood from a Christian Perspective* (San Francisco, CA: Jossey-Bass, 2003); and Heather Montgomery, *An Introduction to Childhood: Anthropological Perspectives on Children's Lives* (Chichester, UK: Wiley-Blackwell, 2009).

[5] 'Mission postures' attempts to describe the various ways the church has sought to 'Christianise' the child in different times and places. 'Posture' can be conscious or unconscious, good or poor, and so refers here to an ecclesial bearing and countenance toward the child. It could be argued that some of what are here called *mission* postures are more correctly described as 'catechetical' or 'instructive' postures, a child being deemed to have been brought into the faith, church or covenant community in different parts of the tradition through infant baptism. However, paedo-Baptist traditions have underlying soteriological and ecclesiological understandings that express themselves in a variety of child-ward actions, from baptism itself through to those catechetical and confirmatory rituals or processes. As Karl Barth, and more recently W. Travis McMaken, have highlighted, whatever else it might be, baptism is in the first instance a missional act. Karl Barth, *Church Dogmatics*, ed G.W. Bromiley and T.F. Torrance, trans. G.W. Bromiley (Edinburgh: T&T Clark, 1969), IV:4, 51; W. Travis McMaken, *The Sign of the Gospel: Toward an Evangelical Doctrine of Infant Baptism After Karl Barth* (Minneapolis, MN: Fortress Press, 2013). For our purposes here, such acts and what they represent are included under 'mission postures'.

of variegated ways in which child has been understood and missionised by the church.[6]

From this survey we will examine how the diversity of historical 'childs' and mission postures poses critical questions for understanding the interrelation of theology, mission and child today, as well as how the many childs of history, in concert with the one set by Jesus amidst the disciples in Matthew's Gospel,[7] can similarly disrupt our settled concepts and help us more self-consciously and self-critically examine deeply held and ostensibly self-evident truths regarding all three of these interacting concerns.[8]

Child in the New Testament

It is beyond the scope of this chapter to offer a detailed analysis of Old or New Testament passages concerning the child. However, particularly influential on later Christian concepts of child are Jesus' welcome and words toward him or her in the synoptic Gospels; in particular, Matthew 18 and 19.[9] Here, like others at the social and theological margins, children were welcomed by Jesus as participants in the blessings of his own mission,[10] which heralded and effected the counter-reign of God amid human kingdoms marked by power, position and prestige. Welcoming children is here exhorted as part of the disciples' continuing mission of witness to Jesus, and his risen, Spirit-mediated presence and lordship. And Jesus' exhortation in Matthew 18 is given with a promise: that receiving the child is an act of welcome to Jesus himself – one interpretation of which is that to welcome and attend to the lowliest, littlest and least (vis-à-vis the grand, wealthy and powerful) is to open oneself to God's own welcome of the lowliest, littlest and least,[11] and thus to live in correspondence with the radical if often hidden way of God's reign as King in the world.[12]

---

[6] I am grateful to Haddon Willmer, Tom Greggs, Beth Barnett and my editorial colleagues for offering constructive feedback on drafts of this chapter. Any merits of the essay are theirs; the shortcomings remain my own.

[7] See Matthew 18:1-5.

[8] On the theme of the child and the divine disturbance, see Bill Prevette's 'The Disturbance of God, Holistic Mission, and Children in Crisis' in Part Three.

[9] See also Mark 9:33-38; Luke 9:46-48. Matthew 18 has evoked commentary throughout the historical record, from Clement of Alexandria and Origen, to Chrysostom and Calvin. Curiously, it has not led to more sustained considerations of 'child' as a topic of theology until recently.

[10] See Matthew 19:13-15, as well as Matthew 18:1-9.

[11] See Corneliu Constantineanu's essay on this topic in Part Five.

[12] Matthew 18:5. See also John Baxter-Brown's contribution in Part Five.

Particularly significant in the centuries since, have been interpretations of Jesus' exhortation to become 'like' little children.[13] Given in the context of a group of disciples arguing about greatness,[14] the long history of diverse interpretations of such passages may suggest that Jesus (or the Evangelists) did not intend this teaching to be readily reducible; instead, Jesus' provocative act and words amid miscontrued understandings of his messiahship seem intended to evoke reflection on the radical difference, otherness, and mystery of God's divine way of reigning; to confound and disturb settled concepts and attitudes, rather than provide straightforward information about the person of the child or 'childlikeness' itself. Whether or not this is true, and whatever else might be intended here, highlighting the incumbency on Jesus' followers of the objective social humility or lowliness of the child does appear to be in view.[15]

In relation to our broader five themes, the child is commonly seen in the New Testament either amid the crowds which followed or encountered Jesus on the street or in the context of their families. While it was soon to be interpreted in this way, there is no overstated sentimentality about the 'innocence' of children in Jesus' teaching or more broadly in the New Testament; but neither is the child ignored, despised or relegated to the margins on account of being inherently sinful, lacking in reason and thus full humanity, as it was in later eras. Rather, children take their place alongside adults in the community of disciples, receiving healing[16] and even their own discipleship instructions in the canonical household codes, as rudimentary as these may have been.[17] Indeed, not all of the 'childs' and

---

[13] Matthew 18:3. For a recent excellent and extended reflection on this text, see Haddon Willmer and Keith J. White, *Entry Point: Towards Child Theology with Matthew 18* (London: WTL Publications, 2013).

[14] In Matthew's account, the disciples come to Jesus with a general question; Mark's version is less charitable to the disciples, who are seen to be arguing about which *of them* would be greatest in the messianic Kingdom. Both accounts suggest the disciples operated with a fundamental misunderstanding of the nature of Christ's messiahship and the nature of God's reign.

[15] Matthew 18:4. A common interpretative mistake in historical and contemporary references to this passage is to propose that Jesus is commending the *subjective qualities* of child – innocence, wonder, joy, purity and so forth. But this assumes these qualities to be true of children to begin with, thus involving a projection of such qualities *onto* the child which Jesus placed in the disciples' midst (while usually ignoring more negative 'childish' behaviours – jealousy, temper tantrums, and plain naughtiness – which as any parent could attest could equally be proposed as common qualities of children). It is difficult to sustain such interpretations exegetically. It is better to see here that Jesus is commending taking on the lowly *objective status* of the child of his day, along with the manner in which that child thus functions as a sign of God's Kingdom.

[16] For example, Mark 5:22 and following; Acts 20:9-12 (note the use in verse 12 of *paida* [boy, child], qualifying *neanias* [young man] in verse 9).

[17] For example, Colossians 3:20; Ephesians 6:1, cf. Eph 6:4.

mission postures of later Christian tradition are directly reflected in the New Testament. This suggests that other social, cultural, philosophical and hermeneutical factors, as well as later theological developments, played key roles in shaping the various images of child which were to follow.

Child in Post-New Testament Church, Theology and Mission

The understanding of child as a person located within and subject to its family (rather than being a rights-bearing individual in the modern sense),[18] along with a somewhat correlative posture of exhorting parents to raise their children 'in the Lord', appears as a key theme in early post-New Testament literature.[19]

The child as vulnerable and at heightened risk – as well as a human person deemed worthy of protection and rescue – can also be seen in the early Christian rejection of abortion and infanticide, and the apparently widespread practice of collections being taken during church services to care for orphans.[20] The formal Christianisation of the Roman empire from the fourth century brought children under stricter legal protection, essentially providing the child an early form of human right which, significantly, cut across classical parental authority, particularly that of the *paterfamilias*.

If innocence was not in view as a characteristic of the child in the New Testament, it soon became a prominent theme in patristic writings; Clement of Alexandria (*c* 150-215) and Origen (*c* 185-254) both use the child as a

---

[18] The location of the child in its family is easily taken for granted today, especially in Western culture. However, Plato for one argued in his *Republic* (V.457d, 464e) that children should be raised communally, without knowing the identity of their biological parents and vice versa.

[19] This is particularly the case in extra-canonical household codes which echo their New Testament counterparts: for example, Clement of Rome's letter to the Corinthians (*c* 96), the writings of Polycarp (*c* 69-155), and the *Didache* (*c* early second century). That children, among other householders including slaves, were subject to intrafamilial witness and discipleship during this period is attested by Aristides in his second-century *Apology*. While Rosemary Radford Ruether and Natalie Watson have demonstrated that the Christian tradition – from Jesus onwards – has had differing and at times ambivalent attitudes towards the family, the location of children within family contexts of some kind continues to be both a Christian and Western social idea into the 21st century. Rosemary Radford Ruether, *Christianity and the Making of the Modern Family* (London: SCM Press, 2001); Natalie K. Watson, 'Expecting or On Being Open to Children', in *Children of God: Towards a Theology of Childhood*, ed Angela Shier-Jones (Peterborough: Epworth, 2007), 1-19.

[20] The rejection of the ancient practices of abortion and infanticide is attested in the *Didache*, Justin Martyr (*c* 100-165) and Athenagoras (writing *c* 177), while the taking up of collections for orphans is attested by Justin and Tertullian (*c* 160-225), among others.

metaphor for the ideal of Christian life before God.[21] This idealisation of the child, especially extolling its ostensible purity, simplicity and faintness of adult passions, sometimes betrays a profound lack of interest in children themselves; however, later church fathers such as John Chrysostom (*c* 347-407) and Jerome (*c* 347-420) were concerned with the proper education of the child in faith and virtue while in this phase of ostensible innocence.[22]

In parallel with this image of child as the ideal of innocence, there runs elsewhere a contrasting acknowledgement of a corrupted humanity derived from Adam, which also infects the child.[23] It was Augustine (354-430) who gave this understanding its enduring doctrinal form and force, such that the child was seen not as innately innocent, but inherently and wilfully sinful, and therefore culpable before God.

Augustine and the Originally Sinful Child

Augustine had a complex, but heavily theologised view of the child.[24] His doctrine of original sin took its most concrete form during the Pelagian controversy, but even as early as his *Confessions* (397), Augustine seems to project onto infantile behaviour what his developing theological views

---

[21] After similar allusions in the *Shepherd of Hermas*, Clement of Alexandria employed an extended symbolic interpretation of childhood in his *Paedagogus* (*c* 198). This idealisation is continued by Origen, for whom the little child is symbolic of greatness in the Kingdom of God precisely because 'it has not tasted sensual pleasures, and has had no conception of the impulses of manhood'. Document 2-11, Don S. Browning and Marcia J. Bunge (eds), *Children and Childhood in World Religions: Primary Sources and Texts* (New Brunswick, NJ: Rutgers University Press, 2009), 105.

[22] The primarily moral concerns of the Alexandrian fathers are echoed in Chrysostom's education treatise, *On Vainglory and the Education of Children*. Chrysostom assumes childhood to be free of strong passions, and stresses the importance of moral and theological education to ensure this childhood 'innocence' is carried into adulthood. Jerome (d 420) similarly assumes the child to be uncorrupted but weak and vulnerable, requiring education in faith and virtue.

[23] This is seen in Tertullian and Cyprian (200-285), who acknowledge respectively a corruption of soul and the contagion of the 'ancient death', though drawing different conclusions regarding infant baptism. Cyprian in particular demonstrates a remarkably high view of children, acknowledging their spiritual and anthropological equality with adults, on that basis arguing for their inclusion in baptism, while Tertullian advocated the delay of baptism.

[24] For a generally sympathetic assessment of Augustine's views on children, see Martha Ellen Stortz, '"Where or When Was Your Servant Innocent?": Augustine on Childhood', in *The Child in Christian Thought* (Grand Rapids, MI: Eerdmans, 2001), 78–102. His views must be located within his wider theological concerns, including the equal need for all of God's grace, and a sacramentology in which baptism is the means of applying the grace of the work of Christ to the individual sinner.

caused him to see.[25] For Augustine even the newborn child is not only infected with the sin of Adam, but liable to condemnation for it. The antidote is baptism, which brings to bear on the individual the work of Christ, and thus the grace of second birth; the unbaptised child, however, is inevitably condemned, though Augustine hopes their torment will be the mildest.

Indeed, Augustine himself was somewhat distressed by the implications of such theology.[26] However, rather than being prompted by this discomforted theological conscience to re-examine his hardening theological commitments, both he and his 'child' remained a prisoner to them. The ramifications have been profound: taken in more extreme directions later, Augustine's theology has, in the words of Stortz, 'formed and informed, transformed and deformed Christian attitudes toward children' in the centuries since.[27]

With Augustine therefore we see both a paedology which owes much of its shape to prior theological commitments, and a glimpse of the complex epistemological issues for adults attempting to perceive the child. In particular, the way (often unrecognised) social and theological lenses shape how adults see the child – and the resulting hermeneutical circle in which both adult and child can become entrapped.[28]

---

[25] Augustine sees, for example, an infant's apparent wrathful indignation at not having his way – even when what he seeks may be harmful – as a sign of his sinful wilfulness. Augustine suggests that young children should be dealt with leniently because such things 'will vanish as the years pass'. Nevertheless, his theological lenses cause him to read into infant behaviour substantiation for his doctrine of original sin. Augustine, *Confessions and Enchiridion*, trans. Albert Cook Outler (Louisville, KY: Westminster John Knox Press, 1955).

[26] In a letter to Jerome in 415, Augustine in anguish retracts an earlier argument that the Holy Innocents (Matthew 2:16) were martyrs, now conceding that because they were unbaptised, they stood condemned: 'But when we come to the penal sufferings of children, you must believe that I experience great difficulties for which I have no answers.' Cited in Stortz, 'Where or When', 78-79.

[27] Stortz, 'Where or When', 79. As Ferguson notes, Augustine's 'coupling of infant baptism and original sin was the foundation of his reconstruction of baptismal doctrine and practice that was to dominate the western church for subsequent centuries'. See also Everett Ferguson, *Baptism in the Early Church: History, Theology, and Liturgy in the First Five Centuries* (Grand Rapids, MI: Eerdmans, 2009), 804.

[28] This circularity can be seen in the *Confessions*: Augustine writes: 'God, in thy sight there is none free from sin, not even the infant who has lived but a day upon this earth. Who brings this to my remembrance? Does not each little one, in whom I now observe what I no longer remember of myself?' Augustine, *Confessions* I.VII.11, 37.

Innocent, Evil, or under Construction? Medieval Childs[29]

The multiplicity of childs continued in the Christian tradition throughout the Middle Ages.[30] In the high medieval era, Thomas Aquinas (1224-74) sought to harmonise the contesting images of innocence and sinfulness, while incorporating Aristotelian understandings of the child as an adult-in-the-making. For Thomas the young child is without reason,[31] and must develop in wisdom and virtue through the stages of life, away from childhood which is not the 'essence of being human', towards that which is: adulthood, endowed with the full function of discursive reason.[32]

Thus Aquinas recognises childhood as a time of moral and rational development while arguably undervaluing the actual capacities, human wholeness and possible contributions to the community of the young child. Aquinas was a creature of his (by now, formally celibate) ecclesial culture,[33] and the child for him remained a largely alien and abstract category.[34]

---

[29] It is necessary to limit the scope of this survey, after Augustine, to Latin and then European and American spheres. As Cornelia Horn notes, 'While studies of family life and even at times specific studies of children in the Middle Ages have appeared, thus far the geographical focus of these has been almost exclusively the Latin West. Few articles or books on children and family life have moved as far as Byzantium in the East,' let alone further afield. Cornelia B. Horn, 'The Lives and Literary Roles of Children in Advancing Conversion to Christianity: Hagiography from the Caucasus in Late Antiquity and the Middle Ages', in *Church History*, 76 (2007), 262-97 (263-64). There is therefore scope for much further research.

[30] By the time of Bernard of Clairvaux (1090-1153) the idealisation of the child had become associated with the cult of the Christ-child. In sharp contrast, Pope Innocent III (*c* 1160-1216) presents a depressingly negative understanding of humanity in general and child in particular, in his *On the Misery of the Human Condition* (*c* 1195). Shahar has suggested that both competing understandings of innocence and sinfulness drew on different medieval 'commentaries on the same texts'. Shulamith Shahar, *Childhood in the Middle Ages* (London: Routledge, 1992), 6.

[31] Infants, according to Thomas, 'have neither good nor bad conscience since they do not have the use of reason'. 'Baptism and Confirmation', 3a.68.9, St Thomas Aquinas, *Summa Theologica*, trans. James J. Cunningham (London: Blackfriars, 1975), LVII, 109.

[32] Aquinas, 2-2.4.4, *ST*, trans. T.C. O'Brien (London: Blackfriars, 1974), XXXI, 129. Thomas is complex on this point: following Augustine, he holds that all human beings made in the image of God have a rational soul, independent of their capacity for rational thought or higher reason. Nevertheless, like Augustine he struggled to reconcile this understanding of the image of God with the full humanity of the child, writing that the child, 'So long as he has not the use of reason ... is like a non-rational animal', Aquinas, 2-2.10.12, *ST*, trans. Thomas Gilby O.P. (London: Blackfriars, 1975), XXXII, 77.

[33] Though having a long and chequered history, celibacy became a formal discipline for clerics of the Latin church following the First Lateran Council of 1123, which officially invalidated clerical marriages. Certainly, by Thomas' day it was the

Aquinas is not alone in the Middle Ages (or earlier) in understanding the child as a developing person; it was a widely accepted formula that the child passed through the stages of *infantia* (to 7 years), *pueritia* (7 to 14 years, for boys, to 12 years for girls), and *adolescentia* (from 14) towards adulthood.[35] This medieval image of child as adult-in-the-making was accompanied by a growing pedagogical sophistication in which education, the primary goal of which was 'to raise a Christian human being', also began to recognise that children had individual abilities.[36] Parents remained the primary providers of childhood education, and it is likely many went about their child-rearing with little reference to the church's theology, theories or childless priests, but rather according to the cultural mores and practices of the day. Nevertheless, the church sought to play its part, through its exhortative efforts aimed at improving parenting (specifically along moral lines), as well as offering education in cathedral and 'reading' (or 'song') schools'.[37]

At the same time, the child continued to be understood as especially vulnerable and prone to various forms of suffering. Church-founded hospitals, and later special orphanages and foundling homes, cared for sick, orphaned or abandoned children, while monasteries (sometimes reluctantly) received disabled, illegitimate, abandoned or orphaned children. As in recent times, the church has a mixed record in this regard: some – perhaps many – children experienced harm at the hands of their ecclesial or monastic guardians. However, literature from the period also demonstrates

---

sanctioned, official norm, distancing, officially at least, priests and theologians from the immediate experience of child-rearing.

[34] Thomas had been an oblate to a Benedictine monastery from his own childhood; subsequently it may be true, as Berryman suggests, that 'contact with children [in Benedictine monasteries] was limited for the average monk to prevent abusive relationships from developing. There was also a tendency among theologians to rely on authoritative texts rather than actual experience, so even if one were interested in children there would be no need to be engaged with them personally. The authoritative texts were what mattered to interpret them properly.' Jerome W. Berryman, *Children and the Theologians: Clearing the Way for Grace* (Harrisburg, PA: Church Publishing, 2009), 77-78.

[35] Augustine had also followed Aristotle's division of human life into various stages; a number of Aquinas' medieval counterparts did similarly, being cognisant – as are any parents – that children were different in many ways and at different stages, from adults. It is medieval writers such as Thomas whose acknowledgement that childhood involved a process of development towards adulthood, that leads Shahar and other medievalists to reject Ariès' once influential thesis that childhood is essentially a modern discovery. Shahar, *Childhood in the Middle Ages*, 1-5, 31; see note 2.

[36] Shahar, *Childhood in the Middle Ages*, 166ff.

[37] In practice, these provided a limited, but growing, number of children with elementary education, though even in the late medieval period few peasant children received any formal education. Shahar, *Childhood in the Middle Ages*, 225ff, 242.

a concern on the part of the church to wield its available instruments to protect and provide for the suffering or at risk child in the medieval era.[38]

Child in the Reformation Era

By the arrival of the Protestant Reformation, theological images of the child and mission postures towards it were increasingly variegated and interwoven.

With salvation, however tenuous its hold, regarded as bestowed through baptism, the fourteenth to sixteenth centuries saw increasing ecclesial emphasis on educating the child, particularly through catechisms designed to instruct the child in right doctrine, along with training the child for civic responsibility.[39] With the Reformation came an image, not of the child as the ideal of Christian life, but rather of the *ideal* Christian child – a pious, responsible Christian citizen-in-training. This can be seen particularly in Lutheran and Reformed understandings of the child.

The childs of Luther and Calvin

Martin Luther (1483-1546) and his Reformed counterparts, Martin Bucer (1491-1551), and John Calvin (1509-64), all strongly affirmed the importance of the family in the nurture of the child in faith and civic

---

[38] Shahar summarises, 'Christianity, which preached the sanctity of life of all those created in the image of God, emphatically prohibited the murder of infants, including the handicapped and the illegitimate', thus, though such practices undoubtedly continued, monasteries and church bodies were required to take responsibility for children at risk, even if they sometimes objected due to overwhelmed resources. *Shahar, Childhood in the Middle Ages*, 127, cf. 123-25, 184. Abortion and infanticide continued to occur, despite church sanctions – and indeed sometimes within clerical and monastic settings to hide illegitimate births. However, the killing of an unbaptised child is treated in the priestly penitential books as a grave offence – a *magnum crimem* – because both the child's mortal life and its immortal soul were regarded as lost. Rob Meens, 'Children and Confession in the Early Middle Ages', in *The Church and Childhood*, ed Diana Wood, Studies in Church History, 31 (Oxford: Blackwells, 1994), 53-65. Later penitentials also reflect greater demands made of parents to care for the well-being of their children. *Ibid.*, 60.

[39] Along with catechetical materials, the genre of 'Children's Bibles' or books of Bible stories for children emerged in this period. Ruth Bottigheimer has shown how the selection of stories in these books, as well as their emphasis (for example, on Old Testament or New Testament) and how the stories were told, has changed substantially over the centuries, to reinforce the moral, social and theological concerns of the time. Ruth B. Bottigheimer, 'The Bible for Children: The Emergence and Development of the Genre, 1550-1990', in *The Church and Childhood*, ed Diana Wood, Studies in Church History (Oxford: Blackwells, 1994), XXXI, 347-62.

responsibility.[40] Indeed, the rejection of clerical celibacy heralded a significant shift in understandings of the child, as Reformed theologians now had direct experience with children amid their domestic households, responsibility for which many took very seriously. Hints of this new-found parental perspective may well be seen alongside broader social and theological concerns in the Lutheran image of the ideal child, summarised in Veit Dietrich's quip, 'Is there anything on earth more precious, friendly and lovable than a pious, disciplined, obedient, and teachable child?'[41]

Nevertheless, Luther's and Calvin's 'childs' were shaped, at least in some part, by their theological commitments. Both affirmed the Augustinian doctrine that children are conceived and born in sin,[42] and that infant baptism remained a vital institution, though with different emphases: for Luther, the child is made innocent of sin by the mercy of God through baptism, which is nevertheless made efficacious for justification by faith.[43] For Calvin, 'children are baptised for future repentance and faith ... the seed of both lies [hidden] in them by the secret operation of the Spirit.'[44]

---

[40] Luther, for example, declared: 'There is no power on earth that is nobler or greater than that of parents'; similarly, the early Lutheran Justus Menius said of parenthood: 'The diligent rearing of children is the greatest service to the world, both in spiritual and temporal affairs, both for the present life and for posterity.' Both are cited in Steven E. Ozment, *When Fathers Ruled: Family Life in Reformation Europe* (Cambridge, MA: Harvard University Press, 1983), 132.

[41] Cited in Ozment, *When Fathers Ruled*, 132.

[42] Calvin, in particular, strongly emphasises the ontological corruption of the child by original sin, writing: 'Even infants bring their condemnation with them from their mother's womb; for although they have not yet brought forth the fruits of their unrighteousness, they have its seed included in them. Nay, their whole nature is, as it were, a seed of sin, and, therefore, cannot but be odious and abominable to God.' Calvin, 4.15.10, *Institutes of the Christian Religion*, 2 vols. (London: James Clarke, 1949), II, 518. The 'even ...' and 'whole nature' of this passage highlights that Calvin is not here dealing with the child in isolation to broader humanity. Rather, he views it as an integral part of a humanity 'vitiated and corrupted in all parts of [its] nature, [and] held rightly condemned on account of such corruption alone'. His view of the unregenerate child is thus no more pessimistic than his view of unregenerate humankind in general. Nevertheless, Calvin moved beyond predecessors and contemporaries, holding that it must be part of God's active (not just passive) will that some infants and children are reprobate on account of their original sin; later Calvinists were to place still greater emphasis on these points.

[43] Luther allowed that even an infant could have faith; but regardless, 'faith does not exist for the sake of baptism, but baptism for the sake of faith. When faith comes, baptism is complete.' Martin Luther, 'Concerning Rebaptism', in *Luther's Works*, ed Conrad Bergendoff and Helmut T. Lehmann, 55 vols (Philadelphia, PA: Fortress Press, 1958), XL, 246.

[44] Calvin, 4.16.20, *Institutes*, 543. In this way Calvin believes that a child grows into an understanding of his baptism, a sign, comfort and assurance to them and their parents of their forgiveness and adoption by the Father, which simultaneously

Thus, for Calvin, the child should be baptised as a sign of inclusion in the covenant with God, subject ultimately to the inscrutable electing will of God.

Within the generally inward-looking European ecclesial context of the Protestant Reformation, the 'mission' postures of the Lutheran and Reformed churches were somewhat similar: a continued primary concern for the child's salvation commenced in its baptism, though now understood as confirmed, completed or realised by faith, as well as in renewed catechistic enthusiasm; and the pulpit-administered admonishment of parents to raise and educate their children towards the ideals of faith, godliness and social responsibility. In both Lutheran and Reformed realms, the state was also afforded a responsibility to intervene on behalf of children in want of adequate parental provision.[45]

The Anabaptist child: under grace

While both Calvin and Luther have at times a rich and even generous view of the child, both allowing for the possibility that the unbaptised child may not always suffer condemnation, the logic of both their theologies – particularly Calvin's – generally pointed towards a vast number of children globally suffering divine damnation.[46]

By contrast came the assertions of Radical reformers such as Menno Simons (1496-1561) that the child is covered by grace, without the need for baptism until it comes to the 'age of discretion'.[47] For Simons, original sin

---

provides such assurance to their parents. 4.16.9, 22, 32, *Institutes*, 534-35, 544-45, 554.

[45] Luther, for example, called for the establishment of universal public schools, teaching biblical and vernacular languages, and liberal arts, alongside the Scriptures. See Luther's 'To the Councilmen of All Cities in Germany That They Establish and Maintain Christian Schools', in *Luther's Works*, 45: 347-78. Luther was also conscious of the needy child, and the state's responsibility there towards, asking of the German leaders in the lead-up to the Peasants' Revolt of 1524, a question of continuing pertinence today: 'If it is necessary, dear sirs, to expend annually such great sums of firearms, roads, bridges in order that a city enjoy temporal peace, why should not at least as much be devoted to the poor needy youth?' Cited in Byron Klaus, 'Historical and Theological Reflection on Ministry to Children at Risk', in *Transformation: An International Journal of Holistic Mission Studies*, 14 (1997), 15–18 (15).

[46] Calvin's theology was certainly taken more explicitly in this direction by later Calvinists. Strict Calvinists were not alone in holding this belief, however; it remains the logical implication, if not explicit doctrine, of many Evangelicals and others today.

[47] Though not all Anabaptists agreed, Simons was generally representative of Anabaptist doctrine: in 1524 a group of Swiss Brethren wrote, 'We hold ... all children who have not yet come to the discernment of the knowledge of good and evil, and have not yet eaten of the tree of knowledge, that they are surely saved by

predisposes all towards committing sin;[48] however, a person can only be held culpable for their actual sins, and then only after the powers of reason, will, and judgement between good and evil, were fully developed.[49] Contrary to Luther and Calvin, Simons and many of his fellow Anabaptists held that 'faith does not follow upon baptism, but baptism follows from faith'.[50] The primary goal of Anabaptist child-rearing was the young person's knowledgeable request for baptism; in this way, Anabaptism was endowed with its own 'ideal' child.

Thus the Reformation wrought several significant shifts regarding the child: a modification among those at its more radical end to the doctrine of original sin, and among both radical and magisterial Reformers in the understanding of the soteriological status of the child: no longer was a child's salvation secured solely or primarily by the sacrament of infant baptism; a confirmatory or even initiatory public demonstration of faith as a response to the work of grace was now required. Indeed, not all baptised children were necessarily to be considered among the elect, nor the reverse. The Anabaptist child particularly was the catalyst for a shift in mission posture towards the explicit evangelisation of children as they approached the age of discretion, in practice understood as anything from seven onwards.

The Conflicting Post-Reformation Childs

This soteriological ambiguity emerging from the Reformation continued among many late sixteenth and seventeenth-century Puritans, where reports of child conversion experiences were not uncommon.[51] In such accounts, the theological shadows of Augustine and Calvin continued to fall across

---

the suffering of Christ, the new Adam, who has restored their vitiated life.' Cited in Hillel Schwartz, 'Early Anabaptist Ideas about the Nature of Children', in *Mennonite Quarterly Review*, 47 (1973), 102-14 (103).

[48] Simons, 'Foundation of Christian Doctrine', in *The Complete Writings of Menno Simons c.1496-1561*, ed John Christian Wenger, trans. Leonard Verduin (Scottdale, PA: Herald Press, 1966), 130. See also 'Distressed Christians', in *CWMS*, 504-05.

[49] Thus 'little ones must wait according to God's Word until they can understand the holy Gospel of grace and sincerely confess it; and then, and then only is it time, no matter how young or how old, for them to receive Christian baptism as the infallible Word of our beloved Lord Jesus Christ has taught and commanded.' Simons, 'Christian Baptism', *CWMS*, 241.

[50] Simons, 'Foundation of Christian Doctrine', *CWMS*, 120.

[51] In Scotland, a young Mistress Rutherford and a Robert Blair recount childhood conversions, the latter writing that by the age of seven 'the Lord early owned me and caused my conscience to reflect upon me with this query, "Wherefore servest thou, unprofitable creature?"' Recounted by Margo Todd, 'The Problem of Scotland's Puritans', in *The Cambridge Companion to Puritanism*, ed John Coffey and Paul C.H. Lim (Cambridge: CUP, 2008), 174-88 (182).

not only adult understandings of the child, but also on the way children understood themselves.[52]

Such trajectories reached something of their zenith with the eighteenth-century New England Puritan, Jonathan Edwards (1703-58). Intent to defend the increasingly unpopular doctrine of original sin, Edwards argued that inherent human sinfulness caused newborns to commit actual sins 'immediately, as soon as they are capable of it',[53] making all 'by nature children of wrath'.[54] To remedy this, it seems baptism alone was not sufficient; children, like adults, needed to be born again through personal conversion, or risk damnation at the hands of an angry God.

Like Augustine, Edwards wrestled with the implications of this reasoning, but his theological programme could broach no other possibility than that the child is justly subject to God's wrathful condemnation, but for the 'interposition of divine grace' received through personal faith.[55] Like Augustine, Edwards shows how theological precommitments, particularly when hardened amid heated theological disputation, can have grave implications for the child, as well as distorting one's own theological legacy.

Edward's image of the child was losing ground, however, particularly in the face of the broadening impact of the Enlightenment's view of the child as a *tabula rasa* (blank slate).[56] Such a child was in need, not so much of

---

[52] Referring to Mistress Rutherford's narrative, Todd writes: 'Who else but a Puritan child would confess as sin that "after the sermon was done I spent the rest of the day in playing with the rest of the bairns, so great was the strength of my corruption and impenitence" … On the other hand, her rapture when she perceived divine presence was as extreme, as when (still a child) she "sat down upon my knees and prayed to God … [and] was ravished and taken up with joy that I cannot express, so that at that time I may say I tasted of the powers of the world to come".' Margo Todd, 'The Problem of Scotland's Puritans', 182. Such excerpts, and those of Robert Blair, suggest, however, that there were other significant aspects to their self-understanding: that they believed themselves to have direct engagement with God's presence and even voice; that they prayed and played and sought to be serious in their own discipleship before God.

[53] Jonathan Edwards, *Original Sin, The Works of Jonathan Edwards*, ed Clyde A. Holbrook (London: Yale University Press, 1970), III, 134. However, note that Edwards tempers this somewhat, writing all 'commit sin immediately, without the least time intervening after they are capable of understanding their obligations to God, and reflecting on themselves.' Edwards, *Original Sin,*, 135. Nevertheless, Edward's thinking is very similar to Augustine's: 'A young viper has a malignant nature, though incapable of doing a malignant action, and at present appearing a harmless creature.' Edwards, *Original Sin*, 423. He differs from Augustine in regarding infants as culpable before God for their own, actual sins, but that these begin such a short time after birth that the interval was essentially irrelevant.

[54] Edwards, *Original Sin*, 215.

[55] Edwards, *Original Sin*, 109.

[56] This term is commonly associated with John Locke and his epochal *An Essay Concerning Human Understanding* (Kitchener, Ontario: Batoche Books, 2001).

salvation from innate sin, but of a proper modern education, according –
and here Locke echoes something of Aquinas – to the powers and
principles of reason. Both Enlightenment and Puritan images of the child
were confronted, however, by a resurgent image of the child – not as
originally sinful, or as a rational adult under construction – but as both
originally innocent, and indeed the epitome of human life.

In *Émile: or, On Education*,[57] Jean-Jacques Rousseau (1712-78)
propounds a view of the natural child who, he suggests, should be educated
primarily through engagement with the natural world, in accordance with
their inherent goodness and strengths. Evil, for Rousseau, is not an inherent
quality of the child, but rather of bourgeois, adult society, which corrupts
the child as it grows. Rousseau's influence and that of continental
Romanticism general is echoed in the work of the 'father' of liberal
Protestantism, Friedrich Schleiermacher (1768-1834). Schleiermacher
presents the central child figure of his novella *Christmas Eve* as naturally
intuitive of the divine,[58] able to experience piety directly and implicitly, and
in doing so pointing the adult characters back to the purity of true religious
affections.[59] If Schleiermacher's child is the epitome of piety, the child of
the English Romantic poets is the epitome of humanity: 'Heaven lies about
us in our infancy,' wrote Wordsworth; the newborn arrives 'trailing clouds
of glory'.[60] The child of Romanticism has grown in influence to rival and
even surpass both the child of Augustinian hereditary sinfulness and the

---

Locke's *Essay*, which argues that children are not born with innate ideas (contra
Descartes) was followed closely by his educational treatise, *Some Thoughts
Concerning Education* (Oxford: Clarendon Press, 1989).

[57] Jean-Jacques Rousseau, *Émile: or, On Education*, trans. Allan Bloom (New
York: Basic Books, 1979).

[58] Friedrich Schleiermacher, *Christmas Eve: Dialogue on the Incarnation*, trans.
Terrence N. Tice (Lampeter, Wales: EM Texts, 1990). Schleiermacher writes
elsewhere on children – for a fuller treatment, see Dawn DeVries, '"Be Converted
and Become as Little Children": Friedrich Schleiermacher on the Religious
Significance of Childhood', in *The Child in Christian Thought* ed Marcia J. Bunge
(Grand Rapids, MI: Eerdmans, 2001), 329-49; Edmund Newey, *Children of God:
The Child as Source of Theological Anthropology* (Burlington, VT: Ashgate, 2013).

[59] Schleiermacher departs from Rousseau on the relation of the child to religion:
Rousseau argued that religion should not be imposed on the child before the mid-
teens at least, as the child could misconceive the divine, both offending God and
then living with a distorted image of God thereafter. Schleiermacher appears to
refute this view, which is given voice by one of his novella's characters, but
countered by the 'naturally pious' child, Sophie, as below.

[60] William Wordsworth, 'Ode on Intimations of Immortality from Recollections of
Early Childhood', in *Poems, Volume One*, ed John O. Hayden (London: Penguin,
1977), 525. 'Trailing clouds of glory' does not itself intimate a natural communion
between God and child, but as the poem continues, there is a negative assessment of
advancing age – suggestive, if not of a divinised, certainly a prioritised, view of
childhood.

'not-fully human' child of Thomas Aquinas, despite being rife with theological problems.[61]

Sunday schools, and the religious education movement

Through the modern period, the vulnerable and disenfranchised child was far from forgotten. Amid a vibrant era for orphanages, charitable enterprises and evangelical social activism, the late eighteenth century saw the emergence of the British Sunday School movement, initially catering for the children of the Industrial Revolution's urban poor;[62] within a century, Sunday schools had become the major provider of literacy skills in Britain and America, spreading also via missionary societies throughout the British empire and beyond. While there had been from the start a strong emphasis on religious education, Sunday schools often combined this with a conversionist posture toward children; in North America however, Horace Bushnell (1802-76) reacted against Edwards-esque child conversionism, arguing the goal of Christian education is 'that the child is to grow up as a Christian and never know himself [sic] as being otherwise'.[63] Bushnell also highly esteemed the home as 'the seat of religion' and families (echoing John Chrysostom) as 'little churches'.[64]

---

[61] This elevated, if not divinised, child bears a form of humanity and communion with God superior to that of adults, inverting the Thomist error of assuming that adulthood is the true and proper state of being human. This is, of course, problematic Christologically and soteriologically, proposing a communion with God which bypasses the necessity of the incarnation, cross and resurrection of Christ – this, in essence, is Karl Barth's complaint regarding Schleiermacher's child in *Christmas Eve*. Karl Barth, *The Theology of Schleiermacher: Lectures at Göttingen, Winter Semester 1923-24*, ed Dietrich Ritschl, trans. Geoffrey W. Bromiley (Edinburgh: T&T Clark, 1982), 57, 62. It also, in turn, creates its own problematic missional postures to the child by, in effect, objectifying and even idolising the child. While seeming to exalt the child, it nevertheless risks adultifying children in practice, by seeing children prematurely elevated into roles and responsibilities beyond their capabilities. Further, it can promote a tendency to not question, guide or correct the child in relation to its behaviour or understanding of the faith, which may therefore involve all manner of errors and mistaken projections onto 'God'.

[62] Sunday schools were in a sense a modified development of English catechetical instruction, with some common ground with the Charity School Movement. Though debated, the provenance of the Sunday School Movement is usually attributed to Robert Raikes in 1780.

[63] John H. Westerhoff, *Will Our Children Have Faith?*, rev. edn (Harrisburg, PA: Morehouse, 2000), 35. Westerhoff is here slightly paraphrasing Bushnell. A speaker at the St Louis Sunday School Convention in 1893 echoed Bushnell in asserting that 'the natural time to become Christians is in childhood'. Cliff, 'The Rise of the Sunday School Movement', 196.

[64] Horace Bushnell, *Christian Nurture* (New York: Scribner, Armstrong, 1876), 406.

Children, he held, come into the world morally innocent, 'in a sense as a new Adam', betraying similarities to the Romantic vision of the child.[65]

Childs in the twentieth century

Bushnell's child and the associated missional posture of formative Christian education remained influential into the twentieth century. Elsewhere the child continued to be understood as being in need of salvation by conversion, especially among churches with a Calvinist and/or Puritan heritage, and with those identifying with the early twentieth-century Fundamentals movement. In other churches, including some Baptist denominations, the understanding of the child as being under grace before the age of 'discretion', 'accountability', or 'personal responsibility' has also been adopted.[66]

The vulnerable and suffering child, served at home and abroad by charities and mission societies, found a new form of Christian champion in the wake of twentieth-century conflicts in the burgeoning number of Christian relief and development organisations. As the century progressed, global 'child sponsorship' programmes brought images of the distant child 'in need' into churches and the wider public consciousness through mass media advertising.[67] In the late twentieth century this vulnerable child became the focus of 'Holistic Child Development', a mission posture which applies to the child the principle of holistic (or 'integral') mission, in which human development programmes, sometimes following secular development practices, are integrated with church-based evangelism or discipleship of children and families.[68]

The late twentieth and early 21st century has seen a proliferation of missional interest in the child, based on a wide variety of images of child. Groups including the VIVA Network, the Global Children's Forum, and the 4/14 Movement, have respectively championed the 'child-at-risk', the child in need of evangelizing, and the child as a missional agent 'of global transformation'.[69] At the Cape Town 2010 meetings of the Lausanne

---

[65] Bendroth, 'Horace Bushnell's *Christian Nurture*', 361.

[66] See, for example, IV.1 and 2 of the Constitution of the Baptist Union of Victoria (Australia): https://www.buv.com.au/about-us/who-we-are/governance *[accessed 01.09.14]*

[67] For churches in the global North, whereas in previous centuries the needy child had been nearby, even underfoot, this new needy child was separated by often considerable cultural and geographical distance, heightening the degree of otherness, creating even a kind of romanticism of neediness.

[68] See Dan Brewster, *Future Impact: Connecting Child, Church and Mission* (Colorado Springs, CO: Compassion International, 2010).

[69] See, respectively, www.max7.org/resource.aspx?id=cdc66d0d-87cd-4282-88b0-99ba7b695014&creatinguser=1 and www.viva.org [both accessed 25 March 2014];

Congress on World Evangelisation, the child was, for the first time, the focus of a plenary meeting of Congress delegates.[70]

.   This rapid growth in missional interest has been paralleled, though not directly always accompanied, by a growing corpus of theological reflection on child and childhood.[71] Alongside this theological consideration of the child *per se*, the early 21st century also witnessed the emergence of the Child Theology Movement, which moves beyond theologies centring upon children to rethinking theology more broadly with child (particularly that placed by Jesus amid his disciples) in mind.[72]

Some bodies such as Scripture Union which have a long history of working with children, continue to wrestle with theological and missional questions concerning the child;[73] other groups are driven by tacit, unexamined and potentially even conflicting understandings of theology, mission and child. This is not a new development; indeed, as we have seen, it is arguably as old as the church itself. However, the need to bring theology, mission and child together into a deeply considered trialogue is as urgent as it has ever been: hence the particular value of this volume as a starting-point in that endeavour.

Theology, Mission and the Many 'Childs'

What, then, are we to do with this history of many 'childs'? How might such a brief and limited survey serve us today?

The fact of the many 'childs' of history, like the individual child in Matthew 18, poses to us a set of significant questions concerning our own understandings of theology, mission and child. The first and most obvious of these is, how in the light of these many childs of history are *we* to understand the child? One response is to simply choose from among those presented here (and potentially others); that is, to accept and assimilate those images of child which resonate most closely with our own, and ignore or reject the others.[74] But upon what basis or criteria do we justify

---

also Luis Bush, *The 4/14 Window: Raising Up a New Generation to Transform the World* (Colorado Springs, CO: Compassion International, 2009).

[70] The resultant *Cape Town Commitment* also includes a statement on children: The Lausanne Movement, *The Cape Town Commitment: A Confession of Faith and a Call to Action* (Cape Town, RSA: The Lausanne Movement / The Didasko Files, 2011).

[71] See this volume's Bibliography for a listing of many such materials.

[72] See, in particular, Willmer and White, *Entry Point*.

[73] See, for example, the International Council of Scripture Union paper of September 2003, published as William Andersen et al, 'Theology of Childhood: A Theological Resource Framed to Guide the Practice of Evangelising and Nurturing Children', *Journal of Christian Education*, 46 (2003), 5-31.

[74] Indeed, this is in many ways a common and default reality, for we all stand in social and theological traditions, and tend to adopt what we receive, including our notions of child.

such decisions? If we do so uncritically, without examining the assumptions upon which those images have been built, might we simply perpetuate past problems in how we regard, treat and undertake mission with the child?

A second option is to hold all the images in tension, accepting that the multiplicity is representative of the complex, multifaceted nature of the child.[75] However, *are* all the historical images acceptable? Can the child really accommodate all manner of ways in which it has been imagined throughout history, including conflicting visions? Does taking this option risk failing to grapple with the implicit assumptions, and even conflicting underlying theologies? Resolving the question of what we are to make of the many childs may thus involve rejecting some images, while holding others together (in harmony or tension), in a complex but consciously and cautiously selective understanding.

Perhaps it is better still to build fresh conceptions of the child, conceptions that are historically and theologically informed, which acknowledge that we are beholden to cultural, social, and theological traditions. In other words, to acknowledge the many childs of history, yet – based on our own concrete experience with children – ask afresh 'who, today, is the child, in relation to itself, and others? In relation to God? And in relationship to the work of God in the world in Christ and by the Spirit?' This is indeed a work for theologians and missioners to undertake; it is not in the scope of this chapter to achieve it; however, this volume as a whole may again make a contribution here.

The fact of the many childs of history, however, alerts us to the deeper epistemological issues involved in doing such work. Particularly it highlights how we, like those before us, can readily become captive in hermeneutical circles and, like Augustine, find in the child that which we seek, or as Kennedy observes, impose on children 'a view of reality for which we then use them as examples'.[76] This raises deeper questions: how possible is it, in seeking to understand the child, to lay aside our own preconceptions, deeply embedded as they are? To what extent can we avoid constructing an understanding of children and childhood projected from our own recollections now rendered distant, and reinterpreted through adult lenses, with all their collected social, cultural, theological presuppositions?

---

[75] This approach seems to commend itself from Karl Rahner's observation that the human (and thus the child) is an 'inwardly plural being', which, when inverted, suggests that it is outwardly plural as well; that is, a child can be understood in multiple ways, like different facets of one diamond. Karl Rahner, *Theological Investigations*, trans. Edward Quinn (London: Darton, Longman & Todd, 1984), 184.

[76] David Kennedy, 'Images of the Young Child in History: Enlightenment and Romance', in *Early Childhood Research Quarterly*, 3 (1988), 121–37 (122). This is the mistake of Augustine, reading into infants' behaviour evidence of his doctrine of original sin.

Edmund Newey alerts us to our constructivism when he says: 'The child always eludes adult pretensions to objectivity. As portrayed by the mature human being, the child is an imaginary construct, never innocent of the author's cultural preconceptions.'[77]

In making his point, Newey may overstate the distance and discontinuity between adult and child, reverse-reifying and re-objectifying the child in the process. The work of the French dialectical phenomenologist and one-time professor of Child Psychology at the Sorbonne, Maurice Merleau-Ponty, may offer some assistance and balance here.[78] Merleau-Ponty speaks of the child as a 'polymorph', able to assimilate and be assimilated into various cultural (and by extension, theological) possibilities. He insists however that while the child is not precisely the same as the adult, nor is it to be conceived as absolutely 'other',[79] elsewhere he adds that childhood is never radically liquidated in the adult.[80] In other words, there is a genuine continuity, not absolute discontinuity, between child and adult. Further, through a process of critical reflective interaction, Merleau-Ponty argues that something actual and real of the child can be known:

> This circular relationship, even if it implies a danger of illusion, cannot be evaded. There is no other way to access the child's world. One must slowly extricate what comes from oneself and what properly belongs to the child. In summation, the connection between observation and action, between theory and practice, is never a matter of pure knowledge, but one of existence. With a sufficient amount of critical thought, one can hope to constitute a real understanding.[81]

The key point here, it would seem, is doing the difficult work of self-critical disengagement of one's own preconceptions to make space to encounter the child on its own terms – achieving not a 'pure' objective knowledge, and yet a real, existential understanding all the same. Being alert to our tendency to constructivism, and to viewing the child as self-evident, must be the first step: discarding the assumption that because we exist in and around children, we know objectively who and what a child is; yet at the same time realising it is indeed through being with and around children that real understanding – a relational knowing – can occur. That the child in Christian history has been conceived so differently – in fact, in such diametrically opposite ways – suggests that we assume too much

---

[77] Newey, *Children of God*, 2.
[78] Maurice Merleau-Ponty, *Child Psychology and Pedagogy: The Sorbonne Lectures 1949-1952*, trans. Talia Welsh (Evanston, IL: Northwestern University Press, 2010).
[79] Merleau-Ponty, *Child Psychology and* Pedagogy, 377.
[80] Maurice Merleau-Ponty, *The Primacy of Perception: And Other Essays on Phenomenological Psychology, the Philosophy of Art, History, and Politics*, ed James M. Edie, Northwestern University Studies in Phenomenology and Existential Philosophy (Evanston, IL: Northwestern University Press, 1964), 138.
[81] Merleau-Ponty, *Child Psychology and Pedagogy*, 69.

when we assume we understand the child, unless we are prepared to do the difficult work of identifying, acknowledging and as far as possible bracketing our presuppositions – social, cultural, and theological.[82]

Thus, as Jesus' welcome and words concerning the child in Matthew 18 defied his disciples' understanding of the child,[83] so the many 'childs' of our historical survey unsettle our settled conceptions, compelling us to examine not only the way we understand child, but also the presuppositions upon which that understanding is built. It challenges us to self-critically, self-consciously and indeed prayerfully reflect afresh upon the questions, 'Who do I understand the child to be? In relation to itself, to others, to God, and to God's work in the world in Christ and by the Spirit? Am I doing the necessary work to understand not just who is *the* child, but who is *this* child with whom I am interacting?'

For these are not abstract questions. Much of this chapter has been written with an (equally delightful, distracting) toddler sitting on my knee, colouring bits of scrap paper, demanding different coloured pens, and obliviously interrupting my train of thought. The child on our knee, her sister in the next room, along with those in our churches, next door or on our television, compel us to make decisions about how we understand and live with and amongst children, as well as how we understand them to be encountered by God and Gospel. Such decisions must not be made lightly. As we have seen from history, how we ultimately decide to understand 'child' and thus individual children (who are people, not just members of an abstract category, theological or otherwise), has profound consequences, including how we as the church today regard, treat and seek to conduct mission with and among children.

However, the childs of history, in concert with the child of Matthew 18, pose questions not only to our understanding of 'child', but also to our understandings of theology and mission. Who is the God before whom we exist together, as child and adult? To whom is it that we bear witness as we live with, among (and, for some, as) children? In the light of the many childs, we are prompted to ask, is God the wrathful God that Edwards understood him to be? Or the God who, despite Augustine's otherwise lofty theology of love, would assign even the Holy Innocents to condemnation

---

[82] There are limits on the extent to which this is possible; we cannot escape our situatedness, or consciously identify all aspects of the lenses through which we see life. But Merleau-Ponty is right to challenge the subject-object divide that is inherent in constructivist dualisms of adult and child. It is important, perhaps, to remember ultimately that children are *people*, fellow human beings who in the dialectical mystery of shared humanity are both similar and different to those of us further along the timeline of human ageing.

[83] The child amid the disciples was of low status, socially and theologically unimportant (cf. Matthew 19:13-15); Jesus' welcome, words, attention and blessing elevate the child in relation to his Kingdom, and in relation to his community of disciples.

(however mild) because they were unbaptised? Or the God of Rousseau, who should not be foisted upon children in case they misconstrue and thus offend him?

Just as we assume too much when we assume we know the child, the childs of history reminds us we too may assume too much when we presume we understand God and his Kingdom. This is in essence the challenge of the child placed by Jesus into the midst of his disciples in Matthew 18: God's Kingdom, and therefore the God *of* the Kingdom, was not as the disciples assumed (that is, like human Herods and Caesars). For the disciples, there was no way they could come under the reign of this God-King as he is in his actual, rather than imagined, Godness, short of a radical shift in thinking – a rebirth, of sorts.[84] The child placed in their midst thus became a pointer, a sign, to the other-ness, the upside-downness (or the right-way-upness) of God and his way of reigning, and simultaneously the possibility in Christ of a new beginning; a turn to a new way of thinking, being, and knowing which corresponds to that Kingdom and its God. Immersed as we are in kingdoms of earth and clay, amid gods of our own making, the child points to the radical different-ness of God and his reign, to which we must be continually converted. Both the many childs of history and the individual child of Matthew 18 point to the importance of holding open our theology, which is a finite human attempt to speak truly about a God who can and must be truly spoken of, yet who transcends and is not confined by all such attempts even as he may meet us in them. As the child unsettles our unexamined conceptions of child, so it unsettles our theology, behoving us to allow our theology to retain dialectic, paradox, loose ends, and mystery; and to allow ourselves to be turned back in our understanding of God to begin again at the beginning,[85] like the disciples – and like a child.[86]

---

[84] Matthew's language comes close to the Johannine idea of being 'born again', in 18:3 – 'change and become' is *straphēte kai genēsthe*, the latter verb (*ginomai*) potentially suggestive of a 'coming into being' reminiscent of the birth of a child.

[85] As Haddon Willmer writes, 'Becoming as the children means beginning again, always at the beginning, eagerly entering into the enlivening grace of a new start in freedom. The child in the rule of God is little and vulnerable, but more, is the power of new life, the startling arrival of fresh possibility in an old and dying world.' Haddon Willmer, 'Ant and Sparrow in Child Theology', in *Faith and Thought*, 2013, 20-31 (30).

[86] In a related way, the child also challenges our theological method. As we see from history, theology has often been forged in the crucible of conflict, then dogmatically defended across polemical battle-lines. Undoubtedly, by the grace of God, important theology has emerged in the process. But the finiteness of (our own) theology, the multiplicity of 'childs' in history, as well as the lowliness-therefore-greatness of the child in Matthew 18, challenges our tendency towards conflict-driven discourse as a means for doing theology. Indeed, the disciples' arguments alone did not produce a better understanding of God's Kingdom, driven as they were by their own ambitions, anxiety and mistaken theological starting-points

Finally, the childs of history, and that of Matthew 18, challenge our understanding and practice of mission. Just as we need to be self-conscious and self-critical of our conceptions of child, God and God's Kingdom, so the many ways mission has been conceived, and the many ways it has treated and at times mistreated the child (and others) in the process, is cause to examine our missiological presuppositions as well. What is mission? Whose task is it (ours, the church's, or God's)? What ethical constraints does the gospel inherently place on those who would proclaim it? What is mission's goal?

In our mission practice the many childs and the child of Matthew 18 confront tendencies to power, control, autonomy, 'success' and 'impact'. The childs of history have too frequently been objectified, instrumentalised, abstracted or even overlooked in ecclesiological enterprise distracted by such concerns. Indeed, as the disciples postured for position, power and pre-eminence, it was the insignificant child given greatest place by Jesus that highlighted the illegitimacy of these values in their witness to God's reign. Similarly, when our strategies, structures and attitudes, like those of the disciples, are at odds with the nature of God and therefore his reign, it is possible we too may be excluded from acting as witnesses.[87] The child next next to Jesus humbly confronts models of mission in which there are 'right- and left-hand men', silently testifying instead that Jesus' mission is marked by little-ness, least-ness, easy-to-overlook-ness, welcome and blessing as the standards of operation. Theological reflection informed by the many and the one child can help mission avoid being in effect just another secular undertaking, albeit in the name of God; and repeating the mistakes of crusades which betrayed the very cross they bore – the Cross of the

---

(Matthew 18:1-3; cf. Mark 9:33-37). Rather, it took Jesus' disturbing their thinking by placing the child in their midst, to quieten and correct it. It is noteworthy too, that in this context of dispute he exhorts his disciples to welcome the lowly one (and in so doing, to welcome Jesus himself). The sacrificing of various historical childs upon altars of theology forged amid inhospitable polemics compels us to ask whether there is a more hospitable way of furthering theological discourse. This need not mean facile agreement; it does behove a recognition of the humanity of the other person or party – in fact, of Jesus represented in the other – and a concern not just for being right, but for being in *right relationship*. The many childs and the one in this way remind us that it is not just the content but the process of doing theology matters. Perhaps the product of theology done from the lowly place may itself prove to be truly great in the Kingdom of God?

[87] In particular, this may prompt us to consider the legitimacy of the corporatisation of mission, of building churches and mission bodies on business models from contemporary capitalist enterprise, with CEOs, organisational hierarchies, marketing strategies, as well as secular frameworks of thinking which, for example, aim to foster economic development while potentially ignoring other aspects of human flourishing. For a valuable further reflection along these lines, see Sam and Rosalee Ewell's chapter in this volume.

Crucified One, who came not to lord it over others, but to welcome, serve and, in dying, give life.

To our settled assumptions about mission, too, the many childs of history, like the child of Matthew 18, may be the grain of sand, which in aggravating the oyster produces something of value in our theology and praxis.

Conclusion – the Many Childs and the One

Passing on faith to future generations, in and beyond the existing bounds of the church, has been a vocation and necessary task of the Christian church since its earliest decades. How the church today and tomorrow should understand the child and participate together with him and her in God's outreaching and indrawing through Son and Spirit is an open question – but one worthy of historically informed, theologically reflective and self-consciously critical consideration. To this ongoing process, the many childs of history, those around us, and the unnamed child of Matthew 18, can provide potentially constructive questions, if we welcome them to do so. As we do, we may just come to realise that it is us, and our ostensibly self-evident conceptions of child, God and mission which, despite usually being uncritically idealised as innocent and pure, are in fact vulnerable and suffering – even sinful – and certainly still under construction. In the situated context of God's family, our conceptions of theology, mission and child may indeed be in need of continual conversion, of returning again to the beginning, and being born again to new understandings, and new possibilities.

That is, of becoming again like a child.

CHRISTIAN MISSION: CONTEMPORARY THEOLOGY AND PRACTISE WITH REFERENCE TO CHILDREN

Mark Oxbrow

On a warm summer afternoon in 2013 I found myself witnessing the baptism of two children in a small village in Albania. As the priest prayed for them and submerged these ten-year-olds in great plastic buckets, they were surrounded by forty other excited young people and parents, all anxious to confess their faith in a living God. Shortly before the baptism, the priest who had taught these families to follow Christ told me privately that he had lived most of his life 'knowing that God was dead'. As I stood and prayed for these two young lives, I recalled a picture I had been sent earlier that year, a picture of very similar plastic buckets in a prison in Nepal – prisoners being baptised in a country where two decades previously anyone conducting a baptism could face imprisonment. Through the waters of baptism, day by day, in the most unexpected corners of our world, lives young and old are being transformed and shaped by the love of God.

I was in Albania in September 2013, not primarily to witness this baptism, but to facilitate a consultation on 'The mission of God'[1] which brought together several Orthodox (Oriental and Eastern) patriarchs, archbishops and theologians; senior representatives of the World Evangelical Alliance, the Lausanne Movement, and the World Council of Churches; and evangelical theologians and mission practitioners from twenty different countries. After a particularly intense discussion on proselytism, one North American evangelical said to me over coffee, 'I am beginning to think that if I had been born in Greece, I would have been sitting here this morning as an Orthodox believer struggling to understand evangelical missionary zeal, rather than the other way round.' Our birth circumstances, our upbringing within a particular faith community, and the history of each Christian tradition, all deeply affect how we understand the mission of God today.

When, in Matthew 18:2, Jesus calls a child to stand and confront the religious ambitions of his disciples, he does so within the particular context of Judaic election theology. The scandal of his action was that Jesus hereby declares this (perhaps even female) child, quite apart from its family, elect in the Kingdom of God – not only elect but the pattern for election! Today, we too must stand ready to have our theology, our understanding of the

---

[1] See www.loimission.net

mission of God, challenged by those who are the children of other Christian traditions. For this reason, we begin by looking briefly at contemporary mission theology within four different strands of our Christian tradition, and then examine how these might come together and influence our mission praxis.

Mission as the Nature of God

The first strand in our contemporary understanding of mission, God's redemptive act towards creation, relates to the nature of God, the triune God of all Christian theology. As three persons in eternal community (and here I deliberately skip over centuries of debate about the terms we use to describe the divine three-in-one), it is of the very nature of God to reach out, to express love, to build relationship, to desire to include, to encompass in glory. Because God loves, God is by nature missionary. The Orthodox mission theologian, Archbishop Anastasios Yannoulatos, goes on to say, 'Since the Christian mission is incorporated into God's mission, the final goal of our mission surely cannot be different from his. And this purpose, as the Bible (especially Ephesians and Colossians) makes clear, is the "recapitulation" (*anakephalaiosis*) of the universe in Christ and our participation in the divine glory, the eternal, final glory of God.'[2]

Following this dynamic, most contemporary Orthodox mission theology flows out of our understanding (but highly limited comprehension) of the inner life of the Trinity. As we reflect on the Father's sending of the Son, we see more clearly why *we* are sent; as we meditate on the Son's cry of dereliction, 'Father why have you forsaken me?'[3] we glimpse the deep pain of humanity's alienation – from the Creator, creation, our fellow human beings and innermost self; and as we see the Spirit descending upon the Son, we know in whose power we must step out in mission.

The 'child placed in the midst'[4] reminds us by her very presence of what we have lost. The child, once conjoined with her mother by the umbilical cord, and for so much longer self-identifying herself as just one part of a great whole, the family,[5] stands in contradistinction to the individualisation and alienation of adulthood. In God there is no 'being' alone – the child knows that physically, psychologically and spiritually. As God is three persons in one 'being', so the child experiences, and calls us, as adults, to

---

[2] A. Yannoulatos, *The Purpose and Motive of Mission from an Orthodox Theological Point of View*, in *Porefthendos* 9 (1967), 2.

[3] Matthew 27:46.

[4] Matthew 18:2.

[5] In most Western cultures a child will not use the word 'I' until the age of two, and in some non-Western cultures this usage is delayed even further as the child understands himself to be totally part of the family. A child will only understand himself to be a totally autonomous individual much later in life, a process that in some cultures is encouraged by appropriate (or inappropriate) 'rites of passage'.

rediscover life in community, and that we can only fully 'be' in and with others, and ultimately in and with God.

Seeing mission birthed in the internal life of the Trinity gives a certain 'direction' to all Orthodox mission. There is no sense of 'taking God' to the unreached but rather an invitation to a 'journey of return' which we undertake together, prodigals returning together to the Father, drawn by his glory, his love.

Mission as the Nature of the Church

Although none of the four strands is restricted to a particular tradition or denomination, the second is particularly associated with the Roman Catholic Church, post-Vatican II. In this view, the church exists for mission and mission exists for the church. In contemporary Roman Catholic thought, according to Bevans and Schroeder, 'Mission is not only the "mother of theology" … Mission might also be called the "mother of the church," the great task believers have been given that binds them together, provides them with nourishment, focuses their energies, heals their sinfulness and provides them with challenges and vision.'[6] As this pre-eminence of mission as the guiding principle of theological debate becomes more widely acknowledged, other authors have gone on to speak of mission as the life-blood of the church.

For those who adopt this particular approach to mission, the Christian nurture of children has been highly significant, hence their heavy investment in education. Children are to be seen as full members of the community of faith (reflected in the practice of infant baptism) and take their place in witnessing to that faith alongside their parents and elders.

This understanding of mission has implications both for missiology and ecclesiology. In the first case, it focuses the missional endeavour on the ultimate gathering of God's people, not just in a human institution with its *curia* in Rome, but in the heavenly gathering from every nation, tribe, and tongue that stands before the throne of God.[7] Salvation gains a communal quality: it is within the community of the faithful that we experience the love and redemption of God. There are also implications for ecclesiology: what we understand the church to be. If the very nature and purpose of the church is mission, then its liturgy, its shared life, its ecclesial structures must all be shaped for mission. The church must be 'world-facing' and equipped to build communities of redemption. Bevans and Schroeder go on to say, 'If to be church is to be in mission, to be in mission is to be responsive to the demands of the gospel in particular contexts, to be continually "reinventing" itself as it struggles with and approaches new

---

[6] S.B. Bevans and R.P. Schroeder, *Constants in Context: A Theology of Mission for Today* (New York: Orbis, 2004), 11.

[7] Revelation 7:9.

situations, new peoples, new cultures, and new questions.'[8] What, for example, is the gospel for a Muslim girl whose religious identity, but perhaps not her faith, lies beyond her own capacity to determine?

Tobias was the nine-year-old son of a missionary couple working in a majority Buddhist community. He attended the local school and had many friends there. One Sunday morning he announced to his mother, "We have to collect Farid on the way to church." "But isn't Farid a Buddhist?" was his mother's natural response. "Oh, that's OK, he's bringing his own incense with him and some rice to give to Jesus," replied Tobias. And so it happened: Farid brought rice and burning incense to place before the picture of Jesus, and a missional friendship continued quite naturally – while Tobias' mother struggled to explain to her Christian friends what on earth was going on!

Interestingly, this second understanding of mission, which closely links mission and church, can also be seen amongst some of the most radical contemporary Christian communities. I refer to the increasing number of communities of Jesus-followers (who sometimes choose not to be known as Christians because of the Western associations of that name) emerging within Islamic, Hindu and Buddhist communities. As gathered (ecclesial) communities following in The Way of Jesus,[9] they self-define as a witnessing (missional) community in what is often a hostile environment.

Mission as the Nature of Human Fulfilment

'Mission ... must be an every-member mission, from everywhere to everywhere, involving every aspect of life in a rapidly changing world of many cultures now interacting and overlapping ... Local congregations are called to be places of hope, providing spaces of safety and trust wherein different peoples can be embraced and affirmed.'[10] So runs the Conference Message from the Conference on World Mission Evangelism (CWME) in Brazil in 1996. This, the third, strand of mission thinking relates primarily to the human condition. We live in a world of division, exploitation, poverty and greed, a world without hope, and mission is about restoring hope, granting dignity, guaranteeing justice, and seeing 'Thy will be done on earth as it is in heaven'.[11] At the risk of over-generalising, I would suggest that this is the strand most often encountered today within Protestant churches.

Under the slogan 'Justice, Peace and the Integrity of Creation' (JPIC), many such Christians seek to live lives that reflect the life of Christ and

---

[8] Bevans and Schroeder, *Constants*, 31.
[9] Acts 9:2.
[10] *CWME Conference Message*, in *International Review of Mission*, 86:340-41 (January-April 1997), 7-11.
[11] The title of the previous CWME in San Antonio in 1989 was 'Your will be done – Mission in Christ's Way'.

minister to those in need in a Christ-like way. In practical terms, this has led to the emergence of mission programmes to address everything from poverty to creation care, and the exploitation of child labour to post-genocide counselling. For a while, a gulf appeared to be developing between Christian 'social action' and 'mission', with exponents on both sides making an exclusive claim on the term mission, respectively rejecting 'evangelism' (or 'proselytism') or, conversely, 'social ministries', as illegitimate aspects of mission. In recent years, however, exponents of 'holistic' or 'integral mission'[12] have sought to bring these different aspects back together in ways that mutually enhance each other.

In Kampala, Uganda, a network of Christian children have used their mobile studio to record more that fifty short videos, songs and skits about the problems they face and what they think can be done about them.[13] This is part of a global movement of child advocates – children addressing the missional needs of their community. In some cases, this goes beyond advocacy to children themselves establishing small actions or projects to bring changes in their neighbourhood which speak of the in-breaking of the reign of God.[14]

The motivating force behind this stand of mission ideology is this Biblical vision of the breaking into human history of the promised reign (or Kingdom) of God,[15] and the promise of Jesus that 'I come that they may have life, and have it abundantly'.[16]

The rights of the child and the provision of appropriate relationships, environment and security for childhood development, physically, mentally and spiritually, have been a significant part of this missional concern to see the reign of God in our world. Holistic child development programmes[17] have come to be seen as crucial for the transformation of whole communities in line with the reign of God among his people.

Mission as the Nature of Discipleship

Evangelical – and particularly pentecostal – Christians, while embracing all three of the above strands of mission ideology, will normally place more

---

[12] See, for example, T. Yamamori and C.R. Padilla, *The Local Church, Agent of Transformation: An Ecclesiology for Integral Mission* (Buenos Aires: Kairos, 2004).

[13] For more information, see http://blog.viva.org/index.php/2012/12/17/ugandan-children-speak/ (accessed 8 October 2013).

[14] There are four such stories in B. Budijanto (ed), *Emerging Missions Movements: Voices of Asia* (Colorado Springs, CO: Compassion, 2010), 43-47.

[15] See G.E Ladd, *The Presence of the Future: The Eschatology of Biblical Realism* (London: SPCK, 1974).

[16] John 10:10.

[17] See Dan Brewster, *Future Impact: Connecting Child, Church and Mission* (Colorado Springs, CO: Compassion 2010).

emphasis on the response of the individual, first to the gospel itself and then to the call to mission. Mission is seen as a primary constituent of individual discipleship. It is a matter of obedience and gratitude, as well as a matter of urgency for those who remain outside the community of the 'saved'. In his case study of the growth of Korean missionary movements, Paul Hang-Sik Cho[18] has shown how dispensational pre-millennialism, imported from the USA, has shaped the mission understanding of the Korean church, giving it a characteristic urgency for the 'salvation of souls' but scant concern for ecological, or even justice, issues.

This fourth strand of mission ideology has helped to shape much of the mission strategy, if not the theology, of a very large segment of contemporary mission movements. From the 1910 Edinburgh Missionary Conference onwards, it has led to a concern for 'the evangelisation of the world in this generation'[19] – a phrase sometimes linked to the imminent (or even hastening of the) return of Christ, but also understood as the need for each generation to hear the gospel afresh in its own time. More recently we have seen much effort going into researching 'unreached people groups', and the development of strategies to reach these people with the gospel, scriptures, and initiatives such as The Jesus Film. Allied with this strategic focus has been the use of the concept of the 10-40 Window (the regions of the world where most unreached people live), and more recently the '4/14 Window' (focusing on the need to engage missionally with children aged roughly between 4 and 14).[20]

In an age when plans and strategies for world evangelisation multiply exponentially,[21] our 'child in the midst' again questions our methodologies. While billions of Christian dollars, and countless hours, are spent on these new strategies, most people come to a living faith in Christ as a result of the simple words and actions of friends and neighbours. The church gives children very few resources (money, books, programmes) to facilitate them in mission, and yet they are highly resourceful, using not much more than

---

[18] P. H.-S. Cho, *Eschatology and Ecology: Experiences of the Korean Church* (Oxford: Regnum, 2010).

[19] The watchword of the late nineteenth-century Student Volunteer Movement, famously adopted by Dr John Mott for the 1910 Edinburgh Missionary Conference. See Mott, *The Evangelisation of the World in This Generation* (New York: Student Volunteer Movement for Foreign Missions, 1900).

[20] Editor's note: Some of the questions arising around the so-called '4/14 Window' shaped the discussions that led to this book and its use of the theology-mission-child 'Triangle' motif. Several scholars have noted that this approach to mission with children needs more rigorous theological discussion; the editors support that view.

[21] Todd Johnson and Peter Crossing suggest that by 2013 there had been 2,200 plans for world evangelisation compared with only 250 up to 1900. See Todd Johnson and Peter F. Crossing, 'Christianity 2013: Renewalists and Faith and Migration', in *IBMR* 37:1 (January 2013), 33.

their lives and the natural desire to share that which is good, to bring glory to God.

One positive aspect of this strand of mission ideology, however, has been the understanding that mission is the responsibility and privilege of every Christian. No longer is mission seen as the task of priests, religious orders or 'professional' missionaries, but rather the vocation of every baptised Christian. The Baptist Union of Great Britain, for example, suggests that: 'Baptism as a sacrament of mission for being united to Christ involves witnessing to the faith in the world... in such witness our unity is discovered. The unity of the Spirit is known in mission activity, and the wholeness of the baptismal understanding of unity requires the continued participation in mission.'[22]

With this individual focus on mission, children cannot be regarded as 'future church' or as some sort of appendage to Christian adults, but acquire full rights to both hear and embrace the gospel on their own terms and to become witnesses themselves to the transforming power of God in Christ Jesus.

Four Strands are Stronger than One

The weaving together of different strands of mission thinking can also be found in several contemporary authors from different traditions. Chris Wright in his *The Mission of God* rehabilitates within the evangelical community the *missio Dei* thinking which had been much earlier adopted by Roman Catholics and many in the broader Protestant tradition,[23] while Timothy Tennent returns to an Orthodox Christian heritage to develop his powerful Trinitarian missiology for a more conservative evangelical community.[24] In the other direction, the Roman Catholics Stephen Bevans and Roger Schroeder draw extensively on the work of evangelicals such as David Bosch and Stephen Neill,[25] while the Orthodox missiologist Thomas Hopko encourages those within his own tradition to appreciate the missionary expertise of many evangelical movements.[26]

At the beginning of this chapter there was a description of a gathering of Orthodox, Protestant and evangelical (but sadly no Roman Catholic) Christians in Albania to consider the 'Mission of God'. At that consultation, Dr Darrell Jackson pointed to five theological 'points of

---

[22] R. Hayden (ed), *Baptist Union Documents 1948-1977* (London: Baptist Historical Society, 1980), 85.

[23] C.J.H. Wright, *The Mission of God: Unlocking the Bible's Grand Narrative* (Grand Rapids, MI: IVP Academic, 2006).

[24] T.C. Tennent, *Invitation to World Missions: A Trinitarian Missiology for the Twenty-First Century* (Grand Rapids, MI: Kregel Academic, 2010).

[25] See Bevans and Schroeder, *Constants in Context*.

[26] T. Hopko, *Speaking the Truth in Love: Education, Mission and Witness in Contemporary Orthodoxy* (Yonkers, NY: St Vladimir's Seminary Press, 2004).

intersection' for evangelical and Orthodox missiologists. He highlighted (a) the centring of mission in the love of God and love of neighbour, (b) the return to a robust Trinitarian missiology, (c) the acknowledgement of the priority of the *missio Dei* (God's mission), (d) the strengthened understanding of the role of the church in mission, and (e) our joint concern for creation care, the mission to the whole cosmos.[27] The consultation as a whole reflected this coming together of different strands of understanding of mission, its theology and praxis, as missiologists and mission practitioners draw on the strengths of each other's traditions.

Contemporary Mission Practice
(With Particular Reference to Children)

We now turn our attention from the theology that underpins mission to the ways in which this missiology finds expression within the life of our churches and Christian communities today. In the remainder of this chapter we will not make distinctions between the four strands of thinking we have considered above, which are increasingly interwoven in day-to-day mission.

Witness

As we have already noted, the clear focus of the Edinburgh Missionary Conference of 1910 was world 'evangelisation'. It is therefore significant that when 300 mission leaders returned to Edinburgh a century later, they met under the banner 'Witnessing to Christ Today'. In his closing address at the Edinburgh 2010 gathering, Archbishop John Sentamu chose to quote from Bishop John V. Taylor's book *The Go-Between God*, where Taylor writes:

> The chief actor in the historic mission of the Christian Church is the Holy Spirit. He is the director of the whole enterprise. The mission consists of the things that he is doing in the world. In a special way it consists of the light that he is focussing upon Jesus Christ. This fact, so patent to Christians in the first century, is largely forgotten in our own. So we have lost our nerve and our sense of direction and have turned the divine initiative into a human enterprise. 'It all depends on me' is an attitude that is bedevilling both the practice and the theology of our mission in these days.[28]

Forty years ahead of the 2010 Edinburgh Conference, Taylor was signalling the need to see ourselves less as the instigators, the planners, the

---

[27] D. Jackson "'Love of God, Love of Neighbour": Is This Really an Evangelical Missiology?' (2013). Paper awaiting publication.

[28] John V. Taylor, *The Go-Between God: The Holy Spirit and the Christian Mission* (London: SCM Press, 1972), 3-4.

activists of mission, and more as witnesses to the 'power of God at work in His world, through His Son, by His Spirit'.[29]

Through the dark days of Communism in the Soviet Union, China and Eastern Europe, under the despotic rule of Idi Amin, and in the restrictive contexts of Myanmar and Iran, it has often been impossible to evangelise, even to hold public worship, yet 'God did not leave himself without witnesses'.[30] Above all the lives of the martyrs bear witness to the resurrection love of God, and beside these, in Russian villages grandmothers secretly taught the faith to their grandchildren, in workplace canteens in China men whispered the news of God's love to their friends, and in Iran students watch with interest the silent witness of their Christian classmates.

Witness is powerful because it points to another. But witness is also very demanding. It demands integrity and a life beyond reproach. Sadly, the witness of many Christians today points not to the glory of Christ but to the frailty and depravity of humanity. To adopt a witness approach to mission, rather than an evangelistic programme, is highly demanding but in the end more truly corresponds to the mission of God. Whether at home or in church, children and young people are particularly adept at spotting the difference between a well-packaged religious programme and a genuinely lived faith. When the witness is true and the life of the One to whom the witness points is reflected in the life of the witnesses themselves, only then will a new generation of disciples find their way to the risen Christ.

Ishel was the only member of her class that went to the tiny Baptist church in her town. Her teacher took special pleasure in ridiculing her faith whilst the other children laughed. On the day the teacher crashed his motorbike on the ice outside the school gate, it was Ishel who rushed over and took off her school scarf to bind up a gushing wound. Nothing was said. The ambulance took the teacher to hospital and Ishel went to school. Months later three of the girls in school asked Ishel if they could go to church with her. Now six of them meet to read the Bible at Tuesday lunch break; it was the same teacher who persuaded the school principal to give them a room to meet in.[31]

It is a glorious aspect of the mission of the church today that in every nation on earth there are children, women and men, who daily seek to live

---

[29] It is worth noting here that in 2007 the missiologist David Hesselgrave was deeply critical of Edinburgh 1910 and its focus on human enterprise, saying, 'No other missionary gathering impacted twentieth century missions as did the World Missionary Conference held in Edinburgh, Scotland, in 1910. No single error was as significant as the 'Edinburgh' error.' See D.J. Hesselgrave, 'Will We Correct the Edinburgh Error? Future Mission in Historical Perspective', in *Southwestern Journal of Theology*, 49 (2007), 121.

[30] Acts 14:17.

[31] Name changed. This story is taken from a private email to the author sent in 2011 from a church leader in Kazakhstan.

as witnesses to Jesus Christ – in their families and households, their workplace, their schools and colleges, and in the far corners of our hurting world. In their generosity with time, with a listening ear, binding up wounds, fighting injustice, speaking truth, building peace, and in so many other ways, their lives point to Another whose name they are not afraid to own.

Evangelism

So where does all this leave evangelism? Is evangelism to be equated with proselytism and psychological manipulation, and rejected as unethical? To do so would be highly unbiblical. There are very clear biblical imperatives to 'speak' the Name of Jesus, to 'preach' the Good News, to 'proclaim' liberty to the captives, to 'announce' the year of God's favour. The question for us today is not whether we evangelise but *how* we evangelise. Particular care, of course, needs to be taken when children or vulnerable adults are involved, either as practitioners or recipients, but that should not discourage us from doing the hard work of discovering appropriate and safe ways of engaging evangelistically with, and being evangelistically engaged by, children and vulnerable adults.

In every context the church needs to ask itself how those who do not yet know Christ are most likely to hear and respond. The traditional evangelistic rally continues to be effective in some contexts, whereas in others it draws only the 'four times already' converted. The Jesus Film, first released in 1979, is estimated to have been watched by over one billion people, with organisers claiming at least 200 million viewers indicating decisions to accept Christ as their personal Saviour and Lord.[32] In some parts of the world, radio and TV broadcasts of Christian material provide a very effective platform for the sharing of the gospel with those who have little opportunity of personal contact with Christians. Probably more significant than all of these is the distribution and use of Christian scriptures,[33] which are increasingly being used in innovative ways to enable both readers and oral learners to gain access to the Word of God.

Most evangelism, however, is not programmatic. It is personal, relational, low-key and taking place every moment of the day in myriad homes, shops, offices, bars, streets and trains as very ordinary Christians 'give account of the hope that is within them',[34] speaking of Jesus, his love, and the joy that they have found in his presence. Many – perhaps most –

---

[32] www.jesusfilm.org/aboutus/history (accessed 14 September 2013).

[33] At the offices of the Amity Press is China they proudly display the 100 millionth Bible to roll off their press in 2012, just twenty-four years after the press's foundation in 1988. China is now the world's largest producer of Bibles with the Amity Press alone having a capacity of 18 million Bibles a year.

[34] 1 Peter 3:15.

Christian evangelists are women, unpaid, untrained and, sadly, often unrecognised by their church.

But what of the ethics of evangelism? To engage in evangelism which is exploitative, manipulative or destructive of human dignity is obviously counter-productive because it fails to point to the Christ that it seeks to proclaim. This, however, does not mean that such evangelism does not exist. Sadly, there are those who seek to use evangelism for self-glorification and the acquisition of wealth and status, and there are those whose human dignity has been violated by evangelistic activities. But such abuses do not negate the validity of genuine Christian evangelism. In recent years much work has been done in this area and there are now very useful guidelines on ethical evangelism.[35]

Integral Mission

A feature of Christian mission during the second half of the twentieth century was the rise of Christian agencies specialising in international relief, development and advocacy.[36] Christians have always, of course, been involved in caring for refugees, providing education and medical services, advocating for those who are abused or neglected, and much more; but in the past, at least internationally, these activities had normally been closely integrated with the discipling and pastoral ministries of the churches. With the rise of materialism in the 'Christian West' and a newly awakened consciousness of the darker side of colonialism, leading to a weakening of nerve within many churches for evangelising those of another religion or culture, many Christians began to feel much more comfortable about feeding the poor than they did about sharing the gospel. This trend was particularly noted in North America (where the Vietnam war alerted many Americans to poverty in the wider world) and Britain (where the ending of empire led to a reinterpretation of history which was not always positive for Christian mission).[37] Churchgoers in those countries were often more likely

---

[35] See, for example, E. Thiessen *The Ethics of Evangelism: A Philosophical Defence of Ethical Proselytising and Persuasion* (London: Paternoster, 2011).

[36] There were much earlier examples of such agencies focused on the 'social' needs of a community or on advocacy, but it was not until after World War II that this division of labour became pronounced. For example, although the Shaftesbury Society, and the parliamentary work of William Wilberforce to end slavery, were begun in the late eighteenth century, they were very closely linked with mission movements such as the Church Mission Society (known then as the Society for Missions to Africa and the East) and the British & Foreign Bible Society, their respective founders meeting regularly through the 'Clapham Sect'. See also the chapter by D.J. Konz in this volume.

[37] See, for example, J.A. Cogswell, 'Relief and Development: Challenges to Mission Today', in *IBMR*, 11:2 (April 1987), 72-76.

to give funds to dig wells or vaccinate children than they were to train clergy, distribute Bibles or support an evangelist.

This false dichotomy between relief, development and advocacy on the one side, and evangelism, discipleship and pastoral ministries on the other, continues to plague Christian mission which is funded or directed from the global North.[38] On the whole, however, African, Asian, and Latin American churches continue to have a more holistic view of mission.

The move back towards a more integrated understanding of mission probably began with the World Evangelical Alliance *Grand Rapids Statement* of 1982 and the subsequent *Wheaton Statement* of 1983, which provided, within the evangelical community, the rationale for evangelical aid and development ministries. In 1984 Dr John Stott expressed his view that the Grand Rapids Statement had paved the way for a recovery of a balanced view of mission, which encompassed the transformation of communities and social conditions as well as the spiritual life of individuals.[39] A few years later a number of leaders within Christian development movements saw the need to recover their commitment to addressing the spiritual realities of the communities with which they were working and began to use terms such as 'integral' or 'holistic' of mission. Two of the key leaders in this movement were Bryant Myers, then of World Vision, whose book *Walking with the Poor: Principles of Transformational Development*[40] has influenced many, and the Latin American theologian René Padilla, who founded the Kairos Community in Buenos Aires, Argentina.[41] Padilla went on to become the President of the Micah Network for Integral Mission,[42] established in 2000.

For those working with children and young people, this recovery of an holistic understanding of mission is mirrored in the growth of interest in 'Holistic Child Development'[43] as a way of working with children to enable them to develop every aspect of their humanity and to contribute at each

---

[38] One small example of this occurred in the Anglican Communion as late as 2008 when, at the end of that year's Lambeth Conference, the worldwide gathering of bishops called for two new international instruments, an Alliance for Relief, Development and Advocacy, and an Initiative for Evangelism and Church Growth, with little thought about how the two might relate to each other (although they were both formally part of the Communion's Mission Department).

[39] John Stott, 'Ten Years Later: the Lausanne Covenant', in E.R. Dayton and S. Wilson (eds), *The Future of World Evangelisation: Unreached Peoples '84* (Monrovia, CA: MARC, 1984), 65-70.

[40] B.L. Myers, *Walking with the Poor: Principles and Practices of Transformational Development* (Grand Rapids, MI: Orbis Books, 1999).

[41] Most of Padilla's books are available only in Spanish but see, for example, T. Yamamori and C.R. Padilla, *The Local Church, Agent of Transformation: An Ecclesiology for Integral Mission* (Buenos Aires: Kairos, 2004).

[42] www.micahnetwork.org (accessed 20 September 2013).

[43] See Keith J. White, *Introducing Child Theology: Theological Foundations for Holistic Child Development* (Colorado Springs, CO: Compassion, 2010).

stage of their development to the community of which they are a part. If we deny children a place in mission (as in the church), we will distort the image of God we are called to reflect in our world. God comes to us as much as a child as he comes as an adult, as much woman as he does man, as much Kenyan as he does as Canadian. To engage in mission as the Body of Christ without the child (or the Canadian) is to walk with one leg or to see with one eye. If our mission, or witness to the transforming power of the reign of God, is characterised as 'adult' or 'childless' or even 'child deprecating', then our witness will be flawed and it will be no surprise if the church in which we then find ourselves is limited and emaciated by its adultness.

Missionaries

It is a mistake, of course, to think that missionaries have always been the central plank of Christian mission. Before the eighteenth century the concept of a person being a missionary hardly existed. A few of the first-century Christian apologists were deliberately sent to other communities and cultures by their mother church, but for the next seventeen centuries most 'gospel carriers' were making journeys for other reasons – to trade,[44] to flee persecution,[45] war or famine, or to seek a better life. Some, but not all, monastic communities did send out wandering monks, and there were always individuals whom God raised up to take the gospel to foreign lands; however, the concept with which we are now so familiar, of a Christian sent and supported by his or her church or a mission agency, to act as a full-time missionary in another culture for many years, is relatively modern.

I rehearse this history because a realisation that the gospel reached so many parts of the world[46] without the aid of full-time, trained, 'professional' missionaries can open us up to the possibility that things might also be different in the future. In fact, things are already changing.[47]

As the churches of the global South grow and those in Europe and North America decline, the average Christian (if it makes sense to speak in such terms) is now a poor young mother from Africa. She may be called into cross-cultural mission but she is very unlikely to have a church or agency

---

[44] In the fifth to ninth centuries the gospel was carried and churches established all the way from the Middle East, through Central Asia to China itself by Nestorian traders, and in later centuries other traders were responsible for taking the gospel across northern Europe.

[45] Saint Nina, the evangelist and founder of the church in Georgia, arrived in that country fleeing from the persecutions of King Tiridates of Armenia.

[46] With the possible exception of sub-Saharan Africa.

[47] One of the first people to document the rise of global South missionaries and the new ways in which missionaries were being sent was Larry Pate; see *From Every People: A Handbook of Two-Thirds World Missions with Directory/Histories/Analysis* (Monrovia, CA: MARC, 1989).

behind her able to pay her airfare, let alone a monthly stipend. However, thousands of such young women (and men) are already in mission across the world. How? They have gone to the Gulf States as housemaids, to India as students, to Malaysia as migrant workers, while some have gone to Kenya as refugees or Canada as asylum seekers. In the Philippines the churches became aware that so many of their members were working overseas, sometimes in contexts where it would be impossible to send a 'missionary', that they now offer specific training for such migrant workers, both before they go and online whilst they are overseas.

Other Christians are deliberately training as 'tentmakers' after the pattern of St Paul,[48] and looking for places where they can work and gain opportunities both to serve the local community and share the gospel. The rise of the *Business as Mission* movement takes this concept one stage further with the 'quadruple bottom-line' principle, Christian entrepreneurs establishing businesses in local communities that make a profit; provide employment and improve social conditions for workers; protect or even enhance the environment; and bring a spiritual benefit to workers and others in the community.[49]

As we free ourselves from a restrictive understanding of who can be a missionary, we not only create space within the mission of God for young women from Ethiopia and poor workers from Bangladesh, but also for children. No longer are children restricted to sharing the gospel cross-culturally as the children of missionaries, now they have every capacity to be carriers of the good news of Jesus in their own right. I write as someone who fifty years ago was 'evangelised' by a young Ethiopian, my pen-friend, but today the opportunities are so much greater. As a fourteen-year-old, Gebriel handwrote letters to share his new-found faith in Jesus with a boy he thought he would never meet in a country he knew very little about. He waited months for my replies, only to read of my pets and holidays – nothing of faith. But he kept writing until one day I was able to write back and tell him I, too, had met Jesus. Today, Christian teachers and Christian children have children from many different cultures right there with them in their classrooms; they go on school visits; they meet (safely, we hope) people from other cultures on the Internet. The question for our churches is: How we are resourcing our children to help them to be effective witnesses to Christ, 'missionaries', in all these contexts?

---

[48] See J. Lewis, *Working Your Way to the Nations: A Guide to Effective Tentmaking* (Wheaton, IL: IVP, 1996).
[49] See T. Steffen and M. Barnett (eds), 'Business as Mission: From Impoverished to Empowered', in *Journal of Evangelical Missiological Society* (Pasadena, CA: William Carey Library, 2006).

Cosmic Mission

I remember that, as a child, when I was asked to put my address on an envelope at school I once wrote, '33 Cowper Street, Ipswich, Suffolk, United Kingdom, The World, The Solar System, The Universe.' Did I really see myself as a citizen of the universe? Whether I did or not, I am, and more significantly, as a child of the God of the cosmos, I am a steward of that universe. Sometimes we need to be reminded by children, or our own childhood selves, of these things.

Alongside the reintegration of 'social ministry' and 'evangelism' to which we have made reference, recent decades have seen churches taking much more interest in the natural environment and its protection. Creation Care, to which children are often more highly tuned than adults, is increasingly being seen as an essential aspect of mission, and churches are engaging in programmes which link gospel proclamation with environmental care.[50] The A Rocha[51] and Care for Creation[52] movements are equipping churches in this area, and together supported a major Lausanne Movement consultation in Jamaica in 2012.[53]

The cosmos does not just encompass the physical environment in which we live; it is also about the intellectual environment, the legal structures, the scientific community, the world of the arts, and much more. If we are to participate fully in the *missio Dei Trinitatis*, then we will share God's concern for the redemption of these aspects of the cosmos also. Christian scientists who struggle to ensure that new discoveries are used ethically for the enhancement of humanity and not its destruction; Christian artists who work to create music, paintings, drama and dance that contribute to human thriving and the restoration of the image of God in broken individuals; and Christian lawyers who seek to make good law which provides security and the strengthening of communities which reflect the community we see in the Trinity itself – all of these and many more are involved in the Christian mission. The mother who nurtures her child in the faith, and the child who shows Christian love to a classmate, similarly share in God's mission. The challenge for our churches is whether they are going to recognise, resource and bless each of these witnesses to Christ – not forgetting their pastors, missionaries and evangelists.

Earlier in this volume, Haddon Wilmer has written of The Triangle, which connects Theology (knowledge and our speaking of God), Mission and Child in a particular way that links three points of reference in time and

---

[50] One of the early Christian writers to challenge Christians about the care of creation was Sean McDonagh, *To Care for the Earth: A Call to a New Theology* (London: Geoffrey Chapman, 1986). This was followed a few years later by Vincent Donovan (better known for his *Christianity Rediscovered*) in his *The Church in the Midst of Creation* (London: SCM Press, 1991).

[51] See www.arocha.org (accessed 20 September 2013).

[52] See www.careofcreation.net (accessed 20 September 2013).

[53] See www.lausanne.org/creationcare (accessed 20 September 2013).

space. Just as our forebears identified and mapped certain combinations, shapes or constellations of stars as being of greater importance than others (known as the Zodiac), so today we can identify this Triangle of Theology, Mission and Child as an important sign for our human destiny. In our understanding of mission and in our missional practice we have, in recent decades, begun to take more seriously the need to do good theology if we are to do good mission. The challenge now is to understand that we can only do good theology if we are prepared to give space and honour to the theology of the child, and we can only do good mission when that mission reaches out to and invites into itself the child in our midst.[54]

---

[54] Luke 9:47-48.

PART THREE

THREATS AND CHALLENGES

THE MISSION OF CHRIST IN LUKE 4:18-19, HIV/AIDS AND ABUSE OF THE GIRL CHILD IN THE CONTEXT OF BOTSWANA

Rosinah Gabaitse

Introduction

In this chapter I seek to engage in a theological and sociological analysis of the plight of orphan girl children in the midst of the HIV pandemic in Botswana. Patriarchy is a political-social system and ideology that insists on male dominance and superiority, and female subordination. It is a fundamentally flawed system that reflects the fallen nature of human communities, as it imposes suffering on women and children. It does not reflect God's will for how human beings ought to relate in and through mutuality and interdependence. Further, it also contradicts the heart of Christ's mission as recorded in Luke 4:18-19: that of setting children, women and men free from systemic oppression, and all that takes away the quality of life for God's people, including the girl child. Patriarchy represents a threat to the very existence of the girl child because it is oppressive and destructive, treating the girl child as more dispensable and disposable than the boy child, especially in the context of HIV.

HIV has created a large number of orphans in Botswana,[1] and the orphan girl child much more than the boy child faces multiple challenges largely due to the patriarchality of Botswana's culture. The conclusions I draw will demonstrate that, repeatedly in patriarchal contexts, the girl child is sacrificed for the survival of men, and is subjected to violence for the maintenance of the patriarchical social system. Patriarchy imposes its will in many and varied ways.

The material is presented in two broad sections. The first interprets the meaning of Christ's mission announced in Luke 4:18-19. The second offers a lament based upon what is done to the girl child in patriarchal Botswana

---

[1] In Botswana, an orphan is a child under the age of eighteen who has lost one or both parents, whether biological or adoptive. A child whose parents cannot be traced because he or she has been dumped or abandoned is also classified as a social orphan. Orphans, regardless of cause, are also classified as vulnerable: vulnerable children are those who live in abusive environments, with a sick parent, with HIV or some form of disability, who heads a household and lives in a poor family with no access to basic needs, or on the streets beyond the reach of family care. See *User-Friendly Guide to the Care of Orphan and Vulnerable Children* (Gaborone: Ministry of Local Government, Botswana Department of Social Services, 2010), 2.

in the midst of an HIV pandemic. Lament itself is a time-honoured way of unsettling and critiquing patriarchy, and is better than silence. Lament leads to ways of breaking down and critiquing patriarchal oppression for denying the girl child the God-given gift of freedom from oppression: the core of Christ's mission. The chapter concludes with five recommendations:

> (1) deconstructing patriarchy; (2) speaking out against its ideologies, such as violence against the girl child; (3) reconstructing gender roles; (4) paying special attention to the orphan girl child; (5) urging churches to speak boldly against the violence committed against the girl child in Botswana.

Before reflecting in more detail on how patriarchal values contribute to the vulnerability of the orphan girl child, it is important to note three points. First, Botswana is heterogeneous. The evidence refers to some, not all, orphans, to women, men, and in varying degrees to different cultures within the country. Even though Botswana is patriarchal, not all men are women-abusers, and not all women and orphan girl children are abused. Secondly, although patriarchy makes men powerful, not all men have the same power; some are more powerful and have more status than others. However, I believe that patriarchy is potentially in the interests of all men regardless of class and status because it gives them a basis for claiming superiority over women of any class and status. Thirdly, patriarchy is manifested and maintained differently across different cultures and ethnic groups within the country. The way patriarchy is manifested in Europe and Asia is different from the way it is manifested and practised in most African countries. For example, in some African countries, due to the patrilineal nature of the culture, when a woman loses her husband, a brother to the late husband takes the woman as his wife, with immediate effect. This is done to ensure that wealth remains within the same family, and it is one of the ways in which patriarchy is kept alive.

We can say that a society is patriarchal to the extent that it subordinates women and children to the authority of men. This authority is maintained through many variables, two of which are gender inequality, and unqualified obedience to adults by children. These two variables have social functions: they force women and girls into unqualified submission even to the point of death, while maintaining the domination of men. As a consequence of this submission, women and children are marginalised and violated. These two variables are present throughout the lives of children of Botswana. But the orphan girl child is in an even worse state: she has become synonymous with pain, bondage and suffering, contrary to the will of Christ. Jesus, in his life and ministry, opened up spaces for an almost incredible intimacy with God, and God's love and care for all people, including children.

Part One: The Mission of Christ in Luke 4:18-19
– A Critique of Oppression

Luke 4:18-19 has been described by many commentators as a manifesto; a mission statement of the Gospel of Luke. It sets the tone for Luke's theology of the margins and God's universal Kingdom, which knows no boundaries in terms of (for example) gender, race or age. It is by any standards a core text for understanding the missions of Christ and of the church.[2] In this text, Jesus declares that:

> The Spirit of the Lord is on me, because he has anointed me to proclaim good news to the poor. He has sent me to proclaim freedom for the prisoners and recovery of sight for the blind, to set the oppressed free, to proclaim the year of the Lord's favour.[3]

Jesus spoke these words in the Synagogue of his home town, Nazareth in Galilee, on the day of the Sabbath, and with the anointing of the Holy Spirit. This passage had a mixed impact on the hearers of Jesus, with its reference to the year of the Jubilee: a year that marked real freedom for marginalised groups such as slaves. During the year of Jubilee, spoken of in Leviticus 25:8, debts had to be forgiven, slaves had to be set free, and land had to be redistributed. The year of the Jubilee coincided with the Sabbatical year (Exodus 23:10-13; Leviticus 25:1-7) in which the land, people and animals were supposed to rest. In concrete and tangible ways, the year of Jubilee was intended to bring social justice to the Israelites. If practised, the year of Jubilee would result in real and radical change: debtors were given a break and slaves were set free. In short, human relationships would be mended. For example, the institution of slavery which disempowered and marginalised people of a particular class and status, subordinating them to the élite, would be subverted. Although the proclamation of the year of Jubilee did not eradicate slavery altogether, when slaves were released, inequalities between slaves and slave owners were levelled, at least for a time.

Luke 4:18-19, like the rest of the Bible, is subject to interpretation. Often in Botswana the text is spiritualised. It is interpreted to mean spiritual blindness, poverty or spiritual captivity. Biblical scholars have struggled with how to interpret the concepts of poverty, blindness and captivity: do they refer to spiritual or material realms and activity?[4] I tend to think that there is nothing wrong when the text is interpreted as having spiritual *and* social meanings. The kind of interpretation that perceives Christ's mission as only referring to spiritual issues fails to see the possibility of

---

[2] Two biblical scholars who affirm this are R. Jamieson, *Commentary: Practical and Explanatory on the Whole Bible* (Grand Rapids, MI: Zondervan, 1974), 996-97; and David Bosch, *Transforming Mission: Paradigm Shifts in Theology of Mission* (Maryknoll, NY: Orbis Books, 1991), 84.

[3] Luke 4:18-19, *Holy Bible: New International Version*.

[4] Joel Green, *The Theology of the Gospel of Luke* (Cambridge: CUP, 1997), 211.

transformation that this text can effect in the lives of women and children who inhabit oppressive cultures today.

Coming from an African context where children and women are not only faced with spiritual hunger but actual physical hunger because of poverty, I find it appropriate to see the poor in Luke 4 as those people who are impoverished not only spiritually but also materially and physically, because of corrupt governments and unjust systems such as patriarchy. Through these systems, women and children are denied access to, and control of, economic resources: for a long time women in Botswana could not work in the construction industry or the mines, despite the fact that this is where a lot of wealth is generated. This ultimately throws women into imposed abject poverty.

Therefore, the kind of interpretation that I subscribe to perceives Luke 4:18-19 as having the potential to effect not only spiritual change, but social, political and economic transformation as well. I take it to mean that the mission of Jesus speaks of overturning oppressive systems that enslave people on earth, be they spiritual, social or economic. Further, this reading of the text illustrates that the core of Jesus' mission was to usher in a world driven by inclusive justice, where unjust systems of oppression are critiqued, dismantled and even eliminated.

In Jesus' programme of mission he lists six tasks that his mission entails. He has come to proclaim the good news to the poor, to heal the broken-hearted, to proclaim liberty to the captives, to give sight to the blind, to set at liberty those who are oppressed, and to announce the year of the Lord's favour. To speak of the poor, broken-hearted, captives, and the blind and the oppressed, is to speak of the marginalised: people at the fringes and margins of society. According to New Testament scholar Joel Green, Jesus was making a profound point by directing his good news to the poor, the blind and the oppressed. Green states: 'By directing his good news to people without honour, Jesus indicates his refusal to recognise those socially determined boundaries, asserting instead that even those outsiders are the objects of divine grace.'[5] Christ was dismantling systems and boundaries that oppress and impose suffering on people. Christ eliminates those things that threatened the existence of freedom and quality of life. Further, his 'mission statement' is a call to social action: let those who make others captives, set them free; let unjust and oppressive systems (like patriarchy) also set captives free.

As I interpret it, the programme of Jesus' mission was concerned with justice, restoring honour and dignity to people who had obvious limitations of which they were only too aware, and perhaps received little or no respect or honour from others. The six things Jesus came to announce and to put into practice have to do with the release of those who were burdened by unjust, false circumstances and systems that cause people to suffer.

---

[5] Green, *The Theology of the Gospel of Luke*, 221.

Poverty, slavery and oppression are consequences of trapping people in oppressive systems that favour and marginalise some. The release of slaves, land and possessions was liberation from economic, social and political systems that devalue the dignity and worth of a human being. Slavery as a system benefited the rich while oppressing the poor economically, socially and politically. The rich benefit from cheap slave labour and, at the same time, slavery elevates the social status of the rich while it devalues that of the slave. Therefore, one can argue that the mission of Christ, at least in large part, was to dismantle these economic, social and political systems that enslaved people.

Christ's preaching in the Gospel of Luke along with the other Gospels is accompanied by the healing of actual illness, as well as restoring sight to the blind.[6] These healings and deliverances were a manifestation of his mission statement in tangible and measurable ways: he went about actualising his words. His preaching called for the social change and justice that his healing demonstrated. Christ's restoration of otherwise limited lives (i.e. through restoring sight to the blind) can be used to critique systems such as patriarchy which imposes limitations on people's freedom through oppression. Therefore, one way of understanding the mission of Christ is to maintain that he denounced systems, governments and institutions that made people poor, blind, oppressed and enslaved, thus rendering those people powerless and marginalised.

To 'declare the year of the Lord' was to heal broken relationships caused, for example, by debt. If debt is eliminated, justice, equality and interconnectedness between human beings, young or old, is restored. To allow the earth to rest means the restoration of a relationship between human beings and the natural world; a relationship, characterised by respect for God's environment, is also restored. Therefore at the core of the mission of Jesus there is a healed humanity, and a healed earth, which flourish because systems that imposed suffering have been eliminated. Jesus demonstrates that being poor, captive or oppressed are not permanent ascriptions: these are human states or conditions that can be reversed.

Therefore, I submit that patriarchy should never be seen as a permanent system: it can be unlearned and deconstructed. Children, men, and women in Botswana can learn new ways of relating that recognise the truth that Christ's mission was intended to usher in freedom from oppression, for all. They can discover that God wants human beings to relate in ways that enhance the quality of life, contrary to patriarchy, which does the opposite. Women, men and children can learn new ways of relating that genuinely value the other person as made in the image of God, and therefore as worthy and valuable. If human beings were to relate in this way, violence against the girl child would be perceived as hurtful not only towards the

---

[6] See, for example, John 9.

child, but as also grieving God, who desires freedom from oppression for all.

While the mission of Christ calls churches and institutions towards a freed humanity, in patriarchal Botswana, girl children are denied this life of grace and freedom as patriarchal values oppress and impose suffering on girl children. In Part Two, I will focus on the plight of the girl child in Botswana in context of the HIV epidemic, as a way of critiquing patriarchal systems, values and practices. Such a critique is one way of demonstrating that patriarchy stands in contradiction to the mission of Christ which calls all people into mutuality and equality.

Part Two: Botswana, HIV/AIDS and the Girl Child

Botswana has one of the highest HIV infection rates in the whole of sub-Saharan Africa, after Swaziland.[7] For decades the world has witnessed the devastating impact of HIV and AIDS on the people of Botswana, as thousands of men, women, and children died from AIDS. This was alarming because the population of Botswana is small: in the early 2000s the population was just under 1.6 million.[8] From the early 1990s to the early 2000s, over 26,000 adults died from HIV, leaving children under 17 years of age. One of the most devastating effects of HIV/AIDS has been on children left orphaned when parents, and then sometimes extended family members, died of AIDS. Orphans suffer from a litany of vulnerabilities, ranging from malnutrition, victimisation, emotional and physical abuse, poverty, loss of inheritance, lost opportunities for education and health, depression, early entry into the labour force, an increased risk of HIV/AIDS, and early death themselves.

While orphans, male and female, are classified as vulnerable, the orphan girl child is more vulnerable than the orphan boy child in Botswana because Botswana is aggressively patriarchal. For example, the girl child is at a higher risk of contracting HIV through rape, because older men who subscribe to the more brutal forms of patriarchy have a sense of entitlement towards her body and sexuality. In this way, patriarchy becomes the source of yet more vulnerability for orphan girl child. I will now briefly demonstrate how this happens through violence against women, and especially sexual violence against the girl child in Botswana.

Violence against women and children – a manifestation of patriarchy

Police statistics and research conducted by the Botswana and Women's Affairs Division of Childline both indicate that violence against women and

---

[7] *Report on the Global AIDS Epidemic* (UNAIDS, 2001).
[8] *The Impact of AIDS* (UNAIDS, 2002).

the girl child, such as rape and sexual assault, are on the increase.[9] Part of the reason is that patriarchy gives men licence to violate women. Violence against women and girl children is a manifestation of power imbalances, domination and control.[10] I am aware of research being undertaken in the West that suggests that patriarchy should not be blamed for all the violence committed against women and girl children. Some of these researchers argue that there are men inhabiting patriarchal spaces who do not violate women and girl children, and therefore to blame patriarchy for all violence against women is unwarranted. For example, Alan Rosenbaum and Steven Hoge advance other reasons men commit violence against women: they propose that biological factors such as brain structure, brain function and hormonal changes can cause men to commit violence against women. Further, some men commit violence against women because they are clinically classifiable as psychopaths. These men are not able to sympathise normally like other human beings.[11]

I agree that there are probably many factors, even beyond the biological ones advanced by Rosenbaum and Hoge, involved in male violence against women. However, it seems to me irrefutable that patriarchy provides a fertile environment for other men (i.e. those whose brain structures and functions are 'normal') to commit violence against women. In the context of Botswana, most men who rape women will claim that the woman was 'wearing a short skirt', or 'she tempted me', or 'I bought her a drink'. These are reasons that only make sense to men who believe they have an entitlement towards women. Some men use 'corrective rape' on lesbians and women who are 'cheeky' to teach them how to behave like 'proper women'. These are men who are at pains to maintain the patriarchal status core, which requires that men remain powerful and women remain submissive. I do not deny that there are probably some men who commit violence against women because they are indeed psychopaths, but I contend that most of the violence committed in Botswana is done under the guise of culture: a patriarchal culture.

We can choose to blame individual men for the violence committed against girl children; however, communities must look beyond individuals and challenge the social systems that breed violent men. What is it about our cultures that make some men, and not women, gravitate towards violence against women and girl children? Why is it that violence is likely to be committed by men towards women, and not the other way round?

---

[9] *Annual Report 2008-2009* (Gaborone: Childline, 2009); *Report on the Study of the Socio-Economic Factors Contributing to Girl Child Abuse in Botswana* (Gaborone: Childline, 2005); *The Child Sexual Abuse Communication Strategy 2010-2014* (Gaborone: Botswana Department of Social Services and UNICEF, 2009); *Botswana Police Report* (Gaborone: 2011).

[10] *The Child Sexual Abuse Communication Strategy 2010-2014.*

[11] A. Rosenbaum and S. Hoge, 'Head Injury and Marital Aggression', in *American Journal of Psychiatry* 146, 1048-49.

What is it that makes communities devalue the girl child and not the boy child? In answering these questions, we must affirm that the girl child is created in the image of God. As such, she is worthy to benefit from the mission of Jesus and to participate equally in the realisation of the Kingdom of God here on earth. The Kingdom of God can become a reality when the rights of the girl child are defended, when she is respected and her worth ensured.

According to research conducted among groups of different tribes in Botswana by Women's NGO Coalition and SARDC WIDSAA, it is evident from the data:

> That men use battering and rape to keep women subordinate and maintain their control and dominance. Culture is often used as an excuse to perpetuate violence against women since it apparently gives men the right to 'chastise their wives if they misbehave'.[12]

This finding suggests that men who commit violence against women in Botswana using culture as a disguise are not necessarily psychopaths. The culture they are referring to, the one that entitles them to violate women, is heavily based on the social system of patriarchy. In this culture, patriarchal violence is accepted; some men feel that, because they are men, they are entitled to violate women. This confirms my argument that the girl child's life is sacrificed because she inhabits a system that values her less than a boy, and therefore she can be subjugated at best, and sexually violated at worst.

Sexual violence and the girl child

As a consequence of HIV/AIDS, child-headed households have increased, and most orphans stay alone, making them more vulnerable to sexual abuse and exploitation. Orphan girl children are at a higher risk of being sexually exploited, and most of the time the perpetrators of this abuse are relatives and close family members. According to Tapologo Maundeni, citing research by Fergus and Kebafetoletse, HIV-positive men:

> ... think it is therapeutic for them to have sex with young girls ... in addition, some infected men believe that by engaging in sexual relations with children and young people ... the infected individual is simultaneously cleansed.[13]

Findings of the 1998 *Rapid Assessment of Orphans in Botswana* carry a chilling report about an uncle who raped his niece on the night her mother was buried.[14] These horrendous examples demonstrate that patriarchal

---

[12] Women's NGO Coalition and SARDC WIDSAA (2005), 40.

[13] T. Maundeni, 'Cultural Factors in the Spread of HIV/AIDS among Children and Young People in Botswana', in E. Biakolo, J. Mathangwane and D. Odallo (eds), *The Discourse of HIV in Africa* (Pretoria, RSA: ICT, 2003), 135.

[14] *The Rapid Assessment of Orphans in Botswana* (Gaborone: AIDS/STD Unit, 1998).

values of entitlement by some men make it much more likely that the orphan girl child will be subjected to brutality and violence than the boy child. Sadly, the girl's physiology increases her chances of contracting HIV whenever she is sexually violated.

Since patriarchy places emphasis on the role of the man as a provider, some women, including aunts and even mothers, keep quiet when they are aware a girl child is sexually abused, as they rely on the sexual perpetrator to provide for their basic needs. This should be understood within a culture that identifies men primarily as breadwinners. They, too, are perpetuating patriarchal violence by sacrificing the girl child in order for them to survive, forced to comply with the values of the system, through silence. They are thus forced to handle child sexual violence in a way that protects the perpetrator and does not unsettle male power. This does not in any way exonerate these women, though they are not directly responsible for the violence committed against the girl child; they remain responsible alongside the male perpetrators for the continuing violation of girl children. What I am suggesting however is that such women are also victims of a patriarchal system that co-opts both men and women to participate in its values. When a woman keeps quiet about the abuse of the girl child at the hands of the primary breadwinner, she is caught in a system that is bigger than her. Women and children, and even some men, find themselves oppressed by patriarchy in many ways. These are just some of the ways in which patriarchy causes profound dysfunctionality in households and in society. It stands in contradiction to the mission of Jesus which calls human beings into systems free of oppression.

Another sad manifestation of patriarchy is the ongoing effect of childhood hurts imposed on girls through sexual violence. Often the abused girl child is instructed not to disclose the abuse to anyone. Since patriarchy in Botswana functions through the creation of hierarchies, with adults on top and children at the bottom, children are socialised to remain passive, and blindly obey adults. They are taught unqualified obedience. Children who question parental authority are perceived as bad-mannered and haughty. This explains why the girl child is instructed not to disclose the abuse. Perhaps out of obedience to adults and the shame of the abuse, the girl child keeps silent and is thus implicated in the abuse. The child grows up carrying enormous shame, and as a result she is made a captive of fear and guilt by an unjust and toxic system. The silence of the women, the children, and the larger community, props up the system of patriarchy and continues to fuel male violence and domination.

In such a context, the girl child is 'sacrificed' many times. First, by older men who use her to try to 'cleanse' themselves of HIV (that is, they seek to sacrifice her for their own survival). Secondly, the girl child is sacrificed by adult women who remain quiet about the abuse for the sake of their own economic survival. This does not reflect the will of God who desires that the girl child should thrive in freedom and innocence; hence, thirdly, patriarchy as a system thrives on sacrificing the innocence, freedom and value of the girl child at all costs. Fourthly, patriarchal values inhibit the physical, emotional and economic growth of the orphan girl child, as she is forever bound by childhood hurts which violate her innocence and freedom. Patriarchy in this way inflicts pain and long-term suffering on the girl child, which stands in contradiction to the programme of the mission of Christ, which places emphasis on human wholeness and freedom, and from systems that enslave.

There are two important issues for Christian mission that emerge from the sexual violence of the girl child and the silence that surrounds it. The first is that God, through the liberating mission of Christ set out in Luke 4, desires the freedom and safety of the girl child within a community that cares for her, and eliminates structures that threaten that freedom. It grieves God that a child can be subjected to such brutality and violence. God opposes violence and any system that thrives on violence. Secondly, while it is important for children to receive guidance from their parents, it is equally important for children to know that they can also receive guidance from God. Patriarchy blinds some parents to this truth and thus risks creating a false representation of how God wants children and adults to relate. God's plan for humanity is that human beings mutually relate to each other out of respect, not fear. Further, God desires that children also seek God's guidance as their heavenly Father, while still respecting their parents. Therefore, God opposes patriarchy and patriarchal practices for the violence they inflict on the girl child.

The mission of Jesus clearly defined in Luke 4 should give communities of faith the power to be suspicious of patriarchy, as well as to transgress patriarchal practices by declaring them oppressive. Any system that is oppressive is against God's desire for relationships of mutuality and peaceful existence. Girl children endure abuse, trauma and death at the hands of a dangerously flawed social system which fails to reflect the love and grace of God towards them. It poses a threat to the existence and life of the orphan girl child in the era of HIV and AIDS in Botswana. The mission of Jesus in Luke 4 is a call for churches to write a counter-narrative to the story of the girl child – a narrative that questions the rationale behind communities holding on to oppressive systems that deny God's grace to women and children. Luke 4 can be applied by churches who are the mouthpiece of Christ on earth to challenge injustice and even the illness imposed on children by patriarchy – for example, girls who have contracted HIV when they were very young through rape and defilement, and who have not chosen to engage in sex, but rather have had sex imposed on their young bodies.

The church community in Botswana is not doing enough to be prophetic when the girl child is sacrificed and forced into captivity by an unfair and unjust system. Clearly, the experience of the girl child in Botswana is that of brokenness. She is broken through the suffering imposed on her by patriarchy, and she needs the salvation, healing and restoration which are central to the mission of Jesus. The church, whose mandate is to continue the mission of Christ under the Spirit, is to declare God's saving power and to be agents of life to her. This can be done by creating a system that recognises that God's Kingdom is that of love, grace and restoration, for girl children and boy children equally, as well as adults.

This can propel the church to open and widen a platform of lament for the suffering and poor status of the girl child in Botswana. To mourn with the girl child means dealing with the sources of the trauma she experiences in order to affirm her as loved by God. Christ's liberating power proclaimed in his mission transcends all unjust systems and customs that bind and oppress the girl child. The vision of God towards children is that of freedom and justice. Therefore it must be the role of the church to fight for systems that bring justice for the girl child by effecting social change through the gospel. Preaching the gospel must necessarily be accompanied by change that translates into just and inclusive social policies.

The church as the representative of Christ has a calling to engage in prophetic ministry by reclaiming the vision of Christ set out in Luke 4:18-19. Prophetic ministry involves speaking out against violence directed at children. This can be done not just in some abstract way, but in tangible ways where the girl child is kept safe from sexual violence. Further, the church can call communities to reflect on the relationship of the Trinity, a relationship which values mutuality, interdependence, equality and community in diversity.[15] Reflecting on these aspects of the triune God can help Botswana to correct the injustice done to the orphan girl child, as new ways of relating to each other with love and respect for the dignity of each other are developed.

Relationships defined by patriarchy are limited and limiting; a girl child does not have a relation with adults based on love and respect, but rather their relationship is characterised by fear. There is a need to develop ways of being in relationships that supersedes patriarchy, ways of relating that point girl children towards the freedom, love and grace of God. This way of relating could allow the healing of broken relationship between God and God's people. Patriarchy is inimical to the relationships of mutuality and equality that God calls us to; rather, it is a system that encourages broken relationship between people, and between people and God. It alienates children from their fathers and uncles; the girl child especially is alienated from relating to men because of a fear of sexual abuse as I have shown above. This is not the kind of relationship that exists between the three persons of the Trinity, who co-exist as one God in unity, not alienation, from each other.

---

[15] M. Oduyoye, 'Trinity and Community', in *Hearing and Knowing: Theological Reflections on Christianity in Africa* (Maryknoll, NY: Orbis, 1996); E. Johnson, *She Who Is: The Mystery of God in Feminist Theological Discourse* (New York: Crossroads, 1993), 191-223.

The mission of Jesus must propel churches in Botswana, and other countries, to speak out against injustices committed against the girl child. The declaration by Christ that he had come to set the captives free demands that the church, the mouthpiece of God's vision for a free humanity, demands social justice for girl children. The mission of Christ requires that systems of injustice that steal the life of children be critiqued and dismantled. In modern Botswana, patriarchy can be classified as an oppressive system, one that imposes blindness, poverty from the fulness of life, and captivity. It is incompatible with the mission of Jesus: instead of setting free, it enslaves. It has to be denounced.

There are some churches which have taken the courageous step of denouncing violence against children – especially the girl child. They feed and clothe orphans and offer counselling to girls who have been sexually abused. They have opened their churches to be safe houses for these girls and so they are extending God's mercy and grace to them. By doing this, these churches stand in solidarity with the girls and demonstrate God's liberating power towards them. It offers them hope for the healing of the wounds inflicted on them by the patriarchal practices described above. If the churches continue to hold the girl child by the hand and stand in solidarity with her, the God who sent Jesus to set the captives free will be standing in solidarity with the oppressed girl child in the context of death and hopelessness. And he will, through the church, restore the girl child. God hears the cry of the girl child and is able to heal and restore her into wholeness.

Conclusion

I have argued that a society ordered around patriarchal values inevitably oppresses the girl child. Patriarchy, like slavery, is oppressive and therefore we need every institution, government, as well as individuals, to undermine or deconstruct it by speaking against the pain it inflicts on the orphan girl child in Botswana. Patriarchal societies sacrifice women and the girl child for the survival of males, but also for others trapped in the system too. The sacrifice of women and children takes different shapes and forms. At other times, the sacrifice of the girl child happens through denying them opportunities for education and health; at yet other times it happens when their lives are literally put at risk of contracting HIV through rape and abuse.

In Botswana, it seems communities are implicated in the sacrificing of the girl child. Families are silent when breadwinners who are sometimes HIV-positive rape young girls, sacrificing their innocence and health. Churches are silent when young girls are abused by men who have a sense of entitlement towards their bodies. Where is the God of justice, the God of love, who is father to the fatherless? Perhaps the church with its teaching on the domination of men and submission of women is uncomfortable with unsettling patriarchy because it benefits from maintaining it. The church's mission however is to declare the love of God and Christ who is un-patriarchal and anti-injustice, by protecting the innocence of the girl child.

Men and women, churches and organisations, need to lament the sacrifice of the orphan girl child in Botswana by challenging patriarchal ideologies and values. We need to challenge patriarchal structures that render the girl child powerless, be they inheritance laws and the care-giving responsibilities that burden orphan girl children, or debunking and denouncing the myth that older men can be cleansed of HIV through the abuse of young children. One way of doing this is for gender roles in patriarchal Botswana to be deconstructed so that men and women exist in an egalitarian manner. This includes equal treatment in the workplace, at home and in care-giving responsibilities. In this way both boys and girls will learn to share in caring for sick parents, particularly if they must do so from early on in life. Further, it is essential to have inclusive policies, programmes and cultural practices that recognise that all human beings – male and female, young and old – are equal, so that the girl child is no longer subjected to inhuman practices that cause her such suffering, hurt and shame.

It benefits children, men and women if patriarchy is dismantled and a new social order based on equality and mutuality is created. A social system will not thrive when oppressive structures continue to hurt females, in the face of the deliverance that was ushered in through the mission of Jesus.

Recovering a Gospel of Love through Children: Shattering Faith, Knowledge and Justice

Stephan de Beer and Genevieve James

This paper seeks to consider the themes of justice, faith and knowledge using the South African context as its backdrop. South Africa provides a context fraught with a multiplicity of challenges, many of which were inherited from the exceptional injustices which characterised the apartheid era, dating back to the days of British and Dutch colonisation. Since the emergence of South Africa's democracy, the new government has faced unparalleled challenges entrenched in legacy systems designed to cater for a mollycoddled minority. It is for this reason that children in South Africa cannot be viewed as a homogeneous group, since centuries of disequilibrium and dis-proportionality arising out of state-practised Euro-centrism, racism and discrimination, resulted in some children experiencing First World access to education, health care and public utilities, while others succumbed to hunger, ill-health, neglect, violence and death. South African children continue to reap the poisoned fruit of these vile injustices as the new South Africa, laden with promises of a new and better life, has yielded little in the way of social justice for children.

It is necessary to point out that the apartheid government received the necessary theological underpinning from a legion of astute theologians and academics, whose carefully crafted interpretation of biblical texts provided an ostensible basis for the supposed superiority of the white race. Undoubtedly it was an intellectual project *extraordinaire* by which the architects of apartheid successfully raised generations of white children who were led to believe they were superior, chosen and blessed by God. Meanwhile, in South African black townships, and special locations assigned for black people, those children struggled with self-actualisation and esteem issues because of both implicit and explicit messages, coupled with state propaganda, that white was beautiful, intelligent, strong, made in the image of God, beloved of God and valued. This great intellectual project, grounded in a twisted theological motivation, had far-reaching social, economic and justice implications for the children of the nation.

Against this backdrop, and great opposition, the Black Consciousness Movement and Black Theology[1] had to work with great fervour to rebuild a sense of value in the minds and hearts of the majority of the nation's children. Things began to reach fever pitch when, in 1976, children in the black township of Soweto were mercilessly gunned down during protests against the apartheid government's plan to impose Afrikaans language instruction at black schools. This would have further disadvantaged black children in an education system that was designed to keep black people in perpetual servitude. News of the killings shot around the world and this became another tragic milestone in the already catastrophic history of children in South Africa.

The war against children continued to rage across South Africa in diverse and deadly forms. Many were forced to contend with absent fathers uprooted to work in the profitable gold and diamond mines. Tragically, their children were never the recipients of the profits. Instead they had to contend with debilitating poverty, a poor health care and education system, and the irreversible destruction of their families and communities. Through it all, there were pockets of hope and rays of light, but for the most part the church failed to translate the meaning of the Good News of Jesus Christ to and for the children of South Africa in the spaces and places in which they found themselves. Seeing them only as recipients of 'Biblical' instruction and in need of discipline, the church in South Africa failed to apprehend the awesome and tremendous opportunity of declaring the justice of God.

Mission and theology always takes place in specific contexts. It is against this particular backdrop described above that the next section of this chapter will present an insightful narrative account of poor and vulnerable South African children as interlocutors of faith, knowledge and justice. The personal account to follow emerges from the city of Pretoria, the capital of the Republic of South Africa, a city which hosts the seat of the Presidency and countless international embassies. This narrative is a valuable resource for further understanding the unique mission with and to children in the South African context. The personal story is shared by Stephan de Beer, who is currently the Director for the Centre for Contextual Ministry at the University of Pretoria in South Africa. De Beer's narrative illuminates processes of meaning, traces the course of theological action and reveals a transformed missiology, one that can aid our thinking on mission with children. In this story we will read how children served as poignant and powerful agents of mission, calling for a complete *volte face* in theological discourse, consciousness and action in South Africa.

---

[1] See J.N.J. Kritzinger, *Black Theology: Challenge to Mission* (DTh thesis, Department of Missiology, University of South Africa, 1988), and T.S. Maluleke, 'The Africanization of Theological Education: Does Theological Education Equip You to Help Your Sister?' in E. Antonio (ed), *Inculturation and Postcolonial Discourse in African Theology* (New York: Peter Lang, 2006), 617.

A Catalyst for a New Conversion:
The Story of the Elim Church Fire – Pretoria, South Africa

I was raised in the high-rise inner-city neighbourhood of Sunnyside in Pretoria. When I grew up, and until about 1993, this neighbourhood was 100% white in terms of those who lived there. Since 1993 it has rapidly changed and today is 85-90% black. Today the local residents not only represent the diversity of South Africa's language and ethnic groups, but also the continuous migration from all over Africa into the cities and towns of South Africa. Migrants come from Somalia, Ethiopia, Tanzania, Nigeria, Eritrea and the Democratic Republic of the Congo, to find homes, open shops, attend churches and mosques, and to represent their home countries, in the dense and ever-changing neighbourhood of Sunnyside.

While studying theology in the late 1980s and early 1990s I became aware, with others, of an emerging reality that children were making the busy Esselen Street's retail district, now Robert Sobukwe Street, their home. In the late 1980s, children from as young as eight years old found their way to Sunnyside, and other similar inner-city neighbourhoods around the country, to earn a living, escape violence and abuse at home, and to find a glimmer of hope or perhaps a ray of sun.

About 1990, a friend who ran his own business in another part of the city, approached me and some other university friends, to start an overnight shelter for street boys, from where programmes could be offered that would provide alternatives to life on the streets, and also to assist boys in the process of being reconciled with their families, if at all possible.

The old Elim Church in Jeppe Street, now Steve Biko Street, stood empty, as the congregation had moved to a suburb closer to the university to serve the student population. The new owners of the building did not have an immediate use for the property, and allowed us to use this space to create the first overnight shelter for street boys in the inner city. This was not welcomed by the wider community – even veteran social workers working for local non-profit organisations were initially suspicious because they reckoned a business man and a group of university students lacked the necessary experience and knowledge to open such a facility.

However, since the street boys had nowhere else to sleep at night, permission was given. We opened the doors of the church to accommodate twenty boys per night in shelter accommodation. They were served supper, provided by churches and individuals from across the city, and in the morning, after having something to eat, they would leave the building to do whatever they did during the day: odd jobs, hanging out in the streets, stealing, begging, whatever they could find to make a living.

Not having a budget for the project, some of us took turns sleeping over at night as supervisors to the boys living in the facility. This continued for some months until we were able to employ an adult house father who took responsibility to supervise those boys living on the property and offer spiritual formation to the children.

Initially, all the boys slept next to each other in one big space that had been the church's gallery. After some time, we differentiated between older and younger boys so they could sleep in separate rooms. I remember one of the older boys telling the younger boys stories at night to help put them to sleep. These boys, who had to be brave on the streets, who faced darkness and police brutality night after night, started to become like children once they had a secure shelter off the streets. These tough street boys experienced a normal child's fears at night, needing a shoulder to cry on and a story-teller to put them to sleep.

We soon developed a programme in the shelter which included a literacy component, a life skills component, leatherwork training, leadership training, spiritual formation, and a recreational programme. Since this was not a formal residential facility, the washing facilities were limited. I mentioned the apprehension of professional social workers at the beginning of this project; however, over time, some of them became allies and even co-workers. The presence of the children on the streets of Sunnyside, the opening of an overnight shelter in the midst of what was then still a white neighbourhood, continued to generate negative responses from other sectors of the neighbourhood.

The local business community did not welcome the presence of the street children as they argued it drove their business away. Some members of the South African Police Force went out of their way to harass the children, violating their dignity and childhood. Off-duty policemen would come to the church at night, harassing the boys and those of us who volunteered as overnight supervisors. Sometimes they would threaten the boys. We often heard reports of what was happening on the streets: on one occasion the boys were loaded in police vans and driven thirty kilometres out of town, their shoes taken from them, police dogs set onto them, and they were made to walk back – all this to try and discourage them from living on the streets of Sunnyside.

And yet, the boys would return to the shelter night after night. The risks they faced living on the streets did not seem to match the risks of poverty and abuse many of them faced in their homes. The city streets offered them a strange consolation, even if it was a nebulous dream.

The boys on the streets of Sunnyside became the forerunners of new migrations into South African inner cities – not just South African black people coming from townships, informal settlements and rural areas, but in the 1990s, tens of thousands of Africans coming across the borders from Mozambique, Rwanda, Angola and the Democratic Republic of the Congo. In the last decade migrants have increasingly come from Nigeria, Tanzania, Somalia, Eritrea and Ethiopia. Most of the migrants moving into South Africa's inner cities are particularly vulnerable to poverty and crime.

The harassment of the boys on and off the streets, and of the staff and volunteers of the overnight shelter, continued for the duration of the programme. Then a series of incidents occurred that intensified antagonism between the project, the boys, and the police. On 12 March 1992, a fire destroyed the building that housed the shelter: eight boys died in the fire, the youngest being only eight years old. Some died in their sleep from smoke inhalation.[2]

A Personal Shattering of Faith, Knowledge and Justice: The Reality of South Africa's Vulnerable Children

Recently, I shared about the fire with a friend who had volunteered with us when we started the project. I sensed her surprise at hearing how pivotal the fire at the church has been for me, even twenty years after the incident. She asked if I had dealt with the trauma of the event, or whether I still carried the emotional pain of that night in March 1992.

I have reflected on her question for this chapter of the book, in reflecting about theology, mission and children: what was it about this event that has had such a deep and lasting impact on me? I think it goes beyond 'post-traumatic stress', although I acknowledge that trauma impacts us emotionally at a deep psychological level.

Why do I still draw energy from this story and still relate it to colleagues? I believe this incident became a pivotal experience in my spiritual journey, a personal *kairos* (moment). The fire and loss of the boys led me to alter my perspective of God, life, church, vocation, and the world in which I live. It constituted a theological conversion to 'justice', and not just a vague notion of justice, but to justice that can be concretised in relevant ways for families and children who are denied access to socio-economic, political, educational, legal and spatial justice.

The journey with the children on the streets of Sunnyside, the devastating event of the fire, and my subsequent experiences in Chicago and back in Pretoria, have become a catalyst for a deep personal transformation. This has led me to embrace a theology that seeks integral liberation. That is, not just salvation from personal sin, but a theology that embraces restoration of human dignity, and a struggle against those structures that deprive people of dignity, as well as access to socio-economic-political justice: i.e. freedom from systemic sin and oppression, as Jesus preached in his first sermon in Luke 4, and as Mary sang about when she praised God for the child to be born.

The vulnerable children on the streets of South Africa became the interlocutors of a new way of seeing and knowing – in a sense, my journey with them led me to experience *a shattering* of faith, knowledge and justice as I understood them. I was given an invitation to embrace faith, knowledge and justice from the perspective of the most vulnerable children on the streets. Their lives led me to a conversion from simple compassion for

---

[2] See also similar accounts in David Klatzow and Sylvia Walker, *Steeped in Blood: The Life and Times of a Forensic Scientist* (Cape Town, RSA: Zebra Press, 2010).

material welfare to a compassion with justice; to a realisation that neighbourly love and friendship requires the addressing of the myriad of systemic injustices that exclude my neighbours from full participation in the life of our communities.

Faith, knowledge and justice were re-framed, questioned and presented in a dramatically new way that represented *an epistemological and existential break* from the past. It constituted a deliberate break with an exclusivist 'white perspective' on the world of my youth. Shortly after the death of the boys in the fire, I spent six months living on the south side of Chicago, seeing the world through the eyes of another group of vulnerable children – those growing up in the notorious public housing projects, the Robert Taylor Homes (since demolished). These were the children of 'welfare moms', many with crack-cocaine addicts for parents, others born with foetal alcohol syndrome, most lured into gangs from the age of 12 or 13, born into vulnerability and marginality.

My work with these children led me to read, among others, James Cone, Gustavo Gutierrez, Theodore Walker and Dorothee Sölle. These authors opened me to new perspectives on theology, perspectives that challenged the assumptions I had held about personal sin and conversion. I began to discover what some have described as 'theology from below', from the underside of human experience.[3] I found Jesus there, waiting, struggling, suffering with the millions of outcasts on our cities' streets.

Previously, theology for me had been neatly packaged in orthodox systematic theological constructs, apparently universally applicable to all contexts. But when confronted with the realities of children living on the streets of Sunnyside and Chicago, I found myself at a loss. These ordered theological arguments did not help me to make sense of my new realities. The reality of the children's lives, and the abuse of 'white power' to oppress black children, opened me to the Black Theology of Cone, the liberationist theological perspectives of Gutierrez,[4] the challenge of Christ in the context of blackness and Africanness, particularly as it relates to children and youth.[5] Reading Sölle's book *Suffering* turned my theological constructs upside-down.

I discovered the challenge of doing theology in context, which requires an engagement with human realities, a discovery of theological wisdom

---

[3] This essay does not allow space for an in-depth analysis of these texts; however, see Gustavo Gutierrez, *Theology of Liberation: History, Politics, Salvation*, 15th anniversary edn, trans. Caridad Inda and John Eagleson. (Maryknoll, NY: Orbis, 1988); James Cone, *God of the Oppressed* (San Francisco, CA: Harper San Francisco, 1975); and Dorothee Sölle, *Suffering* (Philadelphia, PA: Fortress Press, 1975).

[4] See also Gustavo Gutierrez, *On Job: God-Talk and the Suffering of the Innocent*, trans. Matthew J. O'Connell (Maryknoll, NY: Orbis, 1987).

[5] Theodore Walker, *Empower The People: Social Ethics for the African-American Church* (Maryknoll, NY: Orbis, 1991).

'from below', from the community, and from many contexts of suffering around the globe. The lives, and the deaths, of children in the city became fertile soil for 'liberating' and more creative theology to find root in my thinking and work.

I recognise now that this personal reorientation probably started on the streets of Hillbrow, South Africa, where I did my practical ministry as a student, and that it had been nurtured in my home with my mother's strong sense of justice and fairness. But now it wears the clothes of children living on the streets, of their black experience; it has become more embodied and not just philosophical and abstract.

On Faith – Towards Practical Obedience to God

This experience could have shattered my faith. I was 24 years old when I chose to follow Christ and we did what we thought was right for the street boys. We gained access to the church and we invited the boys in off the streets, then they died. I never blamed God for what happened, nor did I ask where God was in the tragedy. I believed that God was probably deeply shattered by the premature death of the boys, as we were. But this event did shatter the kind of faith I embraced. It shattered a naïve notion of faith that was shattered already on the Cross.[6]

Suddenly, new questions surfaced for me. I had to ask: Who is God? Who is God with? Who is God for? I realised that God cannot be neutral although my faith previously would have had me believe in a neutral loving God. But now I realised that in a situation such as this, neutrality would be criminal, an evil, a compliance. I asked new questions about whether the church holds to a faith without deeds, a faith without commitment to justice, a faith in a God who was not also the God of the child who suffers or who dies in a fire. The content of my faith was deeply challenged and expanded.

The childlike nature of my faith did not disappear but I started to grapple with Jesus' words that we had to become like children. The experiences with the boys off the streets, who had become my interlocutors, became the voices and lives that God used to change me into someone I was not before. These boys reaffirmed that God embraces the children of the world, and particularly the most vulnerable. God in a special way sides with the children, in the face of those who seek to destroy and violate them.

Mine became a faith of the streets, shaped by the streets and its realities. And the gracious presence of God worked in me a faith in the city, not only practising my faith and seeking to translate it into challenging urban places, but also believing in the city itself and the potential of the city to be home

---

[6] See C.S. Song, *Jesus, the Crucified People* (Minneapolis, MN: Fortress Press, 1996), 98-99.

to the stranger, playground to the child, a hospitable place for all who call it home.

This leads to a question of both faith and obedience in mission: how do our educational programmes, spiritualities and Christian rituals foster such a faith – childlike yet not naïve, a faith of children, of the city streets, of concrete justice?

On Knowledge – To Know as We Are Known

Only three months before the fire I completed a theological degree that enabled me to enter ministry. After six years of theological preparation, generating knowledge to equip me for ministry in the world, the fire and the death of the boys challenged the knowledge I had acquired in my training, because it was not the kind of knowledge that had prepared me for a trauma of this nature.

The knowledge of the classroom can never compensate for the knowledge we gain when we go onto the streets. Practical wisdom is nurtured in the heat of things on the streets and in communities, where knowledge is tested, assessed, purified and refined. If we do not find innovative ways to integrate the intellectual knowledge of university, the academy and practical modes of training with the school of the streets, we will always run the risk of producing sterile, impotent knowledge, uninformed by the wounds of the city. Knowledge has to be refined in the fire of contextual experience.

The debate about theory in itself being 'real' and 'noble' to me seems to be a false debate, as theory in itself can never be the endeavour of universities – our theory needs to be informed and shaped by contextual questions and wounds, and in return theory refined in such a manner can then again inform our practices and interventions. It is an ongoing cycle of praxis that is required if we are to develop liberating engagements with the lives of vulnerable children and other people in our urban communities.

The children as interlocutors helped me to understand theology and mission in new ways: the knowledge of six years of theological preparation was tested, evaluated, and critiqued by working with these street boys. This was knowledge 'from below' – knowledge generated through solidarity and shared experiences with of the most vulnerable of our city; it was knowledge transformed from rational jargon to intimate love expressed in a search for justice and truth. Knowledge, according to Parker Palmer, is best obtained in the experience of being known ourselves.[7] For Palmer, we are known first and foremost by God, as our masks and illusions of self are revealed, as our prejudices crumble, and as our fears diminish, we know

---

[7] Parker Palmer, *To Know As We Are Known: Education as a Spiritual Journey* (San Francisco, CA: Harper One, 1993).

anew. In this way, we might discover afresh the presence of God amongst vulnerable children in the streets of our cities.

A second set of questions emerge for mission with children: how do our educational programmes, spiritualities and Christian rituals foster a knowledge in which we will be known with love, and therefore we will know anew – knowledge translated into practical wisdom, incarnational love, and quest for the truth? Adults working with children on the streets might explore the following: how do we create spaces in which new and liberating kinds of knowledge can be generated, in which existing knowledge can be transformed on behalf of children?

On Justice – To Seek the Peace of the City

At the core of the event that shaped me so profoundly was a conversion to justice.[8] This means a political conversion, not only to God and my neighbour but also to the city in a way that will seek the *shalom* of the city in every sense of the word: liberation from all that deprives the city, its people and its children from wholeness, and an ushering in of the good news of healing, freedom and justice as envisaged in Luke 4:18-19.

Many individuals and churches were involved in the shelter in those months when we fed and housed the children. But when the church burnt down and the boys died and we had to ask what happened, who was responsible for the fire, why were young boys such a threat to establishment society that they were killed in this cruel manner, disturbingly, there was an overwhelming silence from the local churches of our city.

I realised that in our churches and theologies we are often more comfortable with charity than with justice. Our charity can still happen at arm's length but justice requires us to change in encounter with our neighbours. Charity is often one-way traffic, while justice requires mutuality in relationship and a re-ordering of the way things work. Charity can come from within our church premises and circles, but when we deal with justice, it takes us beyond the church to the streets, the boardrooms, the court rooms and the political chambers. Charity deals with the symptoms of sin: exclusion, deprivation, hunger, homelessness. But justice deals with underlying causes – asking *why* people are hungry and homeless. It seeks to address systemic evil and the root causes that lead children to the streets in the first place. Working for justice means examining and

---

[8] For additional reading on justice in theology and mission, see Donal Dorr, *Spirituality and Justice* (Dublin: Gill and Macmillan, 1984); Walter Brueggemann, S. Parks and T.H. Groome, *To Act Justly, Walk Humbly, Love Tenderly: An Agenda for Ministers* (New York: Paulist Press, 1986); Robert McAfee Brown, *Spirituality and Liberation: Overcoming the Great Fallacy* (Louisville, KY: Westminster John Knox Press, 1988).

challenging the structures that support injustice, such as indifference or corruption. Biblical justice seeks liberation in the way society is organised and how social resources are shared. Justice is not satisfied with a surface renewal of the city, which often simply means a clean-up of garbage and a displacement of the poor. Instead of urban renewal, holistic justice will seek to transform the city so that it can be viable, sustainable, and radically inclusive of all those who are weak and vulnerable.

Charity often soothes the conscience and silences the most immediate hunger, but working for justice goes deeper, addressing vulnerability, and celebrating signs of breakthroughs, where God's justice is demonstrated. Justice can seem elusive but at the same time it calls for hope and courage. The children of Sunnyside taught me that justice cannot simply be a vague philosophical concept but it needs to be demonstrated specifically, in concrete situations with living communities. Victims of injustice or those who are marginalised become our friends, translators and interlocutors.

The deaths of those boys over twenty years ago traumatised me and my co-workers, their parents, and families. But their deaths also led me to seek to better understand the lives of children on dumping sites of cities in the global South, from Mamelodi to Maputo, from Addis Ababa to Manila; the orphans and vulnerable children having to fend for themselves in Uganda and the South Sudan; child soldiers in Burma or child prostitutes all over the world.

I propose a third set of questions for mission with children on the streets: how do our educational programmes, spiritualities and rituals foster an agenda for justice? How do they equip us with vision, knowledge and skills to become advocates and activists for change; to stand in solidarity with those who cannot speak for themselves; to name local situations of violation and oppression, to resist and stand against it, to overcome and transform it?

In review, the children of the Elim Church have led me to ask: Is our faith actively engaged in partnership with the most vulnerable children and others in our cities, towns and rural places? Is our knowledge sufficient to enable us to be responsible and liberating companions of the poor? Do we allow the children of our streets to teach us where, when and how justice should roll down?[9]

The Things We Gained in the Fire

For narratives to flourish, there must be a community to hear ... for communities to hear, there must be stories which weave together their history, their identity, their politics.[10]

---

[9] Amos 5:24.

[10] Catherine Kohler Riessman, *Analysis of Personal Narratives*, Boston University, 20 April, 2000. www.uel.ac.uk/cnr/riess1.doc

When carefully considering de Beer's account of his 'conversion' as a result of the children of Elim Church, I was reminded of the pop group *Bastille's* hit song *Things We Lost in the Fire*. Fire has the power to kill, destroy and ravage; yet, from this story of destruction and desolation there are significant gains to be made. Out of this story come some important lessons for our mission with children in the current age.

The burning of the church and the death of the children served as a cataclysmic event that brought new insights, reordered priorities, and reshaped the destiny of those like de Beer who would be changed by its message. The fire shed light on traditional practices, the churches' response, and human nature. Though we may experience cataclysmic events all around us, we may never have the eyes to see and ears to hear what the Spirit is saying to the church. In the case of de Beer, we see the missiological possibility of grief, shock and despair to cause deep reflection and an authentic response to the cries of the children in his city. His missional identity was irreversibly changed as a result of the incident. He grasped the full significance of the event. As a result also, de Beer inspired collective action by establishing a responsive organisation, and infusing the faith community in South Africa and several countries around the world with a new vision for mission as justice, a vision forged in the fire. His missiological reflection led to the establishment of a movement for urban justice, with children as key dialogue partners in this journey. The event served as a critical artefact, and the subsequent shock and trauma mobilised him into a transformed praxis. His personal discourse formed by years of theological training was irreversibly changed by these events, leading to the formation of a *public* discourse rooted in the revealed realities of his city. The event enabled de Beer to proclaim his interpretation of mission as justice, first to himself, and then to the wider faith community.

Through de Beer's narrative we see that mission with and to children is also a serious intellectual exercise, involving not just compassion and heart but also mind, ideas, concepts and interpretation. De Beer discovered a different way of thinking, acting and doing. His openness to what the Spirit was saying to him resulted in a kind of 'Cross' thinking – the ability to critically explore the meaning of the Cross and the Good News in the light of his unique context and experiences, since justice, faith and knowledge do not take place in a vacuum but in specific places with specific people.

The children played a subversive role in this story. They witnessed to a 'new' Christ, a Christ who was impartial with regard to pedigree, race or education. They witnessed to a Christ who dwelt in, and was revealed through, the brokenness, rejection and neglect of the children of the street. In this narrative, children have served as the primary catalysts of conversion. This is a critical departure from the traditional view of children as recipients of mission rather than as agents of mission. Embedded in the stories and life experience of children is the latent power for the conversion of the church. Children have always, and continue, to call the church to a *new* conversion. This is a conversion *from* institutional building, the development of empire and the indulging of the middle class *to* the reversal of human hierarchies of status and power and to establishing the reign of God, which is a reign of love and justice. Residing within the child is the constant interplay between the *not yet but already*. While we wait for the realisation of the full reign of God which is *not yet* – as revealed in the injustice, inequalities, suffering and death of the children – we do observe precious signs of the *already*: love, joy, and hope. The children are therefore authors of a 'new' gospel, urging us on to a renewed and authentic praxis of justice, faith and knowledge.

THE DISTURBANCE OF GOD, HOLISTIC MISSION AND CHILDREN IN CRISIS: LESSONS FROM A STUDY OF PARTNERSHIP IN ROMANIA

Bill Prevette

As I write in September 2014, global media has focused our attention on the political conflicts in the Ukraine and Russia, the escalating humanitarian crises in Syria and Sudan, and other countries experiencing social upheaval. Images of suffering children are often used to 'tell the story' of conflict and suffering, and to solicit aid from international donors. In such places, children are often the ones most vulnerable. In response, governments, NGOs and charities mobilise relief and related interventions. Churches, mission agencies and other faith-based organisations (FBOs) develop similar responses, often with the claim of bringing spiritual as well as physical assistance.[1]

Not so many years ago, as the Soviet Union was breaking apart and Eastern European countries were experiencing the end of the Cold War, a similar crisis for children was made public in the nation of Romania. Following the collapse of Nicolae Ceaușescu's socialist government in 1989, more than 150,000 children were living in state institutions.[2] These 'orphanages' were poorly funded and inadequately maintained by the state. Western news cameras brought the tragedy of Romania's orphans and abandoned children to the world's attention. I spent five years (2002-07) working as a mission practitioner and doctoral researcher living in Romania. My work focused on children, youth, churches, and FBOs.[3] I was

---

[1] Mission statements from large evangelical relief and development organisations illustrate this, for example: 'The purpose of Tearfund is to serve Jesus Christ by enabling those who share evangelical Christian beliefs to bring good news to the poor by proclaiming and demonstrating the gospel for the whole person through support of Christian relief and development.' www.tearfund.org (accessed 12 September 2012).

[2] This number is at best an estimate; there are dozens of studies on this era of Romanian history but two of particular interest are Gail Kligman, *The Politics of Duplicity: Controlling Reproduction in Ceaușescu's Romania* (Berkley, CA: University of California Press, 1998), and Victor Groza, D. Ileana and I. Irwin, *A Peacock or a Crow? Stories, Interviews and Commentaries on Romanian Adoptions* (Euclid, OH: Williams Custom Publishing, 1999).

[3] In this chapter, 'FBO' is an abbreviation for Faith-Based Organisations. There is extensive literature on faith-based work. My usage refers to organisations such as World Vision International, Compassion International, Southern Baptist Mission,

there trying to resolve something of a 'puzzle', which we have termed for this present volume, The Triangle of 'theology-mission-child'.

Some Personal Background

Perhaps it will be useful to share some of my background story, leading to this interest in Romania and mission with children. I was raised in a Methodist children's home in North Carolina, USA. This was not always a pleasant experience; I experienced the shortcomings often associated with institutional care for children: abuse from adults, conflicts with other boys, and a lack of attention from family. I began my work with children and youth as an activist and interventionist, not an academic, theologian or policy advocate. I believed it was important to help children and youth escape danger or exploitation, and learn of Christ's love and have an alternative to life on the streets.

I worked with troubled youth through Teen Challenge in Los Angeles, and later with Teen Challenge in Asia.[4] With my wife and son, I moved to Thailand in 1989 to work with children and families in the overcrowded slums along the polluted *klongs* (canals) in Bangkok, and children from the hill tribes in Northern Thailand who were at risk from sexual exploitation. Moving to Cambodia in 1995, we encountered thousands of children that had been marginalised and abandoned after the end of the Khmer Rouge reign of terror. We served as the country directors with an evangelical mission agency, the Assemblies of God World Mission, assisting about 4,000 children in a number of projects, orphanages, schools, clinics, and community development settings.

Many of us have questioned God about the suffering of children which seems so senseless. My work with sexually exploited and abused children reframed my spiritual, practical and intellectual journey. Cambodia challenged me to articulate deeper theological and missiological questions about Christian work with children such as: What is our response when children challenge our assumptions and paradigms of suffering and pain? What answers do we have for the profound and troubling questions that children themselves ask of God in their abuse or abandonment? How carefully are we listening to their voices? Even the question of God, and how God can be believed in, in a world of this sort of suffering, poses wider theological questions.

---

and similar. These charities or mission organisations have resources and the means to set up and deliver large-scale programmatic responses and interventions.

[4] Teen Challenge was founded in New York City in 1958 by David Wilkerson to help troubled youth who were involved in urban gangs. Teen Challenge now works in over ninety countries with youth and others who have life-controlling addictions. See www.globaltc.org/html/about_us.html (accessed 29 April 2014).

As is often the case in mission and theological work, our questions lead to puzzlement as our 'faith seeks understanding'.[5] Like many mission practitioners, I was familiar with the term 'holistic mission'[6] but the ragged and raw realities of everyday life for most children in Cambodia forced me to think differently about their present pain and suffering. How did the promise of the gospel and our hope in Christ for the healthy human development of children fit together in the aftermath of the devastation left by Pol Pot's Killing Fields?

After Cambodia, I spent four years travelling internationally, evaluating interventions and outcomes in many child-focused programmes. It became evident that the evangelical, charismatic and pentecostal Christians managing these projects generally excelled at getting close to children in need and serving in their local communities. However, simply responding to the immediate perceived needs of children tended to control their actions and thinking. I gathered from experience that various methods were advocated as effective faith-based interventions for children in crisis: some promoted church-planting, some promoted community transformation with the child as the focal point, some maintained that the physical, psycho-social and spiritual needs of 'children at risk'[7] were best addressed in the context of family, while others believed that ministries should be based and carried out in and through the local church. When there is dysfunction in families, communities or society, children are usually the first to show signs of suffering. In some ways, children are like 'canaries in a mine shaft': they provide a focal point for discovery and encounter of perilous aspects of our world that is often ignored.

I moved to Romania in 2002, in part to conduct a structured investigation of the relationship between selected FBOs and Romanian evangelical churches, as revealed in their action for children in crisis

---

[5] I am borrowing from Anselm of Canterbury (1033-1109), the great Christian philosopher and theologian who gave us the phrase *fides quaerens intellectum.*
[6] See Brian Woolnough and Wonsuk Ma, *Holistic Mission: God's Plan for God's People* (Oxford, UK: Regnum: 2010); Tom McAlpine, *By Word, Work and Wonder: Cases in Holistic Mission* (Monrovia, CA: MARC, 1995); Rene R. Padilla, 'Holistic Mission', in John Corrie (ed), *Dictionary of Mission Theology* (Downers Grove, IL: IVP 2007).
[7] The age span of childhood has been variously socially constructed over many centuries; see Hugh Cunningham, *Children and Childhood in Western Society since 1500*, 2nd edn (New York: Pearson Longman, 2005). By the mid-1990s, the term 'children and youth at risk' was being increasingly used to describe a demographic of young people up to eighteen years of age deemed 'at risk' from poverty, abuse, war, ethnic marginalisation, sexual or street exploitation, institutionalisation, lack of access to basic education, social services and health care. See Phyllis Kilbourn (ed), *Children in Crisis: A New Commitment* (Monrovia, CA: MARC, 1996); also Glenn Miles and J.J. Wright (eds), *Celebrating Children: Equipping People Working with Children and Young People Living in Difficult Circumstances Around the World* (Carlisle, UK: Paternoster, 2003).

between 1990 and 2004. The study examined missional assumptions, operative theologies,[8] activities, and patterns that characterised FBO/local evangelical church partnerships.[9]

An Overview of Research Findings

A primary question for the research was: How and to what degree do FBO/church understandings of God's work in Christ enable or hinder their collaboration and actions in relation to children? The research examined the three points of this volume's 'Triangle': the Romanian child, methods of mission practice, and operative theology. However, at each point of The Triangle there was both ambiguity and uncertainty that required patience and humility on the part of both churches and FBOs.

In the early 1990s, more than four hundred NGOs and FBOs responded to the child 'crisis' in Romania. International FBO response was largely reactive, and at times disempowering towards evangelical churches. This led to a 'division of labour' as FBOs responded to human, physical, and psychosocial needs of children while churches provided what they understood as 'spiritual' care. While much positive work was done with children, it became clear that short-sighted agendas of the FBOs, and the substantially different agendas of the churches, tended to undermine collaboration; furthermore, both often neglected the concerns and voices of the children themselves.

The FBOs that came to Romania from the West were influenced by a good and practical 'secularity', shaped in large part by their experience of practising mission with children in other places for up to the past 150 years. Western FBOs take care seriously for children and their human well-being, they are willing to concentrate on the visible and immediate, on the child as a person with 'rights', and the child as one who should have the freedom to enjoy life and personal 'well-being'. Such FBOs value faith in Christ, which in turn values a good and healthy life as a gift from God. But in their encounter with Romania in the aftermath of nearly half a century of Communism, they demonstrated impatience with the forces and factors that continued to prevent this freedom and life. They were willing to work in opposition to the injustices and cruelties of Romanian society; many FBOs tended to be impatient with the local forms of Christianity that did not give the same priority to this quest for life in the here and now.

---

[8] 'Operative theologies' are those observable practices and actions that are carried out by churches and Christians which they say they do in the 'name of God' or, in other words, how their theology is put into action.

[9] For the book that resulted from this investigation, see Bill Prevette, *Child, Church and Compassion: Towards Child Theology in Romania* (Oxford: Regnum, 2012). In this essay, I am drawing on sections of the book and refer the reader to the full text for a more comprehensive discussion, analysis and key findings.

On the other hand, local Romanian evangelical churches (Pentecostal, Baptist and others) were shaped by their own evangelical commitments. These churches had resisted Communism and were prepared to continue to pay the price for their faith and commitment to Christ, even if that required that they remain narrow in their focus toward 'salvation from this world'. They had been forced to the margins of Romanian society; they had learned to know God in Christ in his suffering, abiding in the Cross, and finding patience to live in this present world as a preparation for the world to come. They were tenaciously loyal to God, as they knew him, which led to narrowness and rigidity, mixed with a traditionalism and ignorance of the wider world. Discussion of sin, salvation, eternity, and God's intentions were never far from the surface in conversations and interviews with Christian leaders in Romania They lived with the vision of the 'city set on hill', not of this world, but in the world to come,[10] which led them to build strong communities of faith, not lacking in care for one another, but without a vision for transforming their wider society. As a result, such churches were not sure how to deal with the thousands of children who were marginalised by the Romanian state.[11]

FBOs and local churches are both expressions of Christ's body as described in Romans 12:4-5, where each member contributes according to their gift but all members belong to one another. As outlined above, FBOs and churches are common ways of being actively Christian, in Romania and elsewhere. They relate to Jesus Christ and to the whole Body of Christ, with various expressions and visibility. These two forms of Christ's body remind us that each part on its own is inadequate, and there is work for both to do at each point of The Triangle: theology, mission, and child.

I was fortunate to have access to the insights emerging in the 'Child Theology Movement' during the course of my research. Child Theology suggests that Jesus 'called and placed a child in the midst' of a theological discussion,[12] as a pointer to the Kingdom of God and 'a point of entry into the kingdom'.[13] I examined how FBO and church collaboration might open a dialogue about what God intends when Jesus places a 'child in the midst'

---

[10] See Hebrews 11.

[11] I am thankful to Haddon Willmer for reading my original manuscript and offering insights into this and the preceding paragraph. Haddon supervised my research in Romania and I became a more competent thinker under his tutelage.

[12] Matthew 18:1-3. These phrases, along with the whole text of Matthew 18:1-10, became a focus for the founders of CTM. See Haddon Willmer and Keith J. White, *Entry Point: Towards Child Theology with Matthew 18* (London: WTL Publications, 2013). The authors describe the book as a sustained essay on this text. See also the website www.childtheology.org for other papers and resources.

[13] 'The child is needed as a clue to the way by which [the disciples] might enter the kingdom. Jesus takes them right back to the beginning, where they must see themselves as outsiders who are looking for an entrance. Unless the disciples change their ways of thinking and acting, they will not enter the Kingdom of God' – *Entry Point*, 71.

of a missional partnership. This required 'listening' carefully to the voices of the participants, asking what churches and FBOs expected of God and one another in their work with children, and ascertaining if they were engaged in critical reflection on the 'Evangel' in their pragmatic interventions. I will return to this point later in this chapter.

Western FBOs were initiating and operating programmes, supplying financial resources and providing expertise. Suspicion, overwork, anxiety and competition were suggestive of insufficient attention to the Evangel of peace, or consideration of 'the child as a language of God'; that is, the child signs God's Kingdom as liberation from competition for greatness in missional activity.[14] I surmised that FBOs in Romania had effectively launched a new faith-based sector for children, but sadly with little 'dialogical space' for theological reflection with the local churches. At the programmatic level, thousands of children had been helped; the FBOs made a significant impact (positive and negative) on the evangelical churches, and in turn the churches started shaping FBO agendas, but the effects could have been more positive by holding intentional, theological conversations together.

By 2004, several churches that had been reluctant in the early 1990s to work with troubled children were becoming more socially concerned and engaged. Several key factors had influenced FBO and church response to children, and how the partnerships *described outcomes* in their lives. Further analysis highlighted what can be described as 'from above and from below'[15] approaches in FBO/church partnerships:

- *From above* represents how church leaders described God's ultimate actions toward humanity and their response to God.[16] In the main, church-based interventions were focused on 'saving' souls of children for an everlasting eternity, bringing children into a relationship with God as the churches understood God.
- *From below* represents how FBOs described their transient and human actions in the present towards children. FBO interventions

---

[14] The child as 'a language of God' first appeared in essays and papers from Willmer, White and others working in Child Theology: see John Collier (ed), *Toddling to the Kingdom* (London: Child Theology Movement, 2009).

[15] 'From above and from below' follows a methodological paradigm described by James E. Loder in *The Logic of the Spirit: The Human Spirit in Theological Perspective* (San Francisco, CA: Jossey-Bass, 1998), 5-15. For Loder, 'from below' (following Pannenberg) represents the standpoint of human science and human experience, while 'from above' represents the 'standpoint of God's self-revelation in Jesus Christ in whom it is disclosed what God means by humanity in relationship to what God means by God', Loder, *The Logic of the Spirit*, 4. Loder argues that both are necessary, in what he describes as a 'relational unity', Loder, *Logic*, 13.

[16] God's 'actions towards humanity' can be taken from texts such as 2 Corinthians 5:18-19: 'All this is from God, who reconciled us to himself through Christ ... that God was reconciling the world to himself in Christ, not counting men's sins against them.'

were primarily focused on the physical and psycho-social realities of children, 'saving them from suffering' by addressing moral formation, education, community and human development, family circumstances, and health.

An holistic approach to Christian mission argues for integration of both 'from above' and 'from below' dimensions, including and interweaving both faith and faith-in-action. However, the two have often been separated and held apart; even set over against each other, each laying claim to being the 'proper' expression of mission; Bosch notes that the relationship between the 'evangelistic and the societal dimensions' constitutes 'one of the thorniest areas in the theology and practise of mission'.[17] However, in God we are confronted with the promise of the grace and love of the Creator and Redeemer of all things: 'God has come into the world to accompany men and women as they live fully with and in God. What God gives is not an *add on* to the physical, psychological, and social needs of children, but God is met and accompanied in these forms of caring.'[18]

I found little concrete evidence that either churches or FBOs were working critically or meaningfully to integrate their perceived 'eternal' or ultimate objectives with their concerns for the physical and material objectives in carrying out mission with children. Few had articulated a coherent integrated missiology. The terms 'transformation' and 'holistic' were frequently used by FBOs, but the words were used as tropes – 'catch-all' phrases, when more in-depth theological reflection was required. Children were *objects* of church and FBO intervention, but the act of Jesus 'placing a child in the midst' was not considered as a *theological pointer* to what God might expect of FBO and church if their mission activity was indeed to correspond to God's own missional intentions.

Reflections and Application of Lessons Learned

The research and findings from Romania have wider relevance in mission and theological work with children. I contend that FBO/church partnerships must engage in more missiological reflection, and suggest that Child Theology and Christology, in particular, provide clues to ways forward. If what I labelled as 'from above', that is, the self-disclosure of God in Christ, is not meaningfully integrated with what is 'from below', that is, the physical, material and transient aspects of the humanity of children, churches may remain pietistic and concerned only with vertical dimensions of the gospel; conversely, FBOs which tend to leave the work of salvation and conversion to the churches, focussing on delivering effective social

---

[17] David Bosch, *Transforming Mission: Paradigm Shifts in Theology of Mission* (Maryknoll, NY: Orbis Books 1991), 401. The contrast between these terms in missiology goes back more than a hundred years.
[18] From a conversation by email with Haddon Willmer, 14 April 2014, while editing this chapter.

services for children, run the risk of embracing a 'secular eschatology'[19] rather than a deeply and authentically *Christian* action in the world.

Part of the challenge in drawing together the 'from above' and 'from below' dimensions is a re-visioning of holistic mission for children in a wider context. What follows are reflections, suggestions, and applications, which I offer especially to colleagues engaging in frontline mission with children. These men and women are typically deeply embedded in their work and ministries; I hope we will discover common ground in this discussion that opens us to the mystery and 'disturbance' of God.[20]

A Reflection on 'Transformation and Holistic Mission' with Children

> I beseech you therefore, brethren, by the mercies of God, that you present your bodies a living sacrifice, holy, acceptable to God, which is your reasonable service. And do not be conformed to this world, *but be transformed* by the renewing of your mind, that you may prove what is that good, and acceptable, and perfect will of God.[21]

It is common in Christian mission with children (and in general) to use the term 'holistic transformation' as a descriptor of outcomes.[22] Transformation finds an easy fit with the modern age which celebrates development and progress. 'Child development' as a concept is itself a product of the Enlightenment and modernity.[23] Meanings intended by the term 'transformation' are dependent on the usage or definition of the particular mission organisation, FBO, missionary or local church employing the term, though many may themselves only have a vague sense of what they mean by the word. This means that in order to make sense of what is being said about transformation, we must 'embrace open questions, tensions, and some confusion, while at the same time remaining honest whilst trying to

---

[19] Stephen Plant develops the concept of 'secular eschatology' in *Freedom as Development: Christian Mission and the Definition of Human Well-Being* (Cambridge: Henry Martyn Centre, 2002). Available from the online achives of www.martynmission.cam.ac.uk

[20] We will explore this term further in the coming pages.

[21] Romans 12:1-2 (NKJV). Karl Barth, in his exposition of this passage, inserts in his translation the phrase 'not to fashion yourselves according to the present form of this world, but according to its coming transformation'. Barth, *The Epistle to the Romans*, E.C. Hoskyns, trans. 6th edn (Oxford: OUP, 1960), 424, n. 1.

[22] I am not opposed to the term 'transformation' as a outcome in mission. I currently serve as a research tutor at the Oxford Centre for Mission Studies, where our mission statement is: 'Advancing Holistic Transformation through Scholarly Engagement'. However, we need to continue to think critically about the use of the term 'transformation'; this reflection is part of that discourse.

[23] Cunningham's *Children and Childhood in Western Society* is especially useful on this point.

sort out meaning'.[24] I have yet to find a common definition of 'transformation' in my international work and research with children; rather, there is diversity and ambiguity, though the idea generally indicates hope (even a sense of divinely sanctioned confidence) for change, and practical demonstrations of love, all as signs of God's Kingdom. Included are theological ideas, mixed with categories of social change and human concerns, or even tears.

In mission practice, we do well to ask the question: What realistic expectations *in Christ* best describe the goals and expected outcomes of mission with children? In 2014, after almost 24 years of intentional evangelical mission intervention in Romania and Eastern Europe, there is limited evidence that the transformation 'achieved' for children approximates to the freedom from suffering and evil promised in the Kingdom of God, as shall be revealed in 'a new heaven and new earth'.[25] In frequent travel to Cambodia, South-East Asia, and several countries in Africa, I meet with Christians serving needy children. We recognise that there is more evidence of the 'not yet' than 'already finished', as many FBOs and churches continue to work largely in isolation of one another, and many thousands of children continue to need assistance.[26]

Christian mission and interventions with children demonstrates *in a measure* what God has already accomplished in Christ in redeeming the humanity and spiritual lives of children; this should not be trivialised. But engagement with children in crisis reveals an important theological reality: 'The already in the kingdom and in Jesus is not the holistic transformation of the world or humanity ... the already in Christ includes [much] pain and suffering.'[27] Christian work with children faces the temptation of putting children in the centre in such a way that Jesus himself is marginalised. The child placed by Jesus among the disciples does not displace Jesus, but stands beside him, to point to truths about God's unexpected way of reigning in the now-and-not-yet world: 'Jesus put the child in the midst of the disciples who were arguing about power to [teach them to] follow him in the way to the cross.'[28]

---

[24] See H. Willmer's review of Vinay Samuel and Chris Sugden (eds), 'Mission as Transformation: A Theology of the Whole Gospel', in *Transformation,* 18:3 (July 2001), 194-96; also his 'Transforming Society – or Merely Making It: A Theological Discussion with the Bible in One Hand and a Very Particular Newspaper in the Other', in *Society for the Study of Theology Conference Proceedings* (Leeds, 1995).

[25] 2 Peter 3:12; Revelation 21:1.

[26] I write this after the recent annexation of Crimea by Russia. There continue to be signs of 'groaning for change' in Eastern Europe. Christian young people in Romania posted on social media their solidarity with their counterparts in Ukraine. A conference held recently in Bucharest, *Re-Imagining the Seminary and Child Theology* (September 2013) exemplifies the need for ongoing work.

[27] Haddon Willmer, 'Review: Mission as Transformation', 194.

[28] Collier, *Toddling to the Kingdom,* 116.

Christian churches and mission organisations must continue to watch, pray and act in the knowledge that *God* establishes what is rightfully his. The Holy Spirit broods over the face of the deep and offers hope in the midst of human suffering. This is where much Christian mission has been at its best in history, struggling to bring light in the dark corners of the world. The child who lives in the midst of crisis or pain can call forth this hope for God's Kingdom. We are reminded of the many thousands of Christian churches, residential homes and care centres where the choice to serve children is a lifelong commitment, and of the care-givers who watch and pray 365 days of the year, offering their lives in Christ's service *by and in* serving children.

In summary, concerning the outcomes in the lives of children, their families and communities, I hesitate to evaluate the actions of mission organisations as effecting complete 'transformation'. Rather, I interpret these outcomes as 'critical anticipatory signs and lighting candles in the darkness'.[29] These are pointers to the Kingdom of God, which is both present and coming. These are vital actions of obedience, faith in God, prayers for change; they do not allow space for resting or boasting. All human actions are tentative, temporal, subject to God's own work and glory.

Holistic Mission and the Disturbance of God

Following this reasoning, I will comment briefly on the term 'holistic' as a descriptor of mission with children. 'Holistic' outcomes have been described as meeting the physical, emotional and spiritual needs of children, redeeming whole persons and communities. We hope for a meaningful integration of what is from God in Christ with that which is rooted in our limited human efforts in mission. Justin Byworth, a colleague at World Vision, concedes that much remains to be learned about 'the place of spirituality in a community's sense of hope, and what impact this will have on participation and sustainability'.[30] This comment underscores my point: much of the language one encounters in mission concerning its 'holistic' nature tends to leave 'spirituality' or salvation in Christ, which engages with eternal life with God, to one side.[31] On the FBO side is the validity of caring for the humanity of the child, addressing hunger, abuse,

---

[29] 'Critical anticipatory signs and lighting candles in the darkness' is one of the many metaphors that came from dozens of verbal and written interactions with Willmer in the course of my research project.

[30] J. Byworth, 'World Vision's Approach to Transformational Development: Frame, Policy and Indicators', in *Transformation,* 20:2 (2003), 99–111.

[31] Language for eternity with God varies; the point is that for salvation to mean anything worthwhile, it must take into account the demands of God on the human situation. If left to assumptions and without critical evaluation, then the message of God in Christ is bracketed, not informing the totality of FBO action for children.

or need for family, what some describe as 'Samaritan theology' – helping children make it through another day on earth.

In my ongoing interactions with churches and pastors I hear continued speaking of salvation as a priority for children; FBOs, on the other hand, prefer to speak of 'holistic mission'. Yet these evangelical FBOs have not given up on salvation, eternity or eschatology. How then does Jesus and the call to follow him on his way to the Cross affect their 'Samaritan practice'? Jesus speaks of eternal life with God, and care for suffering neighbours, as integral and serious to life in his Kingdom; in the Matthew 18 text we see him refer to children as a way into the Kingdom and to 'his way of doing things'.

Neither churches nor FBOs have put extensive resources into sorting out such questions or bridging this divide. FBOs tend to use the language of faith and God on a 'spiritual' or motivational level, and then describe as 'holistic' programmatic interventions aimed at bettering child welfare in ways that are little different, in practice, to secular approaches, models and methodologies – perhaps with the addition of being prepared to share their motivations with recipients if asked. We ask, How does this 'holistic activity' interface with the eternal God? Some say it was experienced in prayer, others in times of 'divine intervention'; few explain how reflection and immersion in the life of Christ or the Evangel disturbs their 'holistic agenda'. It is as if 'holistic mission' might somehow be synonymous with the Kingdom of God, even when God is, for the most part, left to one side.

Thankfully, God does not remain 'bracketed' on his side of the equation; God in his freedom goes beyond our predictions and our reasonable expectations. The Cross 'articulates God's odd freedom, his strange justice, and His peculiar power'.[32] God surprises and disturbs. Indeed, this is one of Barth's points in his exposition of Romans 12:1-2:

> Once again we are confronted with this sidedness of the whole course of our human existence ... our life and will and acts are brought into question. For the freedom of God, the 'Other sidedness' of His mercies, means that there is a relationship between God and man, that there is a dissolution of human 'this sidedness' and that a radical assault is being made upon every contrasted, second, other thing.[33]

Children in crisis provide another theological clue at this point: FBOs and churches must do the best they can, taking reasonable action, thinking creatively, at times taking risks in caring for the whole child, but they should remain open to what they cannot plan or predict of God in advance. Children who have been traumatised are experts at upsetting established

---

[32] Walter Brueggemann, *The Prophetic Imagination*, 2nd edn (Minneapolis, MN: Fortress Press, 2001), 99.

[33] K. Barth, *Epistle to the Romans*, 427. I am aware that many of my evangelical colleagues have not carefully read Barth, especially church leaders in Romania. I value Barth's work on God's everlasting covenant with humanity, as his partner in mission and life. I cite him several times in this chapter.

theories, organised programmes, and methodical care-giving; they constantly surprise, challenge and disturb, and in so doing, they speak (or shout) the language of God. Faith-based care entails openness to the prodding and judgement of God,[34] and sensitivity to the experiences and pain of children living in a fallen world.

God is not limited by the limitations of 'holistic' agendas. Most children who have been severely traumatised will always carry the scars of their experience.[35] Any account of holism offered by FBOs must take into account God's freedom and disturbance, and God's 'gift of pain'.[36] There are many children who have suffered terrible abuse and neglect, such as those who are abandoned to live on the streets of our global mega-cities. Yet these children demonstrate remarkable resilience in their ability to cope with a way of life that would be impossible for us who are conditioned by our creature comforts.[37]

> It remains true that God, as creator and Lord, is always free to produce even in human activity and its results, in spite of the problems involved, *parables* of his own internal good will and actions. It is more than ever true then, that with regard to these [actions] no proud abstention but only reverence, joy, and gratitude are appropriate.[38]

This suggests another question: how does 'holism' and its concomitant human development agenda account for the death, burial and resurrection of God in Christ? Brueggemann sees in the crucifixion of Jesus 'the ultimate act of criticism in which Jesus announces the end of the world of death ... and takes the death into his own person';

> The criticism consists not in standing over against but *in standing with*; the ultimate criticism is not one of triumphant indignation but one of passion and

---

[34] By 'judgement of God' in this context I am not referring to a 'Final Judgement', but rather that all human activity is laid bare and open before God, and that God is the arbiter for how these actions will, or will not, reflect his glory.

[35] Here I take issue with those who predict that abused children can be 'completely restored to wholeness'. All children (and human beings) carry signs of both wholeness and brokenness; sin is a present reality and any 'holistic' agenda that does not give a reckoning of sin falls short in describing the life of the Kingdom. The balance, in my thinking, is found in the walk of faith that places trust in God's sustaining love and his unlimited freedom.

[36] See Philip Yancey and Paul Brand, *Pain: The Gift Nobody Wants* (New York: Harper Collins Publishing, 1999). For a piercing study concerning the Christian faith and the problem of evil and pain, see Ulrich Simon's *A Theology of Auschwitz* (Atlanta, GA: John Knox Press, 1979).

[37] Resilience is the ability to cope with difficult and stressful situations. When I worked in Romania, several participants working with street children laughed and said, 'That is not something we need to teach them; every child that comes off the streets or a broken home has learned to cope with difficulty.'

[38] K. Barth, *The Humanity of God* (Atlanta, GA: John Knox Press, 1960), 54-55.

compassion that completely and irresistibly undermines the world of competence and competition.[39]

This is the 'standing with' we see in the acts of those Christian care-givers, parents and missionaries who will not abandon the child or young adult when they show no visible sign of 'transformation'.[40]

Embracing Tensions in Partnership

Mission with children requires more than a 'gospel of sin management' that simply calls for their conversion to a 'life in heaven', or readjusting questionable social systems for 'life in the present'. The gospel offers life in Christ, who fully embraces the 'already and not yet'.[41] FBO/church partnerships are an expression of Christian mission and the love of God for humanity and children. Missional partnerships that engage children in crisis require exchanging the categories of certitude, entitlement and privilege, for categories of fidelity, relationship, and mutual embrace.[42] Following Jesus Christ to work with children or youth in crisis, invites, pulls and pushes FBOs and churches into deeper *koinonia*.

In the final sections of this chapter, I will suggest three theological and missiological methods that can serve to reorient FBO/church partnerships to future possibilities in their love and relationship to both Christ and children in crisis: embracing the Cross in partnership, how a 'child in the midst' serves as a pointer in partnership, and how embracing ambiguity in partnerships can point to fuller life in the Kingdom of God.

---

[39] Brueggemann, *Prophetic Imagination*, 94-95.

[40] Thanks to Keith White for this insight. Keith and his family, along with his father's and grandfather's families, have successively run and lived in Mill Grove, a residential for children and families in the East End of London since the 1890s.

[41] Dallas Willard, *The Divine Conspiracy: Rediscovering our Hidden Life in God* (San Francisco, CA: Harper Collins, 1998), 42. In his notes on this section of his argument concerning a 'gospel of sin management', Willard cites the language of Barth, 'an absorption of Christology into soteriology' and goes on to say, 'there [can be] an entire loss of Christological concern in the preoccupation with personal salvation or that of shaping society'. Willard., 43.

[42] I draw here on a comment in a lecture given by Walter Brueggemann when he addressed a group of 'emergent' leaders who have a hunger for certitude. 'Certitude is a flat and mechanistic category but fidelity is a relational category. We must acknowledge our thirst for certitude and recognise that if we had all certitudes in the world, it would not make the quality of life any better, because we must have fidelity. We face in church ministry a constant confusion of those categories'. Brueggemann, 'Nineteen Theses: Overcoming the Dominant Scripts of our Age', recorded lecture (2005).

'Embracing the Cross' in Partnership

Partnership occurs in community; this is a secular fact, but mission partnerships require a more precise Christian form. A Christian community lives and exists in fellowship and partnership with God and therefore lives in obedience to the work of God in Christ, which includes and centres on the Cross. As Villafane notes, 'The Cross frees us up to enter into legitimate and authentic mutuality – true *koinonia*.'[43] The 'Way of the Cross' calls us to live in the company of Jesus in the way of his Kingdom.[44] The 'cross' in St Paul's influential presentation not only makes clear who God is but teaches Christians how to live together in fellowship. Paul address the divisions in the church in Corinth by reminding his readers of the 'power of the cross for those who are being saved'.[45]

Christian mission acknowledges dependence on God and grace; the transformation the Bible speaks of is dependent on the mercy and action of God. 'We have found the world a great, unsolved enigma; an enigma to which Christ, the mercy of God, provides the answer'.[46] This is revealed through the Cross, especially as it concerns caring for children in crisis.

> The cross points to a choice between addressing pain and suffering from the perspective of order and management by taking control of the public sphere, or building covenant communities which embrace pain and pay the price through their own suffering ... The cross makes possible a new reconciled humanity [and community] (Eph. 2:18-22).[47]

I question if improved social policy or better mission management will completely eradicate the problems that children continue to face in our sinful and broken world. However, the Cross points us to the finality of Christ's work to overcome death in his suffering and resurrection – the great 'krisis', or 'great disturbance'.[48] God in resurrection is what disturbs the world, which thinks that death is final. This should not be misunderstood as a pietistic call to retreat from the world of suffering and evil. There are some who would say the presence of suffering is confirmation that the world is bound for destruction, and therefore retreat from addressing personal and social evil. By no means does the church or FBO passively endure all suffering as it awaits the final consummation.

---

[43] Eldin Villafane, *Seek the Peace of the City: Reflections on Urban Ministry* (Grand Rapids, MI: Eerdmans, 1995), 10.

[44] For my use of the 'Kingdom of God', see N.T. Wright, *The Mission and Message of Jesus* in M. Borg and N.T. Wright, *Mission and Message of Jesus* (New York: Harper Collins, 2000), 31-54.

[45] 2 Corinthians 1:10-25; Philippians 2:5-11.

[46] Karl Barth, *Epistle to the Romans*, 427.

[47] V. Samuel and C. Sugden, *The Church in Response to Human Need* (Oxford: Regnum, 2003), 73-74.

[48] Barth's exposition of Romans 12-15 confronts the 'problem of ethics' in a section he calls the 'The Great Disturbance', saying that 'human behaviour must inevitably be disturbed by the thought of God'. Barth, *Epistle to the Romans*, 424.

Embracing the Cross means a reversal of the common view of power as it is redefined in the light of the crucifixion of Christ.[49] Concepts of power, control and mutuality are especially relevant with regard to mission with children. Power is understood by Paul as resistance to the temptation to dominate.[50] Children rarely dominate adults or compete with adults for control or power in organisations, yet a critical look at ourselves, our organisations and even our churches 'reveals that competition, not compassion, is often a main motivation in life'.[51] In mission, pastors, leaders and organisations are tempted to become immersed in all sorts of competitive moves, even if they would rarely admit it of and to themselves.

When FBOs and churches come together to offer care to a child in crisis, they are 'given up' to one another as the child's pain becomes the centre of their attention. FBOs and churches move *towards* the Kingdom when they leave behind their organisational or confessional assurances, subtle plays at power, prestige, control and competition, to embrace outcast, excluded, ignored, or marginalised children.

Jesus Places a Child in the Midst as a Pointer in Partnership

What does God intend when he places a child in the midst of a mission partnership? He places a child 'in the midst' to refocus their attention on the nature of the Kingdom of God: 'I tell you the truth, unless you change and become like little children, you will never enter the Kingdom of Heaven.'[52] Jesus can be read as saying that children act as a parabolic point of entry into the Kingdom of God. The important matter for the disciples is to 'enter', to be 'in' the Kingdom, not that they strive for recognition and power.

Children represent a paradigm of vulnerability that may serve as a valid starting-point for transforming how power and control are understood in FBO/church partnerships. The disciples were not ready to enter God's reign, so 'becoming a child' required a radical change in their thinking. This change does not mean that they were to go back to being simple children; they are adults and must think and act as adults; they must change their assumptions, their priorities, and their orientation. The text in

---

[49] Literature on 'powers' in the NT is considerable: see Walter Wink, *The Powers that Be: Theology for a New Millennium* (New York: Doubleday, 1998), and Jayakumar Christian, *God of the Empty-Handed: Poverty, Power and the Kingdom of God* (Monrovia, CA: MARC, 1999).

[50] Philippians 2:5-6.

[51] Henri J. Nouwen, D.P. McNeill and D.A. Morrison, *Compassion: Reflections on the Christian Life* (New York: Image Books, 1983), 19.

[52] Matthew 18:3. I return here to insights gained in interaction with the Child Theology Movement which takes this text, Mark 9:33-37 and Luke 9:46-48 as a point of departure from other common NT texts on care for children – Matthew 19:13-14 and Matthew 18:1-3; see Willmer and White, *Entry Point*.

Matthew 18 is sometimes read with the idea that the disciples must be gentle, simple, humble and naïve in order to enter the Kingdom of God. But Jesus is speaking to them in parabolic language; they are hard of hearing. They will have to make a complete change in their orientation toward his Kingdom, something that requires adult courage and maturity. Finding their way into the Kingdom of God would involve a special kind of learning, the kind of thinking that we cannot fully understand 'until we get inside it – and even then not fully; this is conversion'.[53]

Children also serve as reminders of life and hope; there is tremendous potential in the life of a child; there is resilience and hope for becoming. The child brings potential for imagination, play and renewal. 'Unto us a child is given': children are signs of hope for every generation, our children remind us of the power of persistence. The power of the child to bring hope to her family, to the wider community, is great and wonderful. The best power in the world has limits and weakness but in many ways the child has the power to remind us of the positive aspects of life and freedom in Christ.

If children can serve as pointers to Kingdom greatness, then FBOs and churches that compete with one another for recognition, resources or support can learn something from a child's receptivity. Of course, there are children who are hostile and unwelcoming, but they also give clues to the nature of living realistically in the light of the Kingdom, for much work on their behalf is like 'lighting candles in the darkness', hoping and working with little certainty that interventions will be effective. This is how it is with the Kingdom of God: it receives, welcomes, surprises, disturbs and challenges human assumptions and assurances.

Just as the child is on the way, in transition, becoming – often in very painful ways – going wrong or being wronged on the way, then Jesus' disciples must be open to this way of becoming. In their argument about power, they assume they are 'already' part of Jesus' inner circle; their horizon of expectation is 'what do we need to do *in order to be great* in this Kingdom?' Jesus takes their expectations and reframes the horizon. He says the Kingdom is not a matter of 'who you are', 'what you do', or 'what difference you are making'; for on these positive or negative distinctions 'much self-esteem is based and human competition thrives'.[54] In the Kingdom of God it is sufficient simply to be counted as a member: to enter into God's reign. Jesus offers the disciples a new way, but they must give up their fearful clinging and aspirations of greatness to enter his Kingdom and 'live with Him in the fearless life of God Himself'.[55] I know no FBO/church partnerships that have 'already' arrived; they are moving together in approaching the way of God's Kingdom *with* the children they are serving. The Kingdom is both a present and future possibility; as the

---

[53] H. Willmer, unpublished lecture at Oxford Centre for Mission Studies, 2003; see also *Entry Point.*

[54] Nouwen et al, *Compassion: Reflections*, 19.

[55] Nouwen et al, *Compassion: Reflections*, 21.

child lives with expectancy, FBOs and churches can remain hopeful in partnership, and hopeful that their partnership will reflect and enter itself into God's reign.

Embracing Ambiguity in Partnerships that Point to the Kingdom

Embracing tension in partnership may also remind those engaged in mission to children of the reality that everything in human existence – including our love for God, one another, and children – is coloured to some degree by human ambiguity.[56] The more we love, the more our faith is vulnerable to the reality that not all is well with the world.[57] Leading an organisation, helping a child in crisis, working with a pastor, or making decisions about partnership are rarely crystal-clear situations.[58] Human beings sometimes fear ambiguity, but ambiguity can be a gift of grace when it leads to greater discernment of the work of God in Christ and by the Spirit.[59]

Ambiguity serves to test untested assurances, selfish ambitions, and our attempts to control chaotic situations. Ambiguity can save when it leads to repentance, discernment and patience with humanity. Ambiguity means that partners will struggle as they grow in mutual surrender to God's Kingdom ways. Jesus warned the disciples that his mission was not always to spread peace.[60] He described divisions in families, where our most intimate personal relationships are developed. Jesus also told the disciples that 'from John until now the kingdom of God has suffered violence and the violent take it by force'.[61]

There are times when working together in partnership requires that churches, pastors and FBOs embrace this 'violence'. This not a battlefield mentality where partners compete for right or privilege; it is a violence of a radical turning towards the Cross, the Kingdom, and Christ. In embracing this sort of 'Kingdom violence', partnerships will be more discerning of the

---

[56] Pierre Wolff, *Discernment: The Art of Choosing Well: Based on Ignatian Spirituality* (Liguori, MS: Triumph, 2003).

[57] See Jeremiah 45.

[58] Leadership study has begun to use the term 'asymmetrical leadership' to describe action-based learning theory. Faced with rapid global change, 'asymmetrical leadership' is concerned with leading through change, momentum and motion, in a constantly changing organisational environment.

[59] Barth, commenting on Romans 5:1: 'The necessity of passing through the narrow gate which leads from life to death and from death to life, must remain a sheer impossibility and a sheer necessity ... The comfortable and easy manner in which men advance towards this critical point [having faith in God] is the primary curse which lies upon all, or almost all, dogmatic preaching, and is the lie, the poison, which is so difficult to eradicate from the pastoral ministry of the church ... As far as we can see, our hands are empty.' Barth, *Epistle to the Romans*, 150.

[60] Matthew 10:34-36.

[61] Matthew 11:12.

reality of God's leading. Christians who persist in this sort of faith have a chance of 'getting free from the illusionary horizons of perfection'.[62] They may be more inclined to remember, 'there is no creature hidden from His sight, all things are naked and open to the eyes of Him to whom we *must give* an account'.[63]

In their actions to take up the cause of children and identifying with their vulnerability, FBOs and churches must constantly evaluate their interventions and partnerships reflecting on Christ and his Kingdom. 'Power is the freedom to let go of all that hinders the expression of sacrificial love'.[64] The loss of hope and love is a major casualty in situations of poverty and oppression; children in crisis have usually suffered this loss. FBO/church partnerships portend to offer the child in crisis new hope, both in this world and eternity, through opportunity, restoration of human dignity, forgiveness, and a chance to assume responsibility for their futures. Children in crisis serve as reminders to FBO/church partnerships that God is their covenant partner even when their attempts to intervene may run aground or accomplish the opposite of their intended results. After all, it is not so much the FBO/church activity that most interests God, but the human beings who make the attempt, and those who are served.

Tensions in partnership are mitigated when partners are less confident of stubborn assurance and willing to embrace the ambiguity of human actions. Ambiguity serves to question and dismantle arrogance and dogmatism, and leads to open questions, repentance and patience with others. Children remind us that God is committed by covenant and command to partnership with our humanity.

Conclusion

Several years ago, I lived in Romania working with churches and FBOs as both mission practitioner and researcher. I set out to explore a central question: How and to what degree do FBO/church understandings of God's work in Christ enable or hinder their collaboration and actions in reference to children? I explored two of the forms of 'church' in Romania: the indigenous local community churches, and the incoming organisations that specialised in serving children in crisis. Each of these forms of church had 'enough' theology to satisfy itself and to claim its identity and role in Christian mission. Much of the operational theology was directed at identity cohesion and affirming what I have described as either working 'from above' or 'from below'. Holistic mission and transformation were

---

[62] Haddon Willmer, email to the author, May 2008.
[63] Hebrews 13:4, emphasis added.
[64] J. Andrew Kirk, *What is Mission? Theological Explorations* (Minneapolis, MN: Fortress Press, 2000), 196. Cf. Mark 10:42-45; John 10:17-18; 3:1.

examined because these forms of churches claimed to be engaged in some form of each.

I suggest that the research in Romania has wider implications for mission with children, implications explored in this chapter. In many missional contexts, churches and FBOs often use their speech and action for God to maintain their own assurance of being 'right'. Too often there is a limited range of theological curiosity or theological engagement with one another, and with it intentional vulnerability to disturbance, ambiguity or question. I have argued that we might learn to see the action of Jesus placing a child in the midst of mission partnerships as a 'theological pointer' as we explore new ways of doing theology and mission together, with openness to being confronted by the otherness of God's way of reigning. But for this to happen, both churches and FBOs must embrace the actual child, not their preconceived notions of what that child represents for them, as an invitation to follow Jesus on the way to the Cross. Perhaps this might awaken churches and FBOs to the distance we all have to travel as we move towards the Kingdom of God.

PART FOUR

THE HINGE: CROSS AND RESURRECTION

THEOLOGY, MISSION AND CHILD UNDER THE SHADOW OF THE CROSS AND IN THE LIGHT OF THE RESURRECTION

Keith J. White and Haddon Willmer

United with Christ in his death ... united with Christ in his resurrection (Romans 6:5).

Having been buried with him in baptism and raised with him through your faith in the power of God, who raised him from the dead (Colossians 2:12).

A Model of Mission Deriving from the *Missio Dei*

There are many ways of patterning Christian theology so that it encompasses and brings together the truth of God in his revelation in Christ on the one hand, and the actuality of the world and our being in it on the other. No pattern does this job perfectly, and all patterns have their uses as well as their dangers and limitations.

We have chosen here the pattern derived from the way of God in the incarnation of the Word; the way of the Son in the world in oneness with the Father and the Holy Spirit. This is the *missio Dei* which calls, directs and undergirds any mission we might have. It does not point to a mission which is a progressive spread of the word, or of light and love, gradually through the world. Sometimes mission has been seen as spread and expansion. A good example of this approach is Adolf von Harnack's classic study of mission in the early church, *Mission und Ausbreitung* ('Mission and Expansion').[1] It gives the picture of a gradual but irresistible tide rolling over the world. In times of (perhaps overstated) missionary confidence this has been a dominant image. The 1910 Edinburgh Missionary Conference can be seen in just such a light, even if its title, 'The Evangelisation of the World in this Generation' is not wholly representative of its intention and content.

God's way in the world, however, is not such a continuum. It is made up of what seem like disjointed episodes, comings and goings. The biblical narrative tells of repeated exiles and returns, of enslavement and redemption, of setbacks and rescues, of loss and finding. John's Gospel

---

[1] Adolf von Harnack, *Die Mission und Ausbreitung des Christentums in den ersten drei Jahrhunderten: die Mission in Wort und Tat* (University of Michigan, 1906).

makes much of the 'coming' and 'going' of Jesus, and it is a significant part of John's missionary vision.[2]

We have chosen to hinge this book around a brief reflection on the great discontinuity at the heart of Christian faith, which is signified and actualised in the death and resurrection of Jesus. This is reflected and repeatedly rediscovered, newly displayed and entered into, whenever people follow in the way of Jesus. It is shared in baptism and in the Lord's Supper, and in living which has any likeness to what Paul describes, in various ways, as bearing the dying of the Lord Jesus so that his life may be manifest in our mortal bodies, and letting death work in us so that life may work in others.[3]

Cross and Resurrection can be used as terms to describe Christ-like spiritual character; however, they then tend to be abstracted from public historical action and are personal and inward. Apart from anything else, our concern with mission makes that move unhelpful. Without minimising the spirituality of Cross and Resurrection, we hold on to its lived temporality and earthiness: Jesus lived through these, in the body, personally, and publicly. The mission of Jesus, and mission as Jesus defines it for us, is not to be wholly spiritualised.

So now, when we investigate theology, mission and child(ren), we hold on to the historical public action which is mission, and seek to interpret it as the life in which we suffer with Christ in the hope of sharing in his resurrection. Mission in practice is like this: it is often venture which sets out to share the gospel goodness of God in Christ, and runs into difficulties and frustrations, some of them deadly, and so it looks for life through and beyond this dying. It does this not for itself as a self-interested enterprise (making our missionary organisations survive and get bigger as an end in itself) but out of desire for the salvation of the world and the glory of God.

This theological pattern of mission can be traced in many if not all the articles in this book, and sometimes obviously and profoundly. That has not been prescribed for authors. This central part and chapter has been planned, because the outline structure of the whole volume was designed according to the pattern of the way to the Cross and from it in Resurrection. We have chosen to work within The Triangle as a way of disciplining ourselves to hold on to the three points – theology, mission and child – in each paper, and in the volume as a whole. We did not want to end up with a collection that was so strong on any one of the points that the other two were dwarfed or put in the shadow of the others. That was the brief; however, the underlying pattern of mission that can be deduced from the papers is testimony to something other than the editors' brief.

Given this pattern, we asked the authors of the chapters immediately before and after this theological hinge to work under the shadow of the

---

[2] See, for example, John 12:24-26, 34-36.
[3] Romans 8:10-11.

Cross and in the light of the Resurrection, respectively. In Part Three – Threats and Challenges – the focus on children in contexts around the world leads us to see them as reflecting the world of humanity which goes to death in sin. And this is encountered in mission, in its powerlessness of its own accord to change the world. Mission studies rarely if ever chart mission *inability*; they either tell mission history as a success story, or an exhortation to have another go at crusading, this time to win. *Theology* in turn often serves myopic optimism ('with God all things are possible'), though if it is at all close to Jesus, it also prays in the darkness of Gethsemane. So there is some sense of the descent into darkness in these chapters. And none of the chapters in this book is unaware of the darkness in which the light of Christ shines, sometimes flickeringly.

The final two sections – Parts Five and Six – come after this hinge chapter – and we choose to see them in the light of the resurrection of Christ. We thought of structuring the book in this way, not merely to give the darkness of the world its due – and so to share the sufferings of God and children in the world – but so that the gospel of resurrection could burst on the reader like the sun rising; or more than the sun rising, for we expect that to happen each day, whereas the resurrection of Christ is surprise, a new unimagined world coming upon us.

As will become apparent, whether considering the pattern of the book as a whole, or reading individual chapters as stand-alone papers, this structuring is anything but neat, or cut-and-dried. It represents an attempt to be faithful to the revelation of God in Christ, and to put all elements of The Triangle – theology, mission and child – like any activity, in the name of Jesus, at the foot of the Cross and in the service of the risen Christ. Those who are familiar with the work of James Loder will also recognise here an attempt to be alive to the 'logic of the Spirit', which is anything but a linear progression, transformation or development.[4]

The Cross

As indicated, the chapters in Part Three – Threats and Challenges – of the book allow the scene-setting in the first two parts to be shaken, and the reader to be jarred by the rugged encounters with real children and their difficult contexts such as those described in these chapters. We are of course aware that these chapters and their sometimes sombre messages are not representative of children worldwide. That has not been our intention, not least because it is probably an impossible task. But we do know that they are replicated across history and throughout the continents of the world. As we seek to enter by imagination, provoked by the narrative descriptions offered into such situations, and to empathise with those

---

[4] James E. Loder, *The Logic of the Spirit: Human Development in Theological Perspective* (San Francisco, CA: Jossey-Bass, 1998).

children described, we find that we have been disarmed and forced to stop in our tracks. We are, theologically speaking, at the foot of the Cross. We have nothing to say with which we are able to defend ourselves as fellow-Christians, even if we should wish to.

We find ourselves with Luther: there is, again and again, an absence of God, of health, of life, of goodness. And we must not, we dare not, find a way out that resembles what Bonhoeffer called 'cheap grace'.[5] Some might wish to claim the healing of the resurrection of Jesus, the power revealed at Pentecost. But these do not dispel the darkness and the suffering of children who cry out here and now; to believe that they do is a theological fiction. Children are crying out in anguish and chronic pain, victims of manifold forms of abuse and neglect, even in places where churches and Christian organisations have long been active. If confronted by one such child, face-to-face, we would be unable to speak. We must listen in silence until we have begun, in and like Christ, to take their suffering into ourselves, including into our theology and mission.

And this is to re-enact in some small, possibly immaterial way, what the Cross of Jesus Christ is all about: 'My God, my God, why hast thou forsaken this child/me/your beloved Son?' In this experience of trial, affliction and dereliction,[6] and the apparent absence of God in his creation,[7] is it possible that we find him, with the eyes of faith?

There is a huge challenge to assumptions and traditions when the suffering of a Botswanan girl child, or South African street boys, or post-Communism children of Romania, are brought into the very centre of our beings. It can shake or break us to the point of provoking the death of long-cherished beliefs and practices. Our theology and mission are taken to the foot of the Cross. In the Introduction we referred to the IMC meeting at Willingen in 1953. *Missions under the Cross*, the papers of this historic meeting that stands between Edinburgh 1910 and Edinburgh 2010, describe with great feeling and honesty what any true *theologia crucis* entails.[8] But significantly they do not refer to children. In this volume we find perhaps a way in which, in our day and age, we can recapture in the suffering of a single child the weight, pain and doubt that they expressed. If so we have been brought by God's grace once again face-to-face with human sin (that

---

[5] 'Cheap grace is grace without discipleship, grace without the cross, grace without Jesus Christ, living and incarnate.' Dietrich Bonhoeffer, *The Cost of Discipleship* (New York: Touchstone, 1995), 45.

[6] *Anfechtung*, in German.

[7] Described classically in Latin as *Deus absconditus atque praesens* – God hidden and present.

[8] Norman Goodall (ed), *Missions Under the Cross* (Edinburgh: Edinburgh House Press, 1953).

is, a sin which is our own – not just that of others), and what it meant and means for the Lamb of God to bear our sin.[9]

At this very poignant moment we remind ourselves that this book has been engendered and is led by mission. In mission, God comes from light into darkness. Light, love, giving, sending and hope are the origin of mission – enough to send it into the heart of the world, where people are in darkness. There can be no mission where people run away from what is unpleasant, dangerous and resistant, and remain impervious. It is necessary to go to Jerusalem, said Jesus: a prophet presses on with his commission to the crisis, even if it means suffering and death. And those who follow are often afraid.[10]

It is possible to conceive and plan mission so that no one takes risks or gets hurt, but it will not be *Christian* mission. And it will not be much good for human beings who need it. Physical danger to life is not the key issue here; and there is no virtue in missionaries or anyone else recklessly courting death. The Cross in mission is the encounter with sin and evil in its many different forms, in every aspect and institution of life in the world, some of them respectable and some immensely stubborn. Mission brings us face-to-face with it. And along with that, mission involves people in uncertainty about what should be done in mission, and in wondering whether they are fit for it. Mission takes us into new territory and to extreme tests: to Gethsemane, to Golgotha.

Some missionaries like David Livingstone do remarkable things (as well as some questionable things), and are armoured by extraordinary determination and self-confidence. They would not admit they make serious mistakes, but rather leave these to their biographers (who are, however, often hagiographers, playing down their foibles and mistakes to maintain a triumphal narrative of mission). Other missionaries may be broken by struggles with what they ought to do and whether they can do it. So, inwardly and outwardly, mission existence (as memorably described more than once by Paul) goes into the darkness.

The missionary goes into the darkness: she does not simply go as the light to those in darkness. In this she follows the example, pattern and experience of her Master: 'He was made sin who knew no sin.'[11] To see mission in this way is not novel, but it bears retelling, for we would forget it if we could. But to put the child in mission is unusual. That is what we have been doing in the early Sections of this book, particularly the third: looking at child and mission in ways that bring us into the darkness of the

---

[9] In the book *Entry Point* we make the radical suggestion that the child placed by Jesus in the midst of his disciples is not an alternative to the call of the Cross, but rather a restatement of it. This present collection of articles may prompt some readers to consider the same possibility. Willmer and White, *Entry Point* (London: WTL Publications, 2013).

[10] Mark 10:32.

[11] 2 Corinthians 5:21.

'sin and want and sorrow' which 'abound' in the world. True, the darkness does not overcome the light, but the light goes on shining against much resistance and misunderstanding. Mission does not achieve the speedy spread of light across the whole world.

Before mission is sent out by the risen Christ in the power of the resurrection, it consists in being with Jesus, staying with him in his troubles, and going his way in honest encounter with the reality of human being in the world. This world is exposed for what it is in the Cross of Jesus.

Neither this Edinburgh series, nor this book, are intended as devotional aids for the personal spiritual development of the reader, but it may well be, on reflection, that this is a by-product. We are not inviting readers to enter the wilderness of their own spirituality, but it is possible that by empathising with the child or children that we seek to receive as placed in our midst by Jesus, there are intimations of that harrowing experience.

In his reflection on the lectionary readings for the first Sunday in Lent 2014,[12] David Henson wrote, 'It was in this place, in my experience of God's absence and in the darkness of my own doubt, that I found not just abiding faith but, more importantly, compassion.'[13] And it may well be that the chapters that immediately precede this hinge reflection may have the effect of calling readers to follow children into the darkness where they do not experience anything but the absence of God – or any angels, for that matter.[14]

It must be questioned whether any follower of Jesus Christ can be engaged in genuine theology or mission unless and until we have come to comprehend 'the visible and manifest things of God seen through suffering and the Cross'. Children, as we have sought to be honest enough to acknowledge in Part Three, have been routinely humiliated, tortured and abused, and these are exactly the words that the apostle Paul and Luther use of Jesus. When we welcome children in the name of Jesus, we welcome him; when we despise, humiliate and abuse them, then – unavoidably – we do the same to him. God has made himself a worldly reality and we cannot grasp this by standing, as it were, apart from reality in whatever version of an ivory tower we choose to inhabit, so as to view this suffering from a safe distance.

When we are open to receive it, we know that any speech about God is speech about an absence. God is known to us in the Cross: and that is where a beloved Son experiences being abandoned, and dies. We find God here in the complete opposite of his nature. We can only understand the

---

[12] Genesis 2; Psalm 32; Romans 5; and Matthew 4.

[13] David R. Henson, 'Into the Wild: A Lenten Homily Not about Temptation', in *Patheos Progressively Christian Blog*, at www.patheos.com/blogs/davidhenson/2014/03/into-the-wild-a-lenten-homily-not-about-temptation/ (accessed 24 May 2014).

[14] Matthew 18:10.

absolute transcendence of God where the human and worldly mock all that he is and stands for. Thus the Cross, like the suffering of children, can be seen as a hinge (this and all other metaphors crack and strain at this point) that connects the hurt of creation and the heart of God.

Commenting on Luther's theology of the Cross, Rowan Williams writes: 'Here where all theological speculation, all conceptual neatness and controlled-ness fall away, God is simply God. It is an experientially and historically oriented restatement of the tradition of negative theology: God himself is the great 'negative theologian', who shatters all our images by addressing us in the cross of Jesus.'[15]

Given the concern of the present age with children's rights and protection, and the high profile given to child abuse, it may be that the suffering of children is a way of forcing us to revisit the Cross in sharper relief than we do by other means.

We note that Henson, like Luther and the Welsh poet and priest R.S. Thomas,[16] is not denying the absence of God by seeing it as replaced by the resurrection, as dawn disperses the darkness of the night. The experience of the darkness and of the absence brings us closer to Jesus in the wilderness, in Gethsemane, on the Cross, and in the tomb.

There is much genuine and passionate action by Christians on behalf of and alongside children who are hurting: that is Christian mission with children as a focus. But we do well to ponder the motivation of those of us who act and those who support them. Is it possible that such support, even such work can be, *inter alia*, a defence against recognising and embracing the utter terror and repugnance of the Cross as represented by the suffering of children? Like the acts of penitence that Luther came to reject so vehemently, this activity may be a subconscious way of denying the gospel's truth about ourselves as revealed in the Cross of Christ.

The Resurrection

In the fifth part of this book – Signs of Life and Hope – we will explore some of the positive, life-giving insights when children are in the midst. For there is in Christ, and the Christ-pattern, growth, hope; a looking up and forward. However, this does not leave behind the challenges brought to bear upon theology, mission and child in the first half of this book, as if these have been decidedly dealt with, and no longer need trouble us. There is no such thing as scar-less healing, and we do not proceed as if the resurrection has cancelled out in some simplistic way the suffering that has disturbed and shaken us.

---

[15] Rowan Williams, *The Wound of Knowledge: Christian Spirituality from the New Testament to St John of the Cross* (London: Darton, Longman & Todd, 1990), 149.

[16] For example, R. S. Thomas, 'In a Country Church', in *Selected Poems* (London: Granada, 1973), 42; and 'The Answer', in *Later Poems* (London: Macmillan, 1984), 121.

But since we come into the darkness with Jesus, and at the Cross, we are not only in sorrow and brokenness, but are at the hinge, though in that place we may not sense it. Until the hinge creaks on Easter day ('while it was yet dark'),[17] and indeed until sometime afterward, we may not see that it is there. It must move, and let a little light come through, before we can guess that the seemingly solid wall has a door hidden in it.

God in Christ is hinge, breakthrough, and door opening. God in Christ is liberation into newness of life, not a revolution that claims to take us out of this present, ambiguous, imperfect world into an unambiguous perfection, but as love in persistent service, enduring in hope and faith. In the risen life of Christ, we may live again with God as he is in the world in Jesus, doing good, showing truth.

A reading of the letters of the apostle Paul makes it abundantly clear that it is (only) through baptism into the death of Christ that we can be raised into new life, life led by the Spirit, where the Word lives in us. Paul is, of course, writing on this side of the resurrection, but in doing so he constantly refers to his suffering in the name and for the sake of the crucified and risen Lord, Jesus Christ. In fact, the power of the resurrection and fellowship in Christ's sufferings are inseparable.[18] It is a life given to and for others, in the name of Christ, and rejoices in suffering.

In the Orthodox Church in Romania the resurrection of Jesus is proclaimed with the following words: *Hristos a înviat!* Christ is risen! *Adevărat a înviat!* He is risen indeed! Dana Bates reflects on this in the following way:

> Today, which marks the middle of the Lenten season here, and the Adoration of the Holy Cross, we are glimpsing the celebration of the victory of Christ on the Cross, encouraged and reassured to continue fighting the good fight of faith, even as you, our sisters and brothers, are tasting, seeing, drinking and breathing in His glorious Resurrection.

> His Resurrection. All hinges upon it. And from His Resurrection breaks forth all the little resurrections. Broken lives restored, injustices righted, hungers filled, brokenness healed, death defeated. The most treasured reason why we love what we do is because of all the little resurrections we get to witness in the lives IMPACT touches here in Romania and abroad. Watching the lives of these young people break forth through the surrounding darkness and despair to bring hope, healing, redemption, answers to the real problems of others. Thriving in and dispersing the Light of His Resurrection.[19]

Little resurrections: perhaps that is a way of conceiving (if only fleetingly, like a shaft of sunlight that breaks through the passing clouds) Part Five of this volume, and, indeed, of mission in the light of Christ's

---

[17] John 20:1.

[18] Philippians 3:10.

[19] An email from Dana Bates to the author, 31 March 2013. See IMPACT Romania: www.impactromania.com a ministry directed by Dana Bates working to empower youth in Romania with 'Action Learning Clubs'.

resurrection. The marks of the suffering of Christ are still visible post-resurrection, but resurrection is breaking out nonetheless. The Cross is what humanity makes of God in Jesus Christ, and thus of human being – its ultimate human No! to God, and thus each other; while resurrection is what God makes and is making of human being, starting with and centred in Jesus Christ. What God makes is new creation, with hope and forgiveness. This new creation is being made out of the same humanity which ruined itself in what it does to God in humanity – to each other, and to Jesus Christ at the Cross. It is hard, not instantaneous, work. And it is human-wide work, not something done to or in Jesus as a special detached, exalted, individual: the true, full being of Jesus Christ is communal and fully representative, for Jesus is the second Adam. So resurrection means ongoing mission, not as a stately progress towards perfection, but in fits and starts, repeated Cross and Resurrection. In the characteristic formulation of Karl Barth, if the Cross is the great human No! to God and thus to humanity as well, the crucified and resurrected Jesus Christ is God's decisive and greater Yes! to humankind, a Yes which includes a No – not silencing the No, but carrying the No still within it. Resurrection saves the No, both intensifying it and making it bearable. In the process, the Yes is in no way 'limited, constricted, conditioned and therefore weakened or called into question by [the] No.'[20] Witness to, confession and *kerygma* of this Yes, which is Jesus Christ the Crucified and Resurrected One, is the task of the Christian community.[21]

The sixth and final part of our volume, Broader Horizons and Continuing Challenges, looks more determinedly ahead, while revisiting mission and theology in the light of the journey thus far, including the disturbance of the child. It is an attempt to represent some of the particular challenges of mission and theology in the contemporary world where children face situations, some of which are well-known, others completely unparalleled in history. So here it is that we shift, not in a simple step from darkness to light, but towards the light, acknowledging the darkness which still accompanies, and even oftentimes dwells within, theology, mission and the circumstances of children.

Concluding Thoughts

So this hinge chapter has attempted to wrestle with the huge challenges thrown up by the aim of the volume; The Triangle it has sought to embrace; and the relationship of suffering and healing, darkness and light, death – indeed death on a cross – and resurrection, as they are focused and re-focused in and through considering 'child'. It has of course to work within

---

[20] Karl Barth, *Church Dogmatics*, IV.3. Trans. G.W. Bromiley, eds G.W. Bromiley and T.F. Torrance (Edinburgh: T&T Clark, 1961), 797.

[21] Barth, *Church Dogmatics*, IV.3, 795-98.

the self-given and accepted rules of The Triangle, so it cannot work within a single domain, for example just that of mission, or theology. In it we have tried, however inadequately, to hold theology, mission and child in tension, and to show how Cross and Resurrection can be seen in both the parts and the sum of the parts of the volume. And how in any involvement with children in the name of Jesus, and in all contexts, they must be held together, inseparably bound, though as distinct as light and darkness.

These represent the 'sign of the Son of Man', God hidden in the death of Christ, for it is only in encountering the depths and darkness of suffering (as represented in this volume, particularly by the lives of many children) that something of the true scope and depth of the nature of the victory of the resurrection is experienced. The combined effect, holding together Cross and Resurrection in our work with theology, mission and child, is to bring us to our knees in humility and repentance, in order that we might represent Christ more faithfully to others, especially children, through faith, hope and love, having been granted the gifts of the Spirit for this purpose.

PART FIVE

SIGNS OF LIFE AND HOPE

THE WHOLE HOUSEHOLD OF GOD:
HOW CHILDREN CAN DEEPEN OUR THEOLOGY AND PRACTICE OF MISSIONAL ECCLESIOLOGY

Paul Joshua Bhakiaraj

The Church in God's Plan

In common parlance today, as in church history, talk of 'the Church' very often implies a particular church denomination or a particular building in which Christians gather to worship their God. So one may be referring to the Roman Catholic Church, for example, or one may be referring to the building that is located on such and such a street in such and such a locality of the village, town or city.[1] In stark contrast to this practice, the overwhelming force of New Testament teaching on the church points to a community of people who are called and commissioned by Christ to be his people and do his will. The New Testament's conception of the church has to do with the people of God, a corporate Body of Christ's disciples, and not an institution which they create, or a particular physical structure they construct, though that may have its place. This is nowhere more clearly emphasised than when the church is spoken of as the Body of Christ,[2] and as the bride of Christ.[3] As we are taught in those passages of scripture, it is this people of God who form the Body of Christ and who are the bride of Christ.

We also learn from the New Testament that it is this community of Christ's disciples, the church, which is a vital part of God's overall plan for his creation. The church is God's chosen instrument to display and represent his work of redemption and reconciliation.[4] This community of disciples displays both to the world,[5] as well as to 'rulers and authorities in heavenly places',[6] the 'manifold wisdom of God'. That is to say, this

---

[1] This can also be sometimes found even in formal models of 'church'. It is interesting to note, for example, that Avery Dulles, in his *Models of the Church* (New York: Doubleday, 1974), speaks of five models of the church: as institution, as mystical communion, as sacrament, as herald, and as servant. It is only in the 1987 edition that he includes the model of 'the community of disciples' into his scheme.

[2] 1 Corinthians 12:27; Ephesians 1:22-23.

[3] Revelation 21:9.

[4] Ephesians 2:1-10; 2 Corinthians 5:18-21.

[5] Ephesians 2:14-16.

[6] Ephesians 3:10-11.

human community called 'the church' is God's creation in Christ, bearing the hallmarks of his deep wisdom and gracious work, and revealing them equally in earthly and heavenly realms. It thus forms an integral part of his overall cosmic plan. The church is the first of the 'artefacts' of his new creation. It is in this human community that both earthly and heavenly beings are able to see actively demonstrated what God's new creation is about.

In the incarnation of Jesus Christ, when 'the Word became flesh', God genuinely identified himself with human reality and history so as to effect his redemptive plan. However, it is striking to find that, in the establishment of the church, God also attaches himself, though in a qualitatively different sort of way, to human reality and history, by attaching himself to the human community of his disciples. Through this community he continues to further his cosmic redemptive plan for all creation. While in the incarnation it was in the person and work of this human Jesus, this Emmanuel – God with us – that God inaugurated his Kingdom, in the latter it is this human community of Jesus' disciples through whom he chooses to work. (It is vital to note that the former provides the latter with its definitive essence and character.)

The church then, as the Body of Christ, continues the mission of Jesus in the world. Pursuing God's cosmic plan, constituted by the work of Christ and now characterised as the temple of the Holy Spirit,[7] the church is that entity, stamped by a Trinitarian ontology, which exists to fulfil divine cosmic purposes of putting everything under the headship of Christ.[8] While the church may sometimes be reduced to little more than denominations or buildings (often with concentration on its negative traits), she is nonetheless God's chosen instrument to represent and showcase his divine cosmic purposes. Lesslie Newbigin articulates this idea well:

> The whole core of biblical history is the story of the calling of a visible community to be God's own people, His royal priesthood on earth, the bearer of light to the nations. Israel is, in one sense, simply one of the petty tribes of the Semitic world. But Israel ... is also the people of God's own possession ... And the same is true in the New Testament, there is an actual, visible, earthly company which is addressed as 'the people of God', the 'Body of Christ'. It is surely a fact of inexhaustible significance that what our Lord left behind Him was not a book, nor a creed, nor a system of thought, nor a rule of life, but a visible community ... He committed the entire work of salvation to that community ... It was that a community called together by the deliberate choice of the Lord Himself, and re-created in Him, gradually sought to make explicit who He is and what He has done ... This actual visible community, a company of men and women with ascertainable names and addresses, is the Church of God.[9]

---

[7] Ephesians 2:13-16, 21-22.
[8] Ephesians 1:22.
[9] Lesslie Newbigin, *The Household of God* (London: SCM Press, 1953), 27.

For this reason, this community of disciples, the church, is worthy of further contemporary reflection, particularly regarding some aspects of both its theological foundations and its sociological characteristics.

The Church as God's Household

In the previous section we emphasised that the church is both a divinely constituted and commissioned body, as well as a human entity. There is an intriguing and creative human-divine dialectic at play here which draws us further into this reality called the church. For example, the use of the title 'saints' or 'holy people', as the writers of the New Testament epistles often call them, points to the fact that the church is the home of such saints or holy ones. Yet as those very letters always testify, these very saints are really recovering sinners who often fail to be faithful to their calling. That is to say, the church is made up of normal everyday people who struggle with sinful lives, but yet normal everyday people who have become saints by virtue of Christ's action. The reformers of the sixteenth century, particularly Martin Luther, used an aphorism to express this: *simul justus et peccator*.

In order to help us comprehend more fully, and faithfully inhabit, that reality called the church, the New Testament employs a number of metaphors or word pictures. It is said that there are over one hundred metaphors and pictures that are used for the church in the New Testament.[10] Metaphors like 'the body' and 'the bride', as already noted, signify both these aspects of the church. Another evocative and rich metaphor is 'the household of God'.[11] 'The household of God' offers a domestic and relational picture of what the church is, and what it is called to be in the world. Indeed, perhaps it is the use of household terminology to describe the church that sheds most light on Paul's thinking about God's people and their life in relation to God and one another.[12] It speaks of a reality that many of us intimately know and are personally a part of. Yet it goes beyond that human experience of family life, qualifying it at the same time as a divine reality, since it is the household of no less than *God*. While we are, humanly speaking, already members of our own households, we are nevertheless now adopted into God's family, his household, and therefore we are simultaneously part of our human families and also members of God's family.

After using the political metaphor of citizenship in the earlier part of Ephesians 2:19, the author introduces a domestic metaphor that throws light on our identity and the reality that we inhabit. In Christ, we Gentiles

---

[10] Peter O'Brien, 'Church', in Gerald Hawthorne et al (eds), *Dictionary of Paul and his Letters* (Downers Grove, IL: IVP, 1993), 123-31.

[11] See, for example, Ephesians 2:19 and 1 Timothy 3:14-15.

[12] Philip H. Towner, 'Households and Household Codes', in Hawthorne, *Dictionary of Paul and his Letters*, 417-19.

are not only fellow-citizens with Jewish believers under God's rule; we are also children together in God's own family. This new identity is possible because of the Fatherhood of God.[13] The author of Ephesians seeks to convince the disciples of Jesus Christ that they are now an integral part of God's family and can indeed be at home in it.[14] God the Father that we meet in the scriptures, whom Jesus revealed and of whom he spoke, is their Father too. They are now part of God's household. That is why, in the church, members of this household address each other as brother and sister.[15]

Nowhere in the New Testament do we find the practice of addressing each other, and especially leaders, as 'Your Grace' or 'His Holiness'; nor do we find the use of other grandiose honorific titles that have developed over the centuries. There is no clue given to us within the pages of the scriptures of a status differential among members of God's household. Instead we repeatedly find that all Christ's disciples are our brothers and sisters, for we are all God's children. Indeed, we are all one in Christ.[16]

As brother and sisters in God's household, we are stamped with this belonging as our primary identity marker. We belong to and represent God's family. We adopt his family name. Whatever ethnic and linguistic background we possess, we all share a family resemblance, for God is our Father and we are God's children. We enjoy the same freedoms and share in the same responsibilities. We adopt the same patterns of family life and affirm the same loyalties. We pull together, we support each other, we protect each other, we nurture and care for each other. We love each other.

These are some of the household codes for our family life. Household codes are not independent moral standards that we are expected to achieve all on our own.[17] But as we learn (in Ephesians 5, for example), this is really a response to divine grace. Our response to God's lavish grace is to emulate God and Christ in the power of the Spirit.[18] They represent the appropriate human response to God's initial work of creating this family. Enabled by the Holy Spirit, we adopt these, as Paul suggests in 1 Timothy, as appropriate lifestyles befitting the grace-saturated family of which we are now part.

The Whole Household of God and Children

While there is clear evidence that the idea of the household of God, and its associated household codes, are biblical concepts, there seems to be in contemporary practice less clarity about the inclusivity of that household,

---

[13] The writer clarifies this in Ephesians 1:2, 5, 17; 2:18 and 3:14-15.

[14] See also Romans 12:5.

[15] Ephesians 5:23.

[16] Galatians 3:28.

[17] See Towner, 'Households and Household Codes', 417-19.

[18] Ephesians 1:8; 5:1.

particularly as it relates to children. There is clearly a dissonance evident today between our belief in this inclusive household of God on the one hand, and its practical outworking on the other. Perhaps there was a similar dissonance in the early church, which is why such attention has been paid to this idea. Both then and now, children are treated as something less than equal within the household of God: sadly, in practice, we seem to allow our sociology of the congregation to determine our operative theology and ecclesiology.

For this reason I would like to suggest that this theological metaphor of the church as the household of God should shape and mould our practice. Though households are clearly human creations, neither first- nor 21st-century social norms provide for us the framework within which we may fully understand and inhabit that which we really are, the household of 'God'. Rather, the church must be understood and lived out from our grounding in, and flowing out of, divine reality and relationships. It is that Trinitarian ontology which ought to provide for us the shape and character of the church. While the church is surely a human entity, and is expressed and lived out in human and cultural contexts and categories, it is nevertheless constituted and commissioned by divine purpose and enabling, and it is that calling which represents – or at least ought to represent – her charter.

The church derives its character, not from its contextual locus or from its sociological status quo, but from its divine Head, who calls it into being and gives it its nature. It is from that divine source from which it originates, that divine shape which provides its structure, that divine sending which frames its presence in the world, that the church derives its essential nature. Once again, Newbigin is instructive here:

> The congregation of God ... is the company of people who it has pleased God to call into the fellowship of His Son. He chooses its members, and we have to accept them whether we like them or not. It is not a segregation but a congregation, and the power by which it is constituted is the divine love, which loves even the unlovely and reaches out to save all.[19]

In a world where children were generally considered less important than fully grown humans, the inclusivity we find in the Old Testament's treatment of families and the household – as found for example in Genesis 12 and Deuteronomy 6 – may provide valuable insights for us here. There is an undeniable understanding in the Jewish practice of faith of the importance and value of children. In fact, here we find the startling fact that the fortunes of Israel as the people of God are actually tied to her children. Parents are mandated with the task of tutoring their offspring into learning the history and activity of God on their behalf. Children are to be schooled into a traditional practice of knowing and dwelling in God's ongoing activity on behalf of his people.

---

[19] Newbigin, *The Household of God*, 29.

When one looks deeper, however, it is evident that this is not a one-way street, where adults play the role of a guide and the child plays the role of the one being guided. While there surely are aspects of that, the value and importance of the child is central for such a scheme. As mentioned earlier, the fortunes of Israel's faith and life depended on the child. In a sense, therefore, the child represented both the present and the future of Israel in a special sort of way. Indeed, the faith formation of the people of Israel was inconceivable without children as a central part of that process. Faith formation was a family and communitarian affair. That was the way God desired his people to become acquainted with and grow deep in the faith; that was the way God chose for his children to continue in the way of life that God desired.

The Passover meal was a prime opportunity of rehearsing the mighty acts of God within the context of the household. As the household ate and drank together, its members also ate and drank in their faith and trust in God. Their identity as the people of God, whether they were children or adults, was instilled in them at times like these – right within their households. It was natural and everyday, part and parcel of their life. However, we also find that the scriptures are not merely idealistic; they are realistic, for no sooner than we reach Judges 2:6 (and following) do we read of the sad fate that befell Israel as a result of neglecting such priorities. A whole generation grew up with little knowledge of their God and his activity on their behalf. The due attention that was to be given to children as part of the family of faith was neglected, and as a result the very faith and lifestyle of the Jews was at stake.

Such an ethos of inter-generational faith and life formation is picked up in the New Testament, as we have already touched upon. The notion of the household of God where all the family is fed and formed in the faith is further stressed, even as such a priority is impressed on the church, the household of God. The household codes of Ephesians and Colossians, for example, express the importance and value of the entire household in that process. While some scholars tend to declare these codes as problematically patriarchal, it can be asserted that if that were so,

> ... patriarchal culture would have addressed only men, masters, fathers and husbands, whereas these lists include instructions for children, slaves and women, suggesting that they were accepted as equal members of the community.[20]

Some argue that the household codes were listed to prove that Christianity 'did not undermine family loyalties or social stability', but went further by demonstrating that there existed 'a certain tension between

---

[20] John W. Drane, 'Sonship, Child, Children', in Ralph P. Martin and Peter H. Davids (eds), *Dictionary of the Later New Testament and Its Developments* (Downers Grove, IL: IVP, 1997), 1115-17.

the more open relationships of the church and what was culturally acceptable in the household of wider society'.[21]

It was in such alternative and counter-cultural contexts that the people of God's identity as the family of God was moulded. It was here in these expressions of the Kingdom of God that we find God's new creation existing and being expressed through human life and human communities. As a result, this is where family patterns of gratitude and faithfulness were set and practised. This is where the family values of acceptance and love were instilled. This is where the alternative community that the church was called to be was grown and nurtured.

Perhaps it is appropriate to use the relationship between Jews and Gentiles in the church as an analogy of adults and children. In this new creation of God in Christ, there is a new relationship brought about between Jews and Gentiles.[22] Could we extend that thought to include a bridging of the distance between adults and children in the household of God? While there may not have been, nor may there currently exist, outright hostility between adults and children, there may well have been, and still now, exist a wall of superiority or inferiority between adults and children. In a context of harsh suppression of children at one end and benign neglect at the other, could we ask whether the inter-racial reconciliation taught by scripture has something to say to us about this inter-generational reconciliation as well? What would it mean for the church if we were to transpose the terms 'Jew' and 'Gentile' to 'adult' and 'child'? What would reconciliation mean in such a case? This leads us to ask: What does it mean for our church practices to reckon with the fact that in Christ we (adult and child) are all one? If we cannot think of the household of God as the community where ethnic hostilities, forms of discrimination and expressions of superiorities are broken down, then we are not talking about the church of Christ described in the Bible? While it may be true in one sense (to alter the African proverb) that 'It takes a whole church to raise a child', I would like pose that idea differently by suggesting, 'It takes a whole church (which cannot be conceived without children and young people) to raise a Christian'![23] While children surely need the church, it is more biblically and theologically appropriate to stress that the household of God needs her children. Let us not rend asunder what God originally placed together.

The Household of God as an Inter-Generational Community

This line of thinking means that, if we are to engage seriously with this theological concept of the household of God, it may well require, at the

---

[21] Drane, 'Sonship, Child, Children', 1116.

[22] See, for example, Ephesians 2.

[23] Allowing of course for the work of God's Spirit in this process, occurring perhaps precisely in the church as the household of God.

very least, a rethink of our theology and practice of ecclesiology, both gathered and scattered. In their very insistence on the value and role of children in the household of God, the scriptures offer us a valuable model for contemporary practice. Notice how that idea is further stressed when the value and role of children becomes an integral strand of Isaiah's eschatological vision. Just as Isaiah 11:6 speaks of the time when the lamb will lie (peacefully) with the wolf, it also speaks a time when a child will play her or his role in that future reality where a great reversal of nature takes place. The specific mention of children in that eschatological vision strikes us as being rather counter to contemporary practices. Surely it is an upside-down Kingdom that is being envisioned here?

This upside-down Kingdom that Isaiah described is what we find concretely expressed in the life and ministry of Jesus. Matthew 19 and Luke 18 describe for us the instance when Jesus brings that vision to fruition.[24] As Jesus places a child in the midst of the company of disciples, and teaches them how it really is a child who is their leader, he demonstrates what the Kingdom of God is all about.[25] That eschatological vision is expressed in Jesus' act, for the priority given to the child is clearly an expression of the Kingdom of God at work. The Kingdom's radical set of priorities, which among others includes 'a child will lead them', is operative here. Besides being a counter-cultural stance, the priority accorded to the child in the formation of faith in the household is therefore equally a priority of the Kingdom of God.

Accordingly, the church is called to reclaim its inter-generational emphasis and character. For example, while common practice appears to separate, for the most part faith, formation efforts for children from the faith formation of adults, it seems necessary to revisit such a practice. While, on the one hand, we may understand that age-appropriate teaching and attention is necessary, one also ought to keep in mind its disruptive and negative consequences. We need to ask: as a church gathered, how may we facilitate opportunities for children to ask the questions of faith and life that are so necessary for their, and indeed our, growth and maturity? If for most of the week we live segregated lives – children at school and adults at work – do our church practices just further that compartmentalisation of families?

How, as a church gathered, are we seeking to offer an integrated view of faith and life for all of God's household? Lest we just think of this as questioning the practice of sending the children to Sunday School after a bit of singing with the larger congregation, I would like pose the question differently: if the household of God metaphor is to be taken seriously, how may we really facilitate, just as Jesus did in his own ministry, children to

---

[24] See John Baxter-Brown's essay in this volume.
[25] See my 'From Invisibility to Indispensability: Sketches for a Child Theology', *Dharma Deepika: a south Asian journal of missiological research*, July 2008.

set some standards for the household of God? How may we express in practice the truth of what Jesus said: 'The Kingdom of God belongs to such as these'? The point I am seeking to stress is not merely to include children in the practices of the congregation, though that is a good thing, but to go much further and allow them the pride of place that Jesus desires them to have within his body. These are clearly weighty questions that will need to be thought through with all the necessary diligence that is called for. If that is followed through, it is certain that the internal life of the church will see some radical change.

At the same time however, we will need to recognise that the internal life of the church is not its only preoccupation. Its mission, that is, its active and creative external engagement with the world, is equally a priority. While it has been suggested before, surely we do not enjoy the luxury of first reforming our internal practice before engaging with the world? Both pro-active internal correction and passionate external engagement will need to proceed simultaneously. The implications of the household of God for the church's specific missionary engagement with the world therefore require close attention as well. In focusing on the integrative vision of community that the scriptures provide for us which, as we may observe, stands in contrast to much of what the world offers, we are promised a fruitful line of enquiry and action. Indeed, this was what happened in the early church. The community life of the household of God was a magnet in a society that was assailed by natural and human disasters. The sociologist Rodney Stark describes this eloquently:

> Antioch was a city filled with misery, danger, fear, despair, and hatred. A city where the average family lived a squalid life in filthy and cramped quarters, where at least half of the children died at birth or during infancy, and where most of the children who lived lost at least one parent before reaching maturity. A city filled with hatred and fear rooted in intense ethnic antagonisms and exacerbated by a constant stream of strangers. A city so lacking in stable networks of attachments that petty incidents could prompt mob violence. A city where crime flourished and the streets were dangerous at night. And, perhaps above all, a city repeatedly smashed by catastrophes: where a resident could literally expect to be homeless from time to time, providing that he or she was among the survivors ... [However when disciples of Jesus came with the Gospel, this] revitalised life in this Greco-Roman city by providing new norms and new kinds of social relationship able to cope with many urgent urban problems. To cities filled with newcomers and strangers, the Gospel offered an immediate basis for attachments. To cities filled with the homeless and the impoverished, the Gospel offered charity as well as hope. To cities filled with orphans and widows, the Gospel provided a new and expanded sense of family. To cities torn by violent ethnic strife, the Gospel offered a new basis for social

solidarity. And to cities faced with epidemics, fires, and earthquakes, the Gospel offered effective nursing services.[26]

This is equally true in so many parts of the world today. The perception of the church in many places is that of a community that loves their God and a community that loves her neighbours. If,

> The missiology that the church needs today ought to be perceiving the people of God, not as a quotation that simply reflects the society of which it is a part, but as an 'embodied question mark' that challenges the values of the world.[27]

How can the church's engagement with the world signify and portray that new creation which it both points to and is? In a world that is pained by enmities and discriminations of numerous sorts, particularly with regard to children, what purchase does the household of God have?

Conclusion

As we observed, the household of God can be more than just a metaphor. After delineating something of what the idea means, we have focused here on the inclusivity of this theological concept, leading us to appreciate the need for the church, in truth, to represent an inter-generational community of God's people. Such an entity values and encourages the real and visible presence of children within the community. But it goes further in valuing their importance and role as a sign of the Kingdom of God, of which Jesus spoke and personally demonstrated. His Kingdom priority is to be our passion. Children are to be seen as an integral part of that household, for this community has been brought into being by Jesus, her Lord, and represents his new creation, the breaking in of that eschatological reality in the here and now. As co-members in the household of God, we thus find that children can, in truth, deepen both our theology and practice of ecclesiology.

One way in which that is expressed is in the internal life of the church, where she inhabits and displays that reality as a 'church gathered'. As a 'church scattered', her external engagement with the world is another way in which she is a sign and symbol of the Kingdom of God. Unlike human society, the church is a unique entity that is divinely authored and conceived. Therefore, by being what she really is, the church represents the most creative and liberating community of children and adults, living in harmony as one people. This intentionally inter-generational community that worships God together, learns from each other, serves one another and

---

[26] Rodney Stark, *The Rise of Christianity: How the Obscure, Marginal Jesus Movement Became the Dominant Religious Force in the Western World in a Few Centuries* (San Francisco, CA: HarperCollins, 1997), 160-61.

[27] Rene Padilla, *Mission Between the Times* (Carlisle: Langham Monographs, 2010), 169.

the world at large, is what the household of God is called to be by her divine author and sustainer. In being such, as individuals and families, we truly discover our ultimate destiny just as we fulfil the creator and redeemer's purpose for his creation, until one day when he will be all in all.

WELCOME: BIBLICAL AND THEOLOGICAL PERSPECTIVES ON MISSION AND HOSPITALITY WITH A CHILD IN THE MIDST

CORNELIU CONSTANTINEANU

This chapter on 'welcome' forms part of the fifth section of our book: Signs of Life and Hope. In our world of suffering, violence and exclusion, the experience and reality of 'welcome' may indeed become the greatest piece of good news. And this especially in the midst of the tragic and painful realities of our world which whispers to us that we are of little or no value, and that there is no genuine love, lasting joy or reliable hope. In such a context, a simple gesture of welcoming a 'little one' in Jesus' name can be a great act of love with the promise of joy and hope for a desperate world. To welcome someone, to offer a hospitable place for a stranger, is a sign of the new world that Jesus Christ has set in motion. Indeed, our attempts to connect theology, mission and child in a new and meaningful way is an expression of our desire to enable the Christian community to be active players in the great drama of God's redemption – announcing by action as well as word the great news of God's welcoming and reconciling the world in Christ.

The concept of 'welcome' can be seen, on the one hand, as among the central elements of the Christian gospel, as it comprises the very essence of the story of Jesus Christ who accomplished God's reconciliation of an estranged and rebellious humanity. The proclamation and embodiment of this divine welcome is the ultimate goal of theology and mission. As well as this, 'welcome' represents also a practical response to some of the greatest needs of our present world: a world of inequalities, of suffering, of estrangement, of exclusion and violence. The plight of countless children in our world reminds us of how urgently welcome is needed: a welcome that brings thought and action together in our theological and missiological enterprise with and on behalf of children.

The purpose of this chapter is to offer a few biblical and theological reflections on the significance of the concept of 'welcome' for Christian theology and mission. It begins with a brief presentation of the plight of children today, with particular reference to the Romanian context. This underlines the urgency to rediscover 'welcome' as essential for Christian theology and mission. The main part of the paper will explore some biblical texts on 'welcome' and highlight some relevant points for our discussion on hospitality. It is hoped that such reflection will offer some insights on the importance of 'welcome' for child, theology and mission that stimulate further thinking on the subject.

The Plight of Children in our World

Even a glance at the situation of children in our world today will be enough to illustrate just how critical and urgently our attention is needed for welcoming action on behalf of children. From the malnourished and the poor, and children such as the child soldiers of Africa and the abandoned street children of Eastern Europe, to the slum children of Latin America and prostitute and child workers in Asia – in all these we discern a desperate cry of children for help and intervention. It is difficult to find adequate ways of describing the needs of children in our contemporary world: the enormous *number* of children that represent a large proportion of contemporary society in several parts of the world; the tremendous *needs* of these children; a *history* of suffering under slavery, colonisation and racism; the *marginalisation* of children in society and in terms of education; the challenge of *globalisation* and the specific concerns that this particular development brings to the life of the church.[1] The state of affairs in the former Communist context is similarly dramatic. According to a recent UNICEF report, the rate of children being abandoned in the former Communist countries is 15,000 per annum.[2] Romania is a case in point.

No one can forget the disturbing images of the orphans and institutionalised children in Romania made public to the entire world immediately after the collapse of Communism in 1989. There were horrible stories of pain, abandonment, violence and exclusion. Similarly, for many years newspapers worldwide carried the headlines: 'Institutionalised children confined and abused'; 'Romania's lost children: thousands of children in Romania are orphaned or abandoned by their families'; 'Invisible children: Romania's orphan tragedy'; 'Children in distress'; 'The Nameless Children of Romania'.[3] As a Romanian, I wish this described

---

[1] See Victor Nakah and Johannes Malherbe, 'Child Theology – A Challenge to Seminaries' in Keith J. White et al (eds), *Now and Next* (Penang: Compassion International, 2011). For a different angle on some of the material presented in this chapter, see Corneliu Constantineanu, 'Welcoming Children: Biblical Perspectives on Children's Welfare,' in Patricia Runcan (ed), *Applied Social Sciences* (Cambridge: Cambridge Scholars Publishing, 2014), and '"Whoever Welcomes a Little Child, Welcomes Me": Re-Visiting the Doctrine of Reconciliation', in Marcia J. Bunge (ed), *Child Theologies: Perspectives from World Christianity* (Grand Rapids, MI: Eerdmans, 2014).

[2] See the report of Sofia Marie-Pierre, the regional director of UNICEF, in 'Quinze mille enfants abandonnés chaque année dans les pays post-communistes', in *Le Monde*, online edition, 21 November 2012.

[3] See Bill Prevette, *Child, Church and Compassion: Towards Child Theology in Romania* (Oxford: Regnum, 2012), and his chapter earlier in this volume.

only the past, and that we had now dealt with this serious challenge; unfortunately, that is not the case. Almost twenty-five years after the Romanian Revolution, there are still far too many stories of child abandonment and street children, not to mention the plight of Roma (gypsy) children, or the tragedy of the so-called 'eurorphans' – the hundreds of thousands of children left abandoned by their parents who migrated for work elsewhere in Europe.

There is still a perception that state institutions are able to deal adequately with the needs of such children, but this is contrary to the evidence. Such institutionalisation is against the children's interests, and many children in such institutions are left with severe physical, psychological and cognitive impairments. Unfortunately, even churches do not do enough to help this situation. Children are not always welcomed in church services or integrated into the full worship of the community. Even today, Sunday Schools in many churches, along with those involved in them, are perceived as rather second class compared with the 'important' activities in the main sanctuary of the church! There is thus some urgency to reflect theologically and act on behalf of children, in Europe and elsewhere. In such circumstances, churches urgently need to consider the task of serious theological reflection on, and missiological engagement in, welcoming children and creating a fully hospitable space where they can find safety and joy, and develop holistically.

It is not news to say that children have been a rather neglected subject in our theological and missiological thinking and praxis. At last the situation seems to be changing, and it is with some sense of relief that in recent years we have seen concentrated efforts being made on behalf of children by various organisations and networks (the Child Theology Movement, the Global Children's Forum, the 4/14 Window Global Initiative, the Global Alliance for Advancing Holistic Child Development, the Viva Network – to name just a few). These developments have been accompanied by fresh attempts by historians and theologians to deal with the important issues of theology, mission and child. One cannot but appreciate the more recent increasing interest in children and childhood studies in different academic fields, not least in theological studies.[4] I would specially like to note the

---

[4] There are several solid theological books on the subject, among which I would mention a few of the most relevant. Arguably, one of the most valuable and extended endeavours has been 'The Child in Religion and Ethics' project directed by Marcia J. Bunge, and the significant books that have emerged from that project: Marcia Bunge (ed), *The Child in Christian Thought* (Grand Rapids, MI: Eerdmans, 2001); Marcia J. Bunge, Terence Fretheim and Beverly Roberts Gaventa (eds), *The Child in the Bible* (Grand Rapids, MI: Eerdmans, 2008); Don S. Browning and Marcia J. Bunge (eds), *Children and Childhood in World Religions: Primary Texts and Sources* (London: Rutgers University Press, 2009); Marcia J. Bunge (ed), *Children, Adults, and Shared Responsibilities: Jewish, Christian, and Muslim Perspectives* (Cambridge: CUP, 2012); and Marcia J. Bunge (ed), *Child Theologies:*

significant way in which the Child Theology Movement has contributed to the subject by highlighting the profound theological and missiological significance of Christ's action of placing a child in the centre of a theological conversation.[5] All these, including particularly the present book, are excellent efforts towards the appropriate integration of theology, mission and child, towards a solid theological basis on which to build a strong case for action on behalf of little ones.[6]

Welcoming a Child, Welcoming God, and Christian Mission

It is interesting to note that in the two very well known passages in the Gospels which address the issue of welcome (Matthew 18:1-5 and Mark 10:13-16), the evangelists put together child, God and mission (disciples entering and living in the Kingdom of God). In this context, children are seen as significant. Jesus presents them as recipients of the Kingdom of God, an integral part of God's reign, and its intended recipients. Moreover, Jesus points to children as models of entering the Kingdom: 'Whoever does not receive the Kingdom of God as a child will not enter it' (Mark 10:15). It is not easy to determine the exact meaning of Jesus' words and what it means to receive the Kingdom of God as a child. Does it refer to childlike status of being totally dependent on others and/or other childlike qualities such as trust, humility, and openness? Since God's great work of

---

Perspectives from World Christianity (Grand Rapids, MI: Eerdmans, 2014). There are also several other significant books worth mentioning: Bonnie J. Miller-McLemore, *Let the Children Come: Re-Imagining Childhood from a Christian Perspective* (San Francisco, CA: Jossey-Bass, 2003); Joyce Ann Mercer, *Welcoming Children: A Practical Theology of Childhood* (St Louis, MS: Chalice Press, 2005); David H. Jensen, *Graced Vulnerability: A Theology of Childhood* (Cleveland, OH: Pilgrim Press, 2005); Kristin Herzog, *Children and our Global Future: Theological and Social Challenges* (Cleveland, OH: Pilgrim Press, 2005); Keith J. White et al (eds), *Now and Next: A Compendium of Papers Presented at the 'Now & Next' Theological Conference on Children, Nairobi, Kenya, March 9-12, 2011* (Penang: Compassion International, 2011).

[5] For an articulated theological argument for child theology, see the recent book written by the founders of this movement, Haddon Willmer and Keith J. White: *Entry Point. Towards Child Theology with Matthew 18* (London: WTL Publications, 2013). Other relevant works by members of the child theology movement include: Keith J. White and Haddon Willmer, *An Introduction to Child Theology* (London: Child Theology Movement (CTM), 2006); Haddon Willmer, *Experimenting Together: One Way of Doing Child Theology* (London: CTM, 2007); Sunny Tan, *Child Theology for the Churches in Asia: An Invitation* (London: CTM, 2007); John Collier (ed), *Toddling to the Kingdom* (London: CTM, 2009); Bill Prevette, *Child, Church and Compassion: Towards Child Theology in Romania* (Oxford: Regnum, 2012).

[6] For an excellent extended review of some major theological works on children, see Jerome W. Berryman, 'Children and Christian Theology: A New/Old Genre', in *Religious Studies Review*, 33:2 (April 2007), 103-11.

reconciliation and welcome in Christ is an absolute act of divine favour and grace, it is possible to think that Jesus wanted to illustrate exactly this point: that the Kingdom of God is not a human achievement but an act of God's grace and therefore as a child is totally dependent on others, so to enter the Kingdom of God is to be totally dependent on divine grace.[7]

The point that Jesus makes for his disciples in Matthew's narrative is that to be great in the Kingdom of God one needs to 'become *humble* like this child'.[8] This is a true eschatological reversal. The values of the Kingdom of God are radically different from the values of the dominant culture. Adults are constantly in danger of viewing themselves as very important. They tend to think highly of themselves, especially at the expense of the weak, vulnerable and humble – not least vis-à-vis children. To be in the Kingdom is to participate in the eschatological reversal and radically change this way of thinking and being. Children, together with those of marginal social status, are active members of, and participants in 'God's grand reversal of present circumstance: the inversion of power, privilege, and status that marks the realm of God.'[9] The child is thus a pointer to a Kingdom radically different from what people, including the disciples, usually think. The Kingdom of God 'has got absolutely nothing to do with status, hierarchy, or merit, and everything to do with genuine humility. It operates by completely different principles to the organisations, culture, religion, and politics that dominate the life of this world'.[10]

If we read Mark 10 with an eye to Mark 9:35-37, however, we are to understand the reference to the child in the larger context in which *welcoming a child means welcoming Jesus which means welcoming God the Father!* This is a very remarkable idea as we are used to thinking about our salvation more in terms of God welcoming us, accepting us, reconciling us! But Mark 9:35-37 tells us clearly and simply and powerfully: to welcome a child, any little one, is to welcome God. What an extraordinary affirmation of the generosity of grace! He comes and is present at every welcome of a child, of any child! Kosuke Koyama puts it well:

> When we are in a state of astonishment at the generosity of God, we are confessing our faith in God. God's generosity is 'scandalous' (1 Corinthians 1:23). It involves a radical reversal of our assumptions. To welcome a little child 'in my name' is to proclaim the gospel of reversal. 'Whoever would be first must be last of all and servant of all.' This 'upside-down' quality of the gospel is its very essence. It is this disturbing reversal that makes all the

---

[7] So, for example, Hans-Rüdi Weber, *Jesus and the Children: Biblical Resources for Study and Preaching* (Geneva: WCC, 1979), 29.

[8] Matthew 4:18, emphasis ,mine.

[9] John T. Carroll, 'What Then Will This Child Become?', in Marcia J. Bunge (ed), *The Child in the Bible* (Grand Rapids, MI: Eerdmans, 2008), 187.

[10] Keith J. White, '"He Placed a Little Child in the Midst": Jesus, the Kingdom, and Children', in Marcia J. Bunge et al (eds), *The Child in the Bible* (Grand Rapids, MI: Eerdmans), 353-74 (370).

liturgical, ecclesiastical, and doctrinal expressions of the Christian faith evangelical in the original sense. In this simple act of welcoming a child, the generosity of God mysteriously creates the reversal.[11]

If we think that a child is a gift, which most of us do, then to welcome a child is to become aware and grateful for the gifts we receive in life, that life itself is a gift. We may never have thought of this but in the context of Christian theology and mission, welcoming a child becomes a symbol of a powerful reality of welcoming God, of knowing him and his generosity. By welcoming a child we become aware that everything we have is a gift, and that enables us to be opened to others, welcoming them as gifts of God. Again, Koyama is to the point:

> The child is a gift. To welcome the child is a matter of sheer thanksgiving. Life is a gift. Body is a gift. 'I am' is a gift. 'You are' is a gift. The biosphere is a gift. Day/night is a gift. All living creatures are a gift. Intelligence is a gift. Language is a gift. All things are gifts. To know and to appreciate that we are surrounded by gifts is essential for the life of healthy human community. Community ('I am because we are, and since we are, therefore I am' – an African saying) is made up of myriad gifts and is itself a gift. When we welcome a little child, we are engaged in thanksgiving for all the gifts that make life precious. The welcoming of the child is the holy act that will bring 'wholesomeness' (*shalom*) to humanity upon this earth. It is the ecumenical holy mystery to which the whole of humanity is invited.[12]

Peter Spitaler argues that in Mark 10 Jesus wants to teach his disciples that welcoming a child is symbolic of welcoming God's Kingdom, and he suggests that we should interpret Jesus' saying in the light of children's social status in antiquity; thus the ultimate purpose of the saying was to lead to social change. More specifically:

> Comparing welcoming God's kingdom to welcoming a child, the figure motivates social change. The disciples must act like adults, not like children, and demonstrate hospitality toward persons whose status they do not share. Jesus' own actions – embracing (10:16), welcoming (10:15) and blessing children (10:16) – relate welcoming God's kingdom to welcoming a child, not to 'becoming' like a child. That is, Jesus embraces a child to demonstrate that he welcomes God's kingdom; his action does not reveal he is welcoming the kingdom in a childlike manner.[13]

Thus, according to Spitaler, Jesus wanted to teach his disciples that welcoming a child is symbolic of welcoming the Kingdom of God, just as in Mark 9 welcoming a child was symbolic of welcoming Jesus and of welcoming God the Father. Ultimately, what Jesus is asking the disciples is 'to transform the dominant socio-cultural and legal norms for the benefit of

---

[11] Kosuke Koyama, 'A Holy Mystery: Welcoming a Little Child', in *The Living Pulpit* (October-December 2003), 4.

[12] Koyama, 'A Holy Mystery', 5.

[13] Peter Spitaler, 'Welcoming a Child as a Metaphor for Welcoming God's Kingdom: A Close Reading of Mark 10:13-16,' in *JSNT*, 31:4 (2009), 425.

people whom these norms marginalise: children, healers (9:38), the little ones (9:42), women (10:2). Jesus' own actions and teachings reveal the symbolic nature of welc:ming a child: it means welcoming Jesus, God and the kingdom'.[14]

Similarly, Matthew's account points to the same truth: to welcome children is to welcome Jesus; 'whoever welcomes a little child like this in my name welcomes me' (Matthew 18:5). It is probably here that we can see the closest link between Jesus, children and welcome – and the great significance of children in God's reconciliation and welcome. To welcome a child is to welcome Jesus, which is also to say that whoever does not welcome a child rejects Jesus. It could not be clearer that one cannot speak of reconciliation with God without including 'the other' in this reconciliation, particularly the child. It is clear that Jesus points to a particular social practice of welcoming children as a proper response to faith. Faith and practice are intrinsically related, i.e. faith in Jesus determines new forms of life, new social practices. Conversely, the practice of welcoming children is an authentic manifestation of faith, as Gundry correctly points out: 'Jesus' teaching on welcoming children informs social practice towards children and suggests that these social practices serve to strengthen faith in Jesus and are themselves a form of this faith.'[15]

Haddon Willmer, one of the founders of the Child Theology Movement, reminds us that the text in Matthew 18 teaches us something about the way we do theology. He has correctly pointed out that Jesus' intention in placing the child in the midst of a theological argument was that it would make a real difference in the way disciples do theology. As he puts it:

> Jesus placed a child in the midst, with the expectation that the child's presence would make a difference to the theological argument. He expected the child to change theology for the better ... The child would open the disciples to what they were closed against. Taking note of the child would undermine their present ideas and the ambitious, anxious and competitive relationships which spawned their false thinking. And more, the child would be a positive clue to entering the Kingdom of God.[16]

We might ask ourselves how different or enhanced our understanding of welcome wouldbe if we reflected on it through the lens of the child. Jesus' gesture of placing the child in the midst means that the child has significance – in her own right, as well as by showing the way into the Kingdom of God. Thus, *welcoming children is more than 'practical application'*. One of the weaknesses of the church's dealing with children comes from treating the subject as merely a sub-set of 'practical

---

[14] Spitaler, 'Welcoming a Child', 441.

[15] Judith M. Gundry-Volf, 'The Least and the Greatest: Children in the New Testament', in Marcia J. Bunge (ed), *The Child in Christian Thought* (Grand Rapids, MI: Eerdmans, 2001), 29-60 (46).

[16] Haddon Willmer, 'Child Theology and Christology', in John Collier (ed), *Toddling to the Kingdom* (London: Child Theology Movement, 2009), 242.

application' in the theological and religious education curriculum. The insight that 'child theology' brings to the debate is its insistence that the child should not be just an afterthought of theology but rather a lens through which we do theology! And indeed, great new insights come to light if we do that, both for different theological themes as well as for children. But, to be sure, this is not simply theological thinking about children! As Joyce Mercer remarks, 'Theological thinking about children cannot guarantee either more just and loving practices with children or a "better childhood" in the day-to-day experience of any particular child. Put differently, the content of theology does not alone dictate its effects and meanings at the level of practices.'[17] She reminds all of us that the primary motivation for action on behalf of children does not come from ideas but from practice.

That is why it is very important to develop the *practice of welcome* in the church. Mercer makes a strong argument for the importance of helping children develop an alternative Christian identity and become mature in their faith – and not only 'consumers' of a particular ritual. This can be done, she argues, in three complementary ways: 1) by allowing children to be part of communal church worship and to take part in the spiritual practices of the community; 2) by moving beyond the simple and politically correct rhetoric against marginalisation and for welcoming children to the actual practices of welcome; 3) through an integrated approach to theological education in which ideas and actions are to be understood as one whole.[18] By doing these, we bring children not only into the centre of our theological thinking but also into the centre of church life where they properly belong. As we welcome children as participants in the church's worship, a Christian identity will be formed that is an alternative to the dominant cultural identity of society.

'Whoever welcomes a little child, welcomes me' (Matthew 18:5) – this shows just how intimately linked is our acceptance, reconciliation, and embrace of Jesus with the child. Acting on behalf of children, we are, in effect, working for Jesus because he is represented by the child; he dwells in the child, as Willmer observes very perceptively: 'The child received is where Christ is, and is the form and way in which Christ is ready to be received. Christ comes into those who receive a child. Somehow, Christ is present and communicated in and through the child.'[19]

To be reconciled with God, through Christ, is to welcome the child. In other words, we cannot profess we are reconciled with God and yet ignore the child in our midst. When we consider the way God reconciled the world by sending his Son, we cannot miss the real possibility that he has made himself vulnerable to being accepted or rejected by people. And yet, as

---

[17] Joyce Ann Mercer, *Welcoming Children: A Practical Theology of Childhood* (St Louis, MS: Chalice Press, 2005), 27.

[18] See Mercer, *Welcoming Children*, 213ff.

[19] Willmer, 'Child Theology and Christology', 250-51.

Karl Barth might say, God chooses to be God *with* us and not without us, *for* us and not against us. That is why he has objectively accomplished reconciliation, despite human rebellion and rejection. Human beings can trust this God who gave himself for his creation in order to reconcile, redeem and welcome it. Again Willmer captures this thought well: 'Christianity is more than a religion concerned with moral education and good order; it is faith and hope in God the creator and redeemer, to whom creatures are precious. God's answer in Christ is that God is God for and not against creation, including human beings.'[20] This is the content of the gospel and the reason for the church's mission: God has welcomed the little ones, the despised and the marginalised, and Christians are the witnesses to and participants in this great divine welcome. To welcome children, to accept, care and pay attention to them is to welcome Jesus, and therefore God, and thus to embody the welcome.

Gospel, Welcome and Mission in Paul

When we come to the writings of the apostle Paul, we find also that 'welcome' was an integral part of the gospel which he proclaimed.[21] Writing to the believers in Rome, he wanted to communicate a very clear, unambiguous message, namely that their own welcome of God is inseparable from their welcome of 'the other'! And this was not an optional extra but rather an intrinsic part of the very gospel of reconciliation they professed. In Romans 6, for example, Paul presents an argument about the complex dynamic of the incorporation of the believers 'in Christ' through baptism, which signifies a real sharing and participation in the same story of Christ. Christ's story is not only his own story but it includes the story of believers. By virtue of their participation in Christ, believers can live rightly and be active actors as the same story of Christ is being unfolded in their midst. Paul wants the believers in Rome to be aware that they have become themselves an integral part of, and active participants in, the larger and ongoing story of God's reconciliation of the world in Christ. They are themselves an *integral part* of God's mission to redeem the world. Indeed, the logic of the story requires a particular way of living, a 'walk in the newness of life' (Romans 6:4), meaning a life of peace, love, welcome, reconciliation and hope in the midst of suffering and difficulties. The reality of believers' reconciliation with God, and their new identity and status 'in Christ', carry with them the responsibility of engaging in welcome and practising reconciliation – both grounded in, and modelled by, Christ's work of reconciliation. Paul's ultimate vision of the

---

[20] Willmer, 'Child Theology and Christology', 255.
[21] For a full and detailed exegetical and theological argument on welcome and social reconciliation in Paul's theology, see Corneliu Constantineanu, *The Social Significance of Reconciliation in Paul's Theology: Narrative Readings in Romans* (London: T&T Clark Continuum, 2010).

reconciliation of all things in Christ gives assurance and hope, and an irresistible impetus to the believer's mission of welcome and of reconciliation in all its forms and manifestations.

The Pauline imperative for welcome is clear in Romans 15:7: '*Welcome one another*, therefore, *just as* Christ *has welcomed you* for the glory of God' (emphasis added). Christ's welcome is the ground and model for what the church must now do: *just as* Christ welcomed and reconciled the believers. so they also should welcome and be reconciled one with another. The conjunction '*just as*' indicates some sort of comparison, thus highlighting not only the fact of Christ's welcome but also the manner in which he did it. God's reconciliation was an act of pure grace in which Christ manifested his love towards people while they were weak, sinners, even enemies of God. *In the same manner* believers should manifest their love one towards 'the other', to show the same grace to others that they have been shown by God.

Paul's imperative for welcome in Romans is grounded in the story of Christ, developed theologically in Romans 5-8. There are several significant Christological features in the story which Paul emphasises with great care. Thus, most frequent reference is to the death of Christ on the Cross as an expression both of God's love and faithfulness and of Christ's willing self-giving for humanity resulting in the reconciliation of the world. Jesus' personal participation in the drama of reconciliation in his death 'for us', understood as a surrender of love, was used by Paul as an appeal for deliberate action. Indeed, by sharing an intimate union with Christ and his story, believers are reminded that they continue to participate in the same story. Paul goes to great lengths to emphasise *the manner* in which this welcome was realised by Christ: by a costly sacrifice, by an initiative of love, by an offer extended to enemies. His story becomes our story, his way of life becomes our way of life. In this context we find that Paul particularly highlights the faithfulness and obedience of Jesus. Particularly relevant for the community in Rome is that their reconciliation with God is to be reflected by their own unity as a new community 'in Christ' as well as by the practice of welcome towards others modelled on the faithfulness and obedience of Christ. What new light is thrown on the Pauline understanding of welcome by the child placed by Jesus in the midst cannot be discussed here, but the implications for ecclesiology and mission are potentially profound.

Welcome, Hospitality and *Missio Dei*

One of the real downsides of the hyper-technological advancement of our globalised world is the loss of face-to-face community and, with that, the disappearance of genuine personal hospitality and welcoming. Yet, in the midst of a great frenzy on virtual 'social' spaces, we discern a great desire and need for people to connect with real people, to have close fellowship and communion. We see the need of people to be listened to, understood, accepted and welcomed. And this represents a great opportunity and a call to Christians, because offering welcome is both an integral part of Christian identity and an imperative for mission. In such a world like ours, where exclusion and hurt and suffering is the order of the day, the church has a great opportunity of offering a different way of understanding, relating to, and welcoming 'the other'. Christians can and must make a difference but for this to happen, hospitality must become a priority.[22]

If we understand hospitality as 'the practice of God's welcome, embodied in our actions as we reach across difference to participate with God in bringing justice and healing in our world in crisis',[23] then we realise that hospitality and welcome are at the heart of the *missio Dei,* God's mission to redeem the world. This is what we learn from the Old Testament presentation of God's relationship to Israel, in particular, and to all humanity in general: God, as the divine host, welcomes everyone, all human guests in his garden. And the challenge for Israel was to live out in their daily life this welcome and hospitality towards everyone (Abraham here was a prime example). Janzen summarises this well: 'in the Old Testament, God the great host invites his guests into his house, the created world, to enjoy its riches and blessings. But God also expects these guests to follow God's example and share their livelihood, their life, with their fellow guests on God's earth.'[24]

The story of God's hospitality riches its climax in Jesus Christ: in him everyone is welcome! The true redemption, the true and full hospitality of any and all human beings is made possible through Jesus Christ. And he made space in himself for everyone, by emptying himself, by calling everyone to share in his own identity and openness. This is exactly how the New Testament writers present the story of God's welcome in Christ: by highlighting the crucial fact that those who are in Christ are now participants and share in the same story of God's welcome and hospitality, and so are to extend it to their neighbours. Being in Christ is living with Christ, sharing our own lives, just as he shared his, welcoming everyone, extending hospitality to all. This is also the conclusion Andrew Artebury reaches in his fine book on early Christian hospitality, namely that 'the God manifest in Jesus Christ is the true God of Hospitality', and that hospitality thus becomes 'a means of spreading the gospel to the Gentiles.'[25]

One of the greatest challenges for hospitality is our own understanding of the neighbour, of the stranger, of 'the other'. Human beings have been

---

[22] See Matthew Carroll, 'A Biblical Approach to Hospitality', in *Review and Expositor* 108 (Fall 2011), 519-26.

[23] Letty M. Russell, *Just Hospitality: God's Welcome in a World of Difference* (Louisville, KY: Westminster John Knox Press, 2009), 2.

[24] Waldemar Janzen, 'Biblical theology of hospitality', in *Vision* (Spring 2002), 10.

[25] Andrew E. Arterbury, *Entertaining Angels: Early Christian Hospitality in its Mediterranean Setting* (Sheffield: Sheffield Phoenix Press, 2005), 189-91.

created in God's image, as social beings, with an inclination for mutual inter-relationships and inter-dependence, and were meant to live in harmony with God and with one another. But who is 'the other' and how can one welcome and embrace a stranger? The way we understand 'the other' and the way in which we relate 'the other' to our own identity becomes an issue of crucial importance for our Christian theology and mission. This is exactly the point made sharply by Miroslav Volf, who identifies one of the most disturbing realities of our world today as being that of defining *otherness* as something in and of itself evil. Volf calls our attention to the fact that, as Christians, if we want to take seriously the mission of engaging the world with the gospel of healing and reconciliation, we have to find the most appropriate ways to address the hatred of 'the other', to address the issues of identity and otherness. And this, according to Volf, is urgent and of crucial importance:

> It may not be too much to claim that the future of our world will depend on how we deal with identity and difference. The issue is urgent. The ghettos and battlefields throughout the world – in the living rooms, in inner cities, or on the mountain ranges – testify indisputably to its importance.[26]

If we take a closer look at 'the other', we realise that as a person separate in identity – 'the other' – is someone other than me, yet always around me in one way or another; so much so that I cannot live without 'the other'. In fact, I cannot define myself without 'the other'. In a sense, 'the other' is part of me and has contributed to, and shaped, my own identity in so many ways that I am not even aware of all of them. But 'the other' is not only someone who is 'present' within me. Even the working definition of the other – 'as a person separate in identity' – bears reference to me! The other is also, and should be, 'other': different, unknown, mysterious, irreducible, unique. To be sure, it is the 'otherness' of 'the other' that makes my life beautiful, colourful, and exciting, because it is 'the other' who makes 'the difference' in my life. So, 'the other' is a cause of celebration of diversity, a part of me and yet always a mystery, someone I marvel at. Needless to say, 'the other' is not my enemy.

Miroslav Volf, the contemporary Croatian theologian at Yale, has written extensively on, and probably made the most significant contribution to, the topic of reconciliation. In his award-winning *Exclusion and Embrace*, Volf developed his theology of reconciliation employing what he calls a 'phenomenology of embrace'. According to Volf, the Christian understanding and practice of reconciliation is a non-negotiable *willingness to embrace the other*. Volf's whole argument is built around the metaphor of 'embrace', which brings together three central, interrelated, theological themes fundamental for his thesis: the mutuality of self-giving love in the Trinity; the outstretched arm of Christ on the Cross for the 'godless'; and

---

[26] Miroslav Volf, *Exclusion and Embrace: A Theological Exploration of Identity, Otherness and Reconciliation* (Nashville, TN: Abingdon, 1996), 20.

the open arms of the father receiving the 'prodigal.' Here is how Volf states the essence of his thesis:

> *The will to give ourselves to others and 'welcome' them, to readjust our identities to make space for them, is prior to any judgment about others, except that of identifying them in their humanity.* The *will to embrace* precedes any 'truth' about others and any construction of their 'justice'.[27]

Volf describes 'the drama of embrace' in four structural elements ('opening the arms', 'waiting', 'closing of arms', 'opening the arms again'), and puts forward a way to understand identity as a constant interaction between the self and the other. Discontent with one's 'self-closed identity' one *opens* the arms as a sign of the desire for the other, of the fact that he has created space in himself for the other, and as an invitation for the other to come in. But because the self respects the integrity of the other, it will *wait* for the other to come. When the reciprocity of 'giving' and 'receiving' is achieved, the *closing* of arms takes place in a proper embrace. It is important that the embrace itself is a 'soft touch' so that an *opening* of the arms after embrace may occur, since in the event 'the identity of the self is both preserved and transformed, and the alterity of the other is both affirmed as alterity and partly received into the ever-changing identity of the self'.[28]

When we give considerable thought to the idea of otherness and manage to change our views to see the other as being someone who enriches us, then our Christian communities can become the place where God's welcome is experienced, a place where the stranger finds hospitality and welcome. The openness, trust, even the feeling of dependence, are all crucial qualities for the process of welcoming. As we have seen, with their 'infinite openness' children inspire us in our own process and ministry of hospitality, to open ourselves for the other in embrace, waiting for the other to respond. When we understand and acknowledge the other as being created by God with equal dignity and worth, we are effective participants in the story of redemption, in the *missio Dei*.

Volf does not address the implications of the children taken by Jesus into his arms so that he could bless them.[29] This is a subject crying out for exploration and exposition: the disciples were determined to exclude those who brought children to Jesus, but Jesus literally took them into his embrace.

Conclusion

The experience of God's welcome is the greatest incentive and imperative for our offer of hospitality. 'Welcome' thus becomes a key category which

---

[27] Volf, *Exclusion and Embrace*, 29 (emphasis his).
[28] Volf, *Exclusion and Embrace*, 143.
[29] Mark 10:16.

integrates theological reflection and missiological engagement, not least on behalf of the child. There is a great need, however, to continue to reflect theologically on the action of Jesus of placing the child in the midst, to reflect on the place of children in the life and mission of the church, to understand the importance of children.

As we reflect on these key biblical texts, it remains our constant challenge to take seriously the radical teaching of Jesus on children and make it alive in our own contexts. This is particularly urgent in our contemporary world in which children remain a vulnerable, needy and abused group. In our life of faith we have to take seriously the fact that children share fully in the community of believers, in the life of the Kingdom of God. It is noticeable in the writings of Paul (and of Miroslav Volf) that children are conspicuous by their absence. Moreover, in their total vulnerability and dependence, trust and acceptance, children point to us the way we should relate to God and so, in all these, we are in debt to them for the profound insights and realities they illustrate: a lack of false ambition, modesty, authenticity, playfulness. We should never lose sight of the urgent call of Jesus to *change/convert* and become as little children – that is, to rediscover an authentic joy of living in the present, with simplicity and openness, vulnerability and dependence, trust and acceptance. Having nothing to claim for themselves, they model a way for us to expect everything from God. And, very significantly, we can test our understanding and practice of welcome through our appropriate action or lack of it, towards children. The way of the Kingdom of God is radically different from the ways of our culture, and so it remains our challenge not simply to undertake good actions towards children but actually to create a different social world in which the values of God's Kingdom – welcome, peace, reconciliation, forgiveness, humility, vulnerability, and hospitability – are embodied in everyday life. This new world was made possible through the work of Christ and his welcome of humanity. It is up to us to live out this new reality.

God's initiative of welcome, shown in the life, death and resurrection of Jesus, is not only the foundation of God's reconciling the world, but also the model for the mission of God's people. Paul provides an unshakable foundation for both the possibility and the actuality of welcome. God's welcome gives people hope and an irresistible impetus for welcoming the other. To live according to the logic of the gospel, in the light of Christ and in the power of the Spirit, means to be community-oriented – a community where everyone, including every child, is engaged in the ministry of welcome and in the practice of reconciliation, a community which strives after the ideal of living together in harmony and solidarity, love, welcome and regard for others.

'Welcome' is a central element of the gospel and of Christian theology, and represents the very essence of the identity and mission of the church within God's own mission. As the community of those gathered in Christ, the church is the place where everyone is welcomed by Christ and is called, in turn, to be a sign of the new creation in Christ by welcoming the other. Christian theology is reflection upon and an explication of the divine welcome that God has given to a sinful and rebellious humanity. Christian mission is effective participation in the same story of Christ, which is the story of God's redemption and welcome.

Identities: Theology, Mission and Child in the Upside-Down Kingdom

John Baxter-Brown

Introduction: Narratives that Define Us

The baby was born as the Chinese invaded India. He was the product of the union of an English mother and a Scottish father, one of the last Imperial babies. His first two years were spent in that wonderful, colourful and contradictory nation, with servants and privileges he cannot now remember. There are stories of tigers and man-eating leopards he learned on his mother's knee and he can recall the magnificent leopard skin that hung on the wall of his father's study in the suburbs of London. It was the skin of a 'man-eater' that his father had shot after it had attacked some of the villagers near the tea plantation where he lived.

One of the stories he was told – alongside man-eating leopards and learning to swim in a crocodile-infested river – was the rather dramatic story of his birth. His mother and older brother were evacuated from a valley off the Brahmaputra river in north-east India. His mother was at her due date and was driven out of the valley at walking pace. The car had to keep pace with the other women and children who were on a forced march to avoid the invading Chinese army. There we not enough cars for everyone. His mother, a qualified midwife trained in the East End of London, England, had made some preparations for the birth in case the baby came during the march. These 'preparations' consisted of one sterilised jam jar containing a sterilised pair of sharp scissors, and one piece of sterilised string. That was it. But the baby was back to front and breach. Thankfully for the mother and child, he was not born on that long journey. A few days later his mother and the other displaced families arrived in Shillong where there was a mission hospital. The baby was born by Caesarean section after a troubled labour. Without surgical intervention, mother and child would have died, probably beside the roadside in Assam during the Chinese invasion. There are times when being late has its advantages. Without such tardiness, this chapter would never have been written. This narrative has, in part, defined me. It has helped shape my sense of personal identity as all appropriated narratives do.

After a moderately difficult childhood and his parents' divorce, the now-teenage boy experienced what amounts to poverty in the UK. On 6 July 1980, the seventeen-year-old became a follower of a first-century Palestinian subsistence manual labourer. This transformation provided him with another narrative that further developed his sense of personal identity. It is this last narrative that is by far the most powerful and influential. At a personal level, this was his introduction to God's upside-down Kingdom.

This narrative of the Carpenter from Nazareth has been told and retold through the ages. It has the power to transform people's lives as much in the 21st century as in the three years of Jesus' earthly ministry. When I was converted as a young person in July 1980, my life was turned around: my priorities changed and I found my life had a renewed sense of purpose and direction based on the transformation Jesus worked in me through the power of his Spirit. But my conversion left me with a righteous anger that it had taken the church over seventeen years to reach me and tell me Jesus' story. That is many years too long! And still the church largely is failing to re-order her priorities, spending too little time, energy and resources in mission to and with children and young people. If we are to take the gospel message seriously, Jesus' challenge of placing the child in the midst ought to serve as a wake-up call both to individual Christians and to the Christian community. Like the disciples, we run the risk of placing ourselves outside the Kingdom if we fail to be where the child stands.

H. Stephen Shoemaker wrote that humans are *homo narratus* – we are story-formed creatures.[1] As he retells some of the Bible's stories, he does so emphasising the way God works through narrative – transformational scripts that offer us a glance of what God is about in redeeming the world to himself. But it is not just the characters in the Bible whose lives are transformed – the child David who kills a giant, the young girl Esther who saves her people, a teenage pregnancy through which God becomes one of us – those narratives also change our lives today and have the power to lead persons and communities from darkness to light. Yet if we follow Jesus, we must first walk through the darkness, we must humbly submit, emptying ourselves as he did and become like the child in order to enter the Kingdom of God.

Narratives, when they are personally appropriated and owned, help form our identity. Just as they did for the teenager described above, stories shape who we become. How is the narrative of the gospel lived and taught in the church today, such that children and young people see their lives re-oriented towards God? Where are the spaces within Christian communities where youth are welcomed, where their narratives are listened to, where they find encouragement and discipleship in the way of Jesus? The narratives of the upside-down Kingdom challenge our stories about the importance of 'leadership development' and 'market values'. Placing the child in the midst is itself Jesus' way of pointing us to the entry way to the Kingdom.

---

[1] H. Stephen Shoemaker, *Godstories: New Narratives from Sacred Texts* (Valley Forge, PA: Judson Press, 1998), xiii-xvi.

The stories, the scripts of our lives shape our personhood. But bad scripts can bring oppression and devastation. Stories, narratives, matter. And these depend upon the child and upon the child's community. These three actors – script, community (including the family) and the child herself are very powerful shapers of how she will grow and develop if, indeed, the child ever sees the light of day.[2] There are many other scripts around the world, prejudiced against the girl-child, or the boy-child, or all children. These scripts limit human flourishing, forcing millions of children into economic, emotional and spiritual devastation. Such is the world's story and the way powers play out in the world-like Kingdom.

There is another, alternative script which finds its fullest expression in the life and teaching of that first-century subsistence worker: this is God's script, God's upside-down Kingdom. In philosopher Alasdair MacIntyre's terms, the gospel narrative is the better narrative, even if the world does not see it as such.[3] However, though the church professes already to know how the story ends, Christians find themselves living in between that promised completion of God's Kingdom and the darkness of this world. It is still within this darkness that we must learn (i) what it means to serve God's Kingdom – how do we participate in God's mission of reconciliation? (ii) what is the place of children living in this in-between time? And (iii) what sort of theology guides us, shapes and is shaped by both the children and the mission of God's script?

As we consider our participation in God's mission, let us examine some narratives of how the church grew amidst the struggles of Christians in those early centuries and the relation of this growth to the stories of children.

Rodney Stark argues that one reason why this comparatively short-lived Palestinian's narrative became powerful is simply because the gender prejudice of Roman society (which, like modern-day India, placed undue value on boys to the detriment of girls) was undermined by a simple but potent idea: that God made men and women of equal, intrinsic value. [4]

---

[2] In 2012, for example, approximately two million girls were conceived but not born into the wonderful, colourful and contradictory nation of India. They were aborted before ever experiencing the dawn of their birth – for that day never existed for them. In India girl babies are not accorded the same value as boy babies: there is a script that is gender-prejudiced.

[3] Alasdair MacIntyre, *After Virtue: A Study in Moral Theory*, 2nd edn (Notre Dame, IN: University of Notre Dame Press, 1984).

[4] Rodney Stark, *The Rise of Christianity: How the Obscure, Marginal Jesus Movement Became the Dominant Religious Force in the Western World in a Few Centuries* (New York: HarperCollins, 1997). Stark devotes Chapter 5 to 'The Role of Women in Christian Growth' and argues that the Christian narrative, which 'accorded women higher status in Christian circles than elsewhere in the classical world', led to the substantial growth of the early church. He builds his argument on the basis of Christians having greater fertility rates than pagans, and women having

Thus, the early Christian church took in unwanted baby girls for no other reason than they, too, were God's creation and therefore of value to him. The law of unforeseen consequences came into force and, according to Stark, these baby girls grew into desirable young women. But they could only be married to men who followed the Palestinian carpenter. And so the church grew, one couple at a time. Over the course of three hundred years the number of Christians grew until the Roman empire itself was 'converted'.

It is worth asking ourselves three key questions. First, what was so powerful about the Carpenter's narrative that it changed the course of human history? Second, what are the key issues that we, as followers of Jesus, should address in the early 21st century in particular as we think about children and young people? And third, what narratives shape our vision of the future? These questions need to be considered in light of the significance of the child that Jesus placed in the midst.

The Carpenter's Kingdom, Upside-Down

Jesus was radical. His teaching and the life he lived which was consistent with that teaching, was both challenging and comforting. The comfort he gave was almost exclusively towards those who were on the margins of society – the poor, women, children, the sick and demon possessed, sinners and tax collectors. The challenge was almost exclusively directed against the rich and/or powerful: priests, politicians, the privileged rich. The key to understanding how radical this carpenter was – and is – is the narrative of Kingdom of God.

Jesus was born in Bethlehem in an occupied land. He was born on the edge of the Roman empire in a small and, politically speaking, unimportant country. The Roman occupation was brutal as military occupations usually are. The politically astute Jewish rulers of the time, such as Herod, pragmatically chose to side with the Romans. In so doing, they believed that their own positions and power were secured. It is an entirely understandable position to take. Yet, it is a precarious position, for there is always the threat of either falling out of favour with the occupying forces or facing rebellion from one's own people. Thus, when the infant Jesus was born, and news of this event reached Herod, he was in dire peril, much as unborn baby girls in India are today. Herod's personal narrative – of keeping power and ruthlessly destroying all opposition – dictated that he would terminate this 'King of the Jews'. This he attempted in what is often called 'The Slaughter of the Innocents', in which he killed all the male children in and around Bethlehem who were two years old or under.[5] The

---

greater status in family and religious life than pagans. The crucial factor of the girl-child is also a feature of his argument.

[5] Matthew 2:1-18.

baby Jesus was saved because his parents had fled to Egypt with him. Jesus thus became a political refugee in a foreign land and only returned to his homeland when Herod died some time later.

Years later Jesus started his ministry in and around Galilee, with a particular emphasis on the 'Kingdom of God'.[6] This idea of God's Kingdom or reign was the central narrative of Jesus' preaching, but it also cannot be divorced from the narrative of Jesus' life, from his birth, through his work, to his death and resurrection – *all* the stories matter. The evidence for this claim is immense, so we will limit discussion to three highlights.

Jesus was known at his birth as the 'King of the Jews'; it was for this reason Herod wanted him terminated. He was also known thus at his death – indeed, the charge brought against him at the trial was that he had claimed to be 'King of the Jews', the same charge painted on a board placed above his head on the cross. Kingship is central at his birth and death.

In Mark's Gospel, Jesus starts his public ministry by proclaiming that 'the Kingdom of God is at hand'.[7] The same is true of Matthew's and Luke's Gospels: Jesus returned to Galilee from the wilderness and taught in the synagogues.[8] The Kingdom is proclaimed at the start of his ministry, and its significance is assumed during the remaining three years of Jesus' work on earth.

Even a cursory read of the Gospels shows that the Kingdom featured prominently in Jesus' discourse and actions. There are frequent references in the parables: 'the Kingdom of Heaven is like ...' appears numerous times in the three synoptic Gospels. But if this were all there was, it would not be strong evidence for the centrality of the concept in Jesus' ministry. There could be a valid argument for dismissing it as a metaphor. We therefore need to dig deeper. An examination of the Gospels shows that the Kingdom:

1. **Is the content of the proclamation of the Good News**. As noted above, Luke records Jesus saying that he was sent for this purpose: he 'must proclaim the good news of the Kingdom of God'.[9]

2. **Is associated with healing the sick and the casting out of demons**. There are frequent references that link the Kingdom with Jesus' (and the disciples') acts of healing and deliverance.[10]

3. **Can be entered or received**. The Kingdom is not a physical place but it can nonetheless be entered, difficult as that will be for some people.[11]

---

[6] Or its equivalent in Matthew's Gospel, the 'Kingdom of Heaven'.

[7] Mark 1:14.

[8] Matthew 4:17; Luke 4:14-15.

[9] Luke 4:43; 8:1; 16:16; and Mark 1:15.

[10] E.g., Matthew 12:28; Luke 9:2,11; 10:9.

[11] Matthew 7:1; 19:4; 21:31; Mark 4:11; 9:47; 10:15, 24; Luke 13:28; 18:17.

4. **Can be near to people**. Jesus implies that some people are *near* the Kingdom of God but not yet *part* of it.[12]
5. **Grows rather than is built**. Jesus told many parables about the Kingdom of God. They tend to drawn on agricultural rather than construction metaphors.[13] The emphasis within the parables implies that God's Kingdom is organic: it grows mysteriously, from a small seed, or is like something that already exists, such as fish in a lake. There is a clear requirement for human involvement (planting, weeding, harvesting, fishing) but, unlike construction, in which human planning and activity are essential, human agency does not *make* it grow: it is *God's* Kingdom, not ours. God alone gives life, and extends his reign.
6. **Has a different value system (or script) from surrounding political and religious systems**. There are several dimensions within this last category, to which we now turn, before returning to our list:

The exercise of power:

Jesus told his disciples that 'the rulers of the Gentiles lord it over them, and their great ones are tyrants over them'.[14] This is the way power is usually exercised in the world, then as today. For the disciples, however, Jesus said, 'It will not be so among you; but whoever wishes to be great among you must be your servant.'[15] He held up himself as an example: 'The Son of Man came not to be served but to serve, and give his life as a ransom for many.'[16] As we will see below, Jesus also used a child as a way of underlining this same point about the subversive and radically different nature of power within God's Kingdom.

The subjects:

In Matthew 20 Jesus is confronted by the religious leaders of the day. They try to trick him by asking him difficult questions, but Jesus turns this ploy round upon them by telling them a parable. He applied the parable thus: 'Truly I tell you, *the tax collectors and the prostitutes* are going into the Kingdom of God ahead of you.'[17] In Mark 10 it is children who are given preferential treatment: the disciples were rebuking parents who were

---

[12] Matthew 10:7; Mark 12:34; Luke 9:62; 10:9,11.

[13] There is only one parable about house-building, in Matthew 7:24-27, which is not directly about the Kingdom, but rather about the disciple listening to and acting upon Jesus' words.

[14] Matthew 20:25.

[15] Matthew 20:26.

[16] Matthew 20:28; cf. parallels to Matthew 20:20-28.

[17] Matthew 20:31, emphasis added.

bringing their children to Jesus to be blessed: 'But when Jesus saw this, he was indignant and said to them, "Let the *little children* come to me; do not stop them; for it is to such as these that the Kingdom of God belongs. Truly I tell you, whoever does not receive the Kingdom of God as a little child will never enter it." '[18] In Luke 6 Jesus highlights another group of people: 'Blessed are you who are *poor*, for yours is the kingdom of God.'[19] The subjects of the Kingdom of God are the marginalised; they are the least, the last and the lost. The rich, the powerful, the political and religious leaders – these are the ones who have to struggle to enter the Kingdom.

It is counter-cultural:

The Kingdom of God opposes many of the cultural norms (or narratives) we find in most – perhaps all – human cultures. There is a hierarchy within God's Kingdom, but it is based not on age, privilege, education, wealth or power; rather, as we saw above, it is based on servanthood where the greatest will be least and the least greatest; the first will be last and the last first. The Kingdom of God has its own ethical framework: love, joy, forgiveness and self-sacrifice. Priorities are turned upside-down (or the right way up from God's perspective), and seeking God's Kingdom is our primary responsibility. His Kingdom is not ostentatious: our prayers and almsgiving are to be done in secret, quietly, without drawing attention to our piety or generosity.[20] The Kingdom of God calls into being a new human society in which mutual submission, sharing and caring are core features. Relationships are radically rearranged – as they were among the twelve disciples. Loyalty is to Jesus and our sisters and brothers, not to political, economic or ethnic scripts. Conflict with such ideologies and demonic forces is inevitable, and our response to persecution is to count ourselves as 'blessed'.[21] Our King, Jesus, exemplified these qualities in his earthly life, calling us likewise to pick up our cross and follow him.

Finally, we see from an examination of the Gospels that the Kingdom of God:

7. **Has one King, Jesus.** The Kingdom of God is directly associated with the King. It cannot exist without him. The implications of this fact are immense, and will frame the rest of this chapter. For if the Kingdom of God is the core narrative of Jesus' ministry, what is the upside-down power of this narrative?

---

[18] Mark 10:14,15, emphasis added; see also Matthew 18:4.
[19] Luke 6:20.
[20] Matthew 6:1-6.
[21] Matthew 5:10-12.

The Carpenter and Children: Two Encounters

One way of exploring the power of the Kingdom narrative is to consider what happens when Jesus encounters children. There are a number of such encounters in the Gospels and they all point to the upside-down nature of the Kingdom of God, and to ways in which children are signs of how we are called to live in that Kingdom, here and now. That is, children are not just examples in these texts, but are the embodiment of how we are to participate in God's mission of reconciliation. We will highlight two texts.

Greatness, the Kingdom of Heaven, and the World to Come

Matthew uses five major discourses to give structure to his Gospel. At the beginning of the fourth discourse the disciples come to Jesus asking, 'Who is the greatest in the Kingdom of Heaven?'[22] This is a recurring theme in Jesus' teaching in Matthew, suggesting that the disciples were slow to grasp Jesus' point. In chapter 18 Jesus responds to the question by calling a little child 'whom he put among them' (NRSV) or 'in the midst of them' (NKJ). In so doing, as Hagner notes, Jesus 'gave substance to what he was about to teach. The social insignificance, if not the innocent unself-consciousness of the little child, was the very antithesis of the disciples' interest in power and greatness'.[23] The disciples are required to 'exhibit a childlike indifference to greatness' for if they do not, Jesus said, they 'will never enter the Kingdom of Heaven'.[24] They must be 'humble like this child' to be great in the Kingdom. Jesus is not referring to the internal life of the child, her feelings or actions: rather he is referring to the child's lack of status in the society of his time. *The child lacks social, economic and political status* – the very things that so easily lead to the exploitation of children. Thus, the child in this pericope becomes the model for the disciples to emulate. It is precisely by embracing a lack of status in the social hierarchy and authority structures that one becomes great in Jesus' Kingdom and in so doing participates in God's mission. The point is further emphasised two chapters later, in response to parental ambition. The mother of James and John sought advantage for her two boys; what mother would not want the best for her children? Yet even here the Kingdom of God dances to a different tune: Matthew 20:17-28 weaves into the consideration of greatness the suffering that Jesus – and the two brothers – would have to experience. The path to greatness in Jesus' Kingdom is the path of self-sacrifice.

Jesus continues to use the language of the child in Matthew 18. The child is not only a symbol of greatness, but also is a demonstration of

---

[22] Matthew 18:2.

[23] Donald Hagner, 'Matthew 14-28', in *Word Bible Commentary* (Nashville, TN: Thomas Nelson, 1995), 517.

[24] Hagner, 'Matthew 14-28', 517.

hospitality: welcoming 'one such child' is equated with welcoming Jesus himself. This is not about any attitude on the part of the child but about the attitude of adults to children and about our mistaken understanding of the place of power within Christian mission. The child is, in effect, powerless to control or influence how she is welcomed. Rather, Jesus is emphasising that the nature of God's Kingdom is to welcome those on the margins of society – those without power, status or prestige. A core characteristic of the *missio Dei* (God's mission) is this simple hospitality, welcoming all.

Yet there is more. Jesus expands his argument to include the 'little ones who believe in me'.[25] The disciples have been warned that if they do not 'change and become like this child [they] will never enter the Kingdom of God'.[26] The 'little ones' here certainly includes children but can also be interpreted as including those disciples of Jesus who have become like children themselves. The warning includes not placing 'a stumbling block before one of these little ones', and to 'take care that you do not despise one', for 'it is not the will of your Father in heaven that one of these little ones should be lost'.[27] Jesus uses extremely strong language to drive this point home: for those who create for children a stumbling block, he says 'it would be better for you if a great millstone were fastened around your neck and you were drowned in the depths of the sea'; it is better, he warns, to cut off your hand or foot, or pluck out your eye, than 'to be thrown into the hell of fire'.[28] As France observes, 'These verses contain some of the most severe teaching on spiritual punishment in the Gospels. They take hell very seriously.'[29] They take Heaven very seriously also by placing the child – the humble outsider – as the one who is inside this upside-down Kingdom.

Deliverance, Healing and the Dead Restored:
Outcasts Within and Without, Fathers and Children

In Luke 8 Jesus is seen going through towns and villages, proclaiming and bringing the good news of the Kingdom of God. He was with his core of disciples and some women followers, and 'a great crowd gathered'.[30] He taught the crowd in parables, and emphasised the closeness of relationships among 'those who hear the word of God and do it'.[31] There follows four intertwined stories: Jesus stills a storm as the disciples cross the lake to Gerasene; there they encounter a man possessed by demons whom Jesus sets free; Jesus returned from there to be met by Jairus, a leader of the synagogue whose daughter was gravely ill, but as Jesus was going to heal

---

[25] Matthew 18:6-14.

[26] Matthew 18:3.

[27] Matthew 18:6, 10, 14.

[28] Matthew 18:6, 8.

[29] R.T. France, *The Gospel of Matthew* (Grand Rapids, MI: Eerdmans, 2007), 680.

[30] Luke 8:4.

[31] Luke 8:5-19, 21.

the daughter, he had an encounter with a woman suffering haemorrhaging. As Jesus talked with her, Jairus' daughter died. This setback did not stop Jesus. He still went on to Jairus' home and there he raised the girl from the dead. '*Then* Jesus called the twelve together and gave them power and authority over all demons and to cure diseases, and he sent them out to proclaim the Kingdom of God and to heal.'[32]

All this activity reveals what the Kingdom of God is like, set in the context of Jesus' own mission, and the mission he subsequently gave to the disciples. The central figure throughout the narrative is Jesus, the King. He has power and authority over nature, over evil and demons, over illness – even over death – as well as authority to teach. This power comes from God and can be delegated to others to do the same tasks. Jesus' ministry is to everyone: no-one is excluded from the touch of Jesus: men and women; children and adults; those caught up in evil and those who are ill; outcasts who are excluded from, or even within, society; those at the centre and those at (or beyond) the margins; the powerful and the poor. Some are named, most remain anonymous. But each is met by Jesus, often transformed in the encounter, and is sent on their way by Jesus with words of guidance, challenge, and/or encouragement.

Of particular interest for us is the healing of the young girl. She is young according to modern Western cultural norms – twelve years old – and in those of the first century she was not yet an adult, but on the verge of adulthood. It is important to keep in mind the ways in which the narratives of our cultures shape the way we see ourselves and how we think and act towards children and young people because such narratives define us. The church is called constantly to examine the ways in which the Kingdom of God challenges our assumed scripts. It is no different in this text.

The values of God's Kingdom ought to lead God's people to seek such change and we must see that this is a fundamental aspect of the *missio Dei*. At the same time, it is inevitable that the process will be contested, for God's Kingdom requires that the economic, political and legal powers that keep children in bondage be confronted. Jesus was determined to save Jairus' daughter, even from death itself. As Anne Richards comments, 'It seems that the woman [with the issue of blood] has effectively ended the life of the child and claimed the healing miracle for herself.'[33] However, she goes on to note that 'once Jairus had asked for help, nothing stops Jesus from getting through to his daughter, despite interruptions, a crowd pressing on him from every side, a usurpation of his healing power by another, and the news that the child is beyond help anyway ... Jesus finds in her something of complete value, worthy of saving and healing, loved by God ... loved by her father to whom Jesus responds'.[34]

---

[32] Luke 9:1-2, emphasis added.

[33] Anne Richards, *Children in the Bible: A Fresh Approach* (London: SPCK, 2013), 102.

[34] Richards, *Children in the Bible*, 103.

The narrative is compelling for it offers a glimpse not only of Jairus' motivation – that of any loving father desperately seeking help for a child – but of Jesus' own compassion and determination. Luke 8 and the parallel passage in Mark 5 emphasise Jesus' authority, but also show

> that the Gospel extends to all of creation: it is for men and women caught up in evil, for people who are suffering from illness and disease, and for children and their parents. The breadth of the gospel is for those excluded from the community (the demon-possessed man), for those within who are also outcasts (the woman), and also for those in positions of power and influence (Jairus). No one is exempt from the need of God's free and saving grace. Transformation is for all.[35]

Jesus brought a fresh perspective, a new narrative that God's Kingdom was not only a future hope but also a present reality. The Kingdom of God was not to be the socio-religious-political-military theocracy that many of his fellow Jews desired. Rather, it was to be governed by love and established through faith. Jesus was not constrained by the narrative of death and decay. Rather, his narrative of the Kingdom of God brings life, hope and joy. Unlike other healings of children, in which the child is usually a boy, this narrative hints again at the importance Jesus placed on women and girls, and their place within God's mission. Unlike the widow's son who is brought back to life,[36] there is no particular financial or social power associated with a 12–year-old girl. She is simply and powerfully brought back to life – 're-narrated' – within the context of a culture whose script emphasised that both she and the woman Jesus healed en route to her, were of little importance.

The Carpenter's Narrative and Power

There are three main reasons why Jesus' narrative of the Kingdom is powerful and upside-down.

First, it is focussed on the person of Jesus Christ. The Christian faith cannot be distilled into a formula or ideology, although systematic theology and doctrine are important. Neither can mission be reduced to strategy (a mistake rather too common in Western Christianity, and at risk of being imitated by emerging mission movements in the majority world); strategy, too, has its place, of course. Nor yet can the faith be systemised into a particular form of institutional expression, though many have tried to do so. Rather, faith has to be focussed upon a Person. At its heart, the faith is about the King of Kings and Lord of Lords, Jesus Christ. It is this personal

---

[35] 'Evangelism: The Hallmark of Evangelical Faith'. World Evangelical Alliance Theological Commission. Available at: www.worldea.org/images/wimg/files/ Evangelism%20-%20The%20Hallmark%20of%20Evangelical%20Faith.pdf (accessed July 2013).
[36] Luke 7:11ff.

emphasis, and Jesus' lordship over all of creation, that turns the world's scripts upside-down.

Second, the narrative transforms people's lives, especially but not exclusively those on the margins of society. Often the people Jesus encountered came to him with specific problems (such as disease, possession by evil spirits, questions, doubts, hunger, poverty). Many also came with more malicious intent – scribes and Pharisees often came asking questions designed to trap Jesus. Jesus always responded to those who came with genuine need, leading to lives being changed and made whole. It has been the same throughout Christian history: people who encounter Jesus can be transformed just as in the case of the seventeen-year-old at the start of this chapter.

Third, it offers a different view of the future. People can dare to re-imagine life: their future can be different – *better!* – than the current reality they face. In words from a popular recent film, 'The only thing more powerful than fear is hope'.[37] The upside-down Kingdom offers a hope of a re-imagined future that is extraordinarily powerful in situations where the dominant narrative oppresses children in all sorts of ways: the Good News of the Kingdom of God shouts of another narrative, one that brings freedom and delight and that challenges to overthrow oppression. It says 'No More!' – no more child slavery or trafficking; no more child poverty; no more child exploitation. And it says 'Yes!' to life, to hope, to faith.

This brief overview has significant implications for mission with and to children and young people.

What are the Key Issues to Address Now – and with Which Narrative?

Let us return for a moment to the young man with whom I opened this chapter. Many years have passed since I became a follower of the Carpenter, filled with the usual successes and failures that life throws at us. But some things remain constant: I am still angry with the church for failing to tell me the story until I was seventeen, and I am still determined not to make that very same mistake. Indeed, I started out by telling people about Jesus on the streets, in clubs, pubs and bars, in schools and universities – wherever I could find and keep a crowd of people willing to listen to a young evangelist, in my homeland and around the world. But I had too narrow a focus. I have learned that Jesus was not particularly interested in a one-size-fits-all approach to ministry and neither should I be. As we have seen, he dealt with people in their specific context with their particular issues. Likewise, but especially when ministering among children and young people, we must be mindful of the particularities of culture and context. A children's programme that works in New Hampshire is probably

---

[37] *The Hunger Games*, Lionsgate (UK), 2012.

not going to work in New Delhi without radical re-contextualisation. Indeed, the very concept of a 'children's programme' might be inappropriate in some cultures!

The specific issues that face children and young people in today's world are complex and multiple. They range from the grotesque abundance of material resources in some parts of the world to the abysmal poverty in others; from the spiritual poverty in the Western world to the exuberance of faith for many in the majority world. From the sinful and abhorrent abuse of children in wars, slavery and industry, to their exploitation for the gratification of adults or their near-idolisation in other cultures. All of these are sinful. All require that we approach the whole child, within their whole context, working for and with them at many different levels to seek wholesome, life-affirming outcomes. One of those outcomes is, and must always be, sharing with them the story of the life-affirming, life-giving Carpenter.

However, our methodologies need to reflect the gospel we share, particularly with respect to power. Jesus used a child to illustrate the subversive nature of power in God's upside-down Kingdom. He certainly had great power himself and he delegated power and authority to his disciples – and by extension to us today. But the power operated very differently from the manner in which power usually operates – in the church as well as in the world. Power and greatness in the economics of God's Kingdom lead to the 'Way of the Cross': self-giving, inclusive, serving. Therefore, we need to be like the child placed in the midst, totally reliant upon our loving Father, treating power, position and status with the disregard they deserve. Our participation in the mission of God as we work with and for children in God's Kingdom must reflect Jesus' approach to power. By placing the child in the midst, Jesus points us towards the incarnational character of our mission. This character is personal – it has to do with following Jesus himself; it is holistic – it has to do with the transformation of the social order according to God's upside-down Kingdom; and it is missional – it involves service and self-sacrifice as we seek together to witness to the good news of Jesus. The famous hymn in Philippians 2 perhaps best captures both the shape of our mission and its promised outcome, for as we die with Christ, we have hope that we will also be raised with him.

In the mission of the church and her various ministries we must seek to empower children and young people within these narratives of life and hope in God's Kingdom. Children are not just to be objects of our benevolence or charity, but according to Jesus, they are active subjects in the Kingdom – the very ones writing the scripts that lead us to life. This script is focused on Jesus – the Word 'tented' among us.[38] We need to help people, especially children and young people, appropriate for themselves

---

[38] John 1:14 – literally, 'And the Word became flesh and tabernacled among us'.

the big narrative of Jesus and to discover where their own stories actually fit within the bigger picture of his story. It is not enough simply to tell stories: rather we need to help equip children and young people themselves to become participants in the ongoing story of Jesus. It is this story that, above all, brings the hope and power that is so crucial for living this life well and for preparing us for the life to come (cf. Philippians 1:21). This narrative of the King must be pre-eminent in mission, in theology, in life, for it is this narrative alone that brings light into the darkness.

RECOVERING HOPE AND THE FORMATION OF CHILDREN: A THEOLOGICAL CRITIQUE OF INSTITUTIONS

Samuel E. Ewell and C. Rosalee Velloso Ewell

What does it mean to be human? What are the conditions necessary for human flourishing and why has so much of contemporary Christian theology and missiology failed at addressing these questions as they relate to children? The child placed in the midst is a sign of God's Kingdom and a symbol of what discipleship ought to be like. That child is not a cute, white, fat or naked cupid-like creature – nor necessarily a young, innocent, brown child with big eyes that we too often see on fund-raising campaigns for relief organisations. Rather, each child is fully human, a person made in God's image and shaped by the powers, the institutions, the adults, and the society in which it lives. How it grows and learns what it means to be made in the divine image is a matter of formation – the shaping of identity.

There are various ways one can think about the powers that affect children, powers that thus shape the way that child is enabled to participate fully (or not) in God's Kingdom. There are the very visible powers of poverty, war and famine that undermine not just a child's growth, but an entire community's way of being; there are the powers 'behind' the powers – the exploitation, the corruption, the ambition of persons and institutions intent on evil. And there are signs of good news – the often misunderstood power of the prophet, calling the church back to its call to welcome the child and to see in that child characteristics of the Kingdom of God; there are communities and families whose mere presence among the least of these signals the upside-down nature of the power of Jesus.

In this chapter we will draw on the work of Ivan Illich (1926–2002), a Catholic theologian, philosopher and social critic whose works greatly influenced the fields of sociology and education, but who has gone mostly unnoticed in Christian theology. Illich's analyses of the power of institutions (including the church) and the way they shape human lives offer us a lens, or a way to explore the particularities of how these powers impinge upon the lives of children. Through examining the way Illich retells an ancient Greek myth, we will also see the ways in which identities of children are shaped and enabled to flourish in contemporary society.

Formation and the Consumer Way

In the early 1970s, Catholic theologian and sociologist, Ivan Illich, argued 'that the institutionalisation of values leads inevitably to physical pollution, social polarisation, and psychological impotence: three dimensions in a process of global degradation and modernised misery ... this process of degradation is accelerated when non-material needs are transformed into demands for commodities; when health, education, personal mobility, welfare, or psychological healing are defined as the result of services or "treatments" '.[1] He suggested that human beings are oriented towards one another, that giving and receiving are inherent to what it means to be God's creatures, and therefore, if we fail to take account of how one is dependent on the other, we fail in Christian formation. One of the tasks of Christian theology is to enable us to tell the difference between good and bad dependencies, but the problem is that the church has largely given up on what mutual dependency means, and has left the task of 'formation' to its institutional forms, as if Christian virtue were now a commodity made, sold or bought by the church.

Drawing on epic tragedies from Greek mythology, Illich suggested that Christian theology failed to question the rise of dominant institutions to which our culture has handed over the right of formation. We tend to think of dominant institutions (such as health care, schools, transport services) as the primary sites for human flourishing or as catalysts for social progressivism, when in fact, he argued, careful observation suggests that they are crucibles of unprecedented forms of alienation. Why? Because they exchange vital *personal* activities for dependent consumption of *institutional* outputs – that is, scarce commodities. Thus, at the heart of Illich's social criticism in the early 1970s lies this claim: dominant institutions both call forth our trusting commitment and allegiance while at the same time entrapping or colonising domains of human activity in novel and fundamentally disabling ways.[2]

What has this to do with the child or mission? Fundamentally, it is that the formation of identities – how children learn about the Kingdom of God and their place and role in it – is no longer based on the personal growth of love, obedience, humility and mutual dependency through participation in this odd Kingdom. Rather, children become instruments in a system, whether it is the systems of schools and education, of media and a depersonalised virtual universe, or of economics and learning to be productive citizens for the state. The habits and virtues necessary for a life of discipleship are seen as products – commodities that are scarce and which the church must supply.

---

[1] Ivan Illich, *Deschooling Society* (London: Marion Boyars, 1971), 1.

[2] Lee Hoinacki and Carl Mitcham (eds), *The Challenge of Ivan Illich: A Collective Reflection* (Albany, NY: State University of New York Press, 2002), 164.

Illich is not against institutions *per se*, but suggests that too often they go unchecked, and their strengths become their weakest point and the tool for oppression and manipulation. In the best cases, institutions can be convivial – they facilitate human activity and promote mutual dependency, that is, a constructive, enabling space for growth and flourishing. But in most cases, institutions become manipulative, in the sense of holding onto power – for example, controlling the activity of learning and making it an assembly line focused on outputs and results. In this scenario, needs are identified by the institution based on the lack of results or the inadequacy of what has been produced. Therefore, the institution must develop new products or programmes that it then 'sells' back to those in its assembly line (e.g. students and parents) so that they can better fit the system. The dynamics of formation are confused or even equated with a streamlined process.

Such a mentality shapes the way the church thinks about its role in society and how it relates to people. There is tendency to equate church attendance, whether through liturgies or programmes, with spiritual/ personal growth. The church has been lulled into imagining that its role is to provide religious goods and services in the same way that a school might provide educational goods and services – still using the language and the framework of commodities. It is this distorted theology that also shapes the formation of children – they no longer are agents in the story, enabled to discern alongside others what is needed for human flourishing, but are mere recipients of goods produced based upon the perceived (or created) needs the church has deemed necessary. A theology which suggests that simply being, in the midst, with Jesus is sufficient, is not adequate or viewed positively according to this distorted type of formation. Rather, that child must learn and behave in certain ways that are determined not by its proximity to the Lord, but by the disciples or the religious or civil authorities who are outside.[3]

In *The Abundant Community*, John McKnight and Peter Block argue that institutions manipulate and socialise us into being commodity-dependent, thus turning us into 'clients'.[4] Moreover, we are socialised into the idea that the only way to lead a satisfied or a full life is through consumption. This is the notion that the means to a good or abundant life can be purchased. McKnight calls this 'the consumer way' – we cannot discern or meet our own needs and therefore we are not able to lead a full life. One can see the way this mentality shapes the worldview and identity of children in the contemporary world. In many contexts worldwide, children have lost the space or adequate time even to ask questions about discernment or a life of discipleship. There are many reasons for this loss, among them the social powers that press in on kids – media, computers (or other types of screens),

---

[3] Compare this with the scene in Matthew 19:13-15.

[4] John McKnight and Peter Block, *The Abundant Community: Awakening the Power of Families and Neighborhoods* (San Francisco, CA: Berrett-Koehler, 2010).

the socialisation that occurs in schools, on the streets or in church. Amid the pressures to perform and to conform in such spheres, there is rarely room for the question, 'What does it look like to share life together in God's Kingdom?' No one, not even in the church, usually asks where they are or are at in their discipleship, thus reinforcing the point that being close to Jesus is irrelevant for their lives. In the consumer way there is also what McKnight calls the 'professional problem'. This refers to the ways we are taught about need or the formation of desires. In this system an expert (doctor, pastor, priest, educator, therapist) is given the task of identifying 'needs', and imputing them to us/to children. One can see how this notion can unravel and infect the church, whether through leadership programmes or hierarchical structures, through social moulds and the way stories are told, such that children are mere spectators in the machine rather than formed as active participants whose gifts and talents are discerned and enabled to flourish.

The consumer way shows itself also in the manner most Christian parents and parenting programmes work in the church. Reading through the Beatitudes with the lens of parenting, the question might arise, who desires persecution for their child, even if for the sake of justice? Or who desires poverty or mourning? The pressure on the parents is to raise happy, successful, well-educated and well-mannered kids.[5] If your child does not quite fit in, then something in your parenting is wrong (or there is something wrong with your child) and so the church offers more courses, more counselling, more services; just as health care professionals offer more medicine, more therapy, schools offer more tutors, more exams, and so on.

In contrast to the consumer way, McKnight offers the language of 'community competence' and suggests that it is this latter type of life formation we need to recover. While he does not use theological language to explain what he means, the idea is that within the community we discern our needs, relate together, and are enabled for life using the very gifts God has given us, learning to be shaped in the image of Christ. The point is not to turn one's back on services such as health care or education, but to see that those places are not where human flourishing happens, and that too often they end up alienating us from the location, the contexts, the communities, in which the best kind of formation can and should take place.

Every community has gifts, such as the ability to associate, to become interdependent, and the capacity for hospitality. In the consumer way the focus in on lack, on what we do *not* have, and therefore we shift our gaze to those services that can supply the need. The church should be a community

---

[5] For an important essay on this topic, see Stephen Mattson's article (7 May 2014) on the *Sojourners* website: http://sojo.net/blogs/2014/05/07/struggles-christian-parenting

of abundance and a gift for everyone; this is based not only on the God whom we worship as Father, Son and Holy Spirit, but on the very particular way of life and ministry of Jesus of Nazareth, and the mission into which God calls us to participate.

The same Jesus who put the child in the midst is the one who displays the abundance of God's reign in the feeding of the multitudes and the healing of the sick. If we look at the Gospel narratives of these events,[6] one sees that such acts both give us a foretaste of the coming Feast of the Lamb, and in themselves are part of the inauguration of this Kingdom that Jesus has brought. It is a reign of plenty, where bread and fish are shared by all. Yet the disciples are still caught up in the framework of the world, in and of the reign of scarcity. It is the child's fish and loaves that not only signal the Kingdom, but offer a contrast between the two perspectives: one is the disciples' focus on what is lacking and on the services that can fill that void: 'Dismiss the crowd so that they can go into the villages to buy food;'[7] the other is Jesus' focus on staying and sharing: 'Get the people to sit down on the green grass ... and he divided [the bread and fish] among them all.'[8]

Part of learning what it means to be a creature is being shaped into the plentiful reign of God. Yet too often the church has failed and has been more like the disciples than like Jesus or the child who shared the loaves and fish. The church's focus has been on diagnosing needs in the sense of deficiencies and then trying to come up with programmes that meet such needs. The blind spot in this is that it fits hand-in-glove with the consumer way. The alternative is that when communities come together and focus on gifts, association and hospitality, we recognise that children have gifts, people have gifts, and that fulness of life is about cultivating interdependence rather than finding the magic pill or the ideal programme for the formation of children. Ultimately, the danger is that the church becomes commodity-dependent rather than people-dependent.

The process of discerning our needs and gifts within the community is itself an enabling process that allows for interdependence, which in turn disables dependence on commodities (services or programmes in which you have no say and no control). Illich uses the term 'conviviality' to describe this type of people-focused dependence. Built into his argument for conviviality is an account of what it means to be truly human or, more precisely, what it means to be formed into our full humanity. It is this type of formation to which the church should strive as it participates in the formation of children, aiming always to be in that midst where Jesus has called us to be.

---

[6] Matthew 14, Mark 6, Luke 9 and John 6.

[7] Mark 6:36.

[8] Mark 6:39-41.

Prometheus and Epimetheus: Two Rival Versions of Being Human

Though much of modern society and Christian theology, especially in the western world, is caught up in the consumer ideology described earlier, there are ways to think about the formation of children and its relation to a biblical doctrine of creation that offers us an alternative. This alternative is the conviviality of which Illich writes.

In 'Rebirth of Epimethean Man', an essay included as the final chapter of Illich's most famous book, *Deschooling Society*, he challenges the certainties and social conditions generated by dominant institutions, interpreting them in light of Greek epic tragedy. Specifically, Illich turns to the characters of Prometheus, Epimetheus and Pandora as a way of 'demythologising' what he describes as the 'Promethean ethos/enterprise' of contemporary western society – the very ethos that shapes the formation of children and disables them from being the creatures God has made them to be. The Promethean enterprise is 'the degradation of Pandora's myth' and 'the endeavour to forge institutions in order to corral each of the rampant ills'.[9] Illich exposes the false universalism of the myth of modern progress, which extends the 'technological ethos' through the industrialisation of *hubris/nemesis*. At stake is the awareness that the Promethean ideal – while held by a majority of the social élites – operates according to an anthropological fallacy that must be exposed and renounced in favour of the Epimethean alternative. In theological terms, at stake is the renunciation of the powers that deform humanity – notions of development, consumerism, and progress that are commodity-based. The alternative is the turn to an understanding of how a child is formed in the image of Christ, raised in the ethos of the hope and reality of God's Kingdom.

In ancient Greece the story goes that Pandora, the 'All-Giver', was sent by the gods to live among humanity. She carried with her a jar containing various social ills, which then escaped. In her jar, however, she also kept one good gift – the gift of hope. According to Illich, there is a shift between the original account of Pandora and that of the classical Greeks. The former emphasised humanity's incapacity to control or manipulate the cosmos, and therefore, the importance of living in hope. Within the latter view, 'classical Greeks began to replace hope with expectations. In their version of Pandora she released both evils and goods'.[10] As Illich points out, through subsequent retellings of the story – and with a decidedly misogynous bias – the myth in its classical form did not remember Pandora in the same way, and not well enough. That is, it remembered her *primarily* for the ills she brought, while forgetting that the All-Giver was also the bearer of hope.

---

[9] Illich, *Deschooling*, 105

[10] Illich, *Deschooling*, 106.

Prometheus (meaning 'foresight') warns his brother Epimetheus (meaning 'hindsight') to stay away from this woman, Pandora. But instead of disregarding Pandora and her box, Epimetheus marries her, thereby creating a human alliance with this bearer of hope! Prometheus, the (allegedly) foreseeing 'visionary', looks ahead and sees a future of new possibilities for humanity. Then, casting himself in the role of epic hero through a great act of *hubris*, or unbounded presumption, tricks the gods with a false offering and steals their fire to fashion new tools of iron. As the one who acts with 'foresight', Prometheus may have deceived the gods and may even be considered the 'god of technologists' – the one who challenged the gods and enabled humanity to overcome the vicissitudes of necessity. Yet, with or without 'foresight', he did not overcome his mortal condition. He remained 'wound up in iron chains', less free than he was before, bound by the work of his own hands.

In Illich's view, Prometheus and Epimetheus represent more than distant figures from Greek mythology; they represent alternatives ways of regarding the human condition – two rival versions of learning to be human. Epimetheus lives by embracing hope that comes through another; Prometheus merely endures by being bound to his expectation. Recovering the art of living fully human lives depends upon rediscovering the distinction between these two orientations: (i) hope, in its strongest sense, means trusting faith in the goodness of nature; while (ii) expectation means reliance on results which are planned and controlled by humanity. Hope centres desire on a person from whom we await a gift. Expectation looks forward to satisfaction from a predictable process which will produce what we have the right to claim. The Promethean ethos has eclipsed hope.[11] Its rediscovery is the task of Christian theology, especially as the church explores new or alternative ways of participating in God's mission to and with children through being like Christ. Where is *hope* in the shaping of children's identity?

Prometheus tried to transcend or defy his *creatureliness* by transgressing a perceived limit: he, a mortal, took what belonged to the gods. As a result of his transgression, he used fire to forge tools of iron. Similarly, we have tried to transcend or defy our own creatureliness by transgressing the perceived limits to what we can have, need or want. We have done so by forging institutions as our 'tools' of false transcendence. All such needs and wants are the various powers that shape children today. Prometheus' *hubris* provoked *nemesis,* or backlash from the gods; he ended up in iron chains, alienated and captive by the tools of his own hands. In the same way, our *hubris* has provoked a new form of *nemesis,* the backlash of the 'gods' of industrialised progress. In this way, we have chained ourselves and our children to a dependence upon our dominant institutions and our technological artefacts. In this state of *dependence,* we embody the

---

[11] Illich, *Deschooling*, 106.

Promethean ethos. That is, we expect satisfaction from the very conditions that cause our alienation. We are shaped no longer by the sense of trust and surprise that comes from the gift of hope. Within the Promethean ethos, a child's humanity is formed by the double-edged sword of entitlement ('I should have X') and frustration ('I don't have enough of X'). In this way, the child is taught to live enclosed within its own 'great expectations' without any sense of what it means to receive gift, to be placed in the Kingdom by the Lord himself.

The recovery of hope is the energising social force, argues Illich. He suggests that despite the 'Promethean majority', there is a growing minority who do not cling to the expectations of the Promethean enterprise. There are those who relate to modern institutions neither as 'arks of salvation' nor as Weber's 'iron cages' of imprisonment. He describes them is this way:

> We now need a name for those who value hope above expectations. We need a name for those who love people more than products... We need a name for those who love the earth on which each can meet the other ... We need a name for those who collaborate with their Promethean brother in the lighting of the fire and the shaping of iron, but who do so [not to become hyper-human by transcending their creatureliness but] to tend and care and wait upon the other ...[12]

Illich's prophetic imagination seeks to energise 'those who yearned because the old order had failed them or squeezed them out',[13] and he calls the manifestation of 'these hopeful brothers and sisters' the 'rebirth of Epimethean' humanity.

The Mission of Hope in the Formation of Children

Expectation is a counterfeit hope that deforms humanity.[14] Much like the Pharisees who argue with Jesus, the Promethean ethos offers an idealised version of being human, forming children (or disciples) according to laws and regulations that have no room for hope. The Epimethean ethos embraces limits – being in the midst – in order to flourish and live in hope. Thus, as we reconsider the Christian formation of children, one of the main tasks is to discern authentic human flourishing from its (institutional) counterfeits. To do so, Illich argues, we must discern between (Promethean) expectation and (Epimethean) hope. Expectation offers only a mirage of infinite possibilities instead of a real *horizon* by which we might shape and limit our action. In other words, what is at stake is discerning the difference between living by 'great expectations' which are

---

[12] Illich, *Deschooling*, 115-16.
[13] Walter Brueggemann, *The Prophetic Imagination* (Minneapolis, MN: Fortress, 1978), 105.
[14] Illich, *Deschooling*, 29.

false, and living by a 'better hope'.[15] It is the paradox of lowering of Promethean expectations by hoping for something better!

Diagnosing the contemporary symptoms of formation in the Promethean ethos, Illich argues that everywhere 'nature becomes poisonous, society inhumane, and the inner life is invaded and personal vocation smothered'.[16] Still, we cling to rising expectations and in our arrogance we have transgressed and eroded the fittingness of what is good and what is enough. Such *hubris* provokes a new kind of alienation – the 'ethos of non-satiety'. Social formation and inclusion within institutional landscapes of the Promethean enterprise is not the remedy but 'the root of physical depredation, social polarisation, and psychological passivity'.[17] In this view of formation there is no hope for children.

The Promethean formation of humanity is a heroic aberration that has now become the norm within progressive modernity. While, for the ancients, Prometheus represented the (tragically) heroic exception to the 'human rule', now he has become the universal ideal of every person. Whereas the ancients lived with this double awareness that balanced human potential and risk within the bounds of limits, contemporary humanity does not:

> Classical man framed a civilized context for human perspective. He was aware that he could defy fate-nature-environment, but only at his own risk. Contemporary man goes further; he attempts to create the world in his image, to build a totally man-made environment, and then discovers that he can do so only on the condition of constantly remaking himself to fit it. We must now face the fact that man himself is at stake.[18]

This raises the critical issue of what happens to how we imagine human dignity and the formation of children in the wake (and wane) of the myth of modern progress. Recovering hope entails a reorientation towards the vulnerable – a recognition of our own limits and human frailty, and an understanding that we inhabit a world and are creatures of a good God, rather than little gods caught in the chains of our own making. In recognising such limits, we also are turned towards one another and towards the interdependency that characterises life in God's Kingdom. As Jesus draws the disciples closer to himself, he is also drawing them closer to one another, and closer to the child who has been placed in their midst.

In a world shaped by the ideas of progress and development (in the Promethean way), the forces that shape children's imagination argue that 'the good life' – or human flourishing – 'consists in having institutions which define the values that both they and their society need'.[19] Within this imagination, the good – that which is fitting, or proportional, for humanity

---

[15] Hebrews 7:19.

[16] Illich, *Deschooling*, 113.

[17] Illich, *Deschooling*, 113.

[18] Illich, *Deschooling*, 107.

[19] Illich, *Deschooling*, 113.

– comes as an institutional output: 'Man now defines himself as the furnace which burns up the value produced by his tools. And there is no limit to his capacity. His is the act of Prometheus carried to an extreme.'[20] Within this ethos, 'the good life' is indexed by *unlimited consumption*. Such powers shape children today and are the ones that the church must challenge, even as it sees its own complicity and alignment with such powers.

What has happened to how we imagine human dignity? The self-image or identity formation has been refashioned according to the following fallacy: 'A conception of the human person as an organism dependent not on nature and individuals, but rather on institutions. The institutionalisation of substantive values, this belief that a planned process of treatment ultimately gives results desired by the recipient, this consumer ethos, is at the heart of the Promethean fallacy.'[21] In exposing the fallacy, Illich diagnoses how we have come to imagine dominant institutions – again, examples of technological artefacts – as the bearers of hope and good news, when in truth these structures undermine personal relatedness, corrupt the human self-image, and therefore, end up being fundamentally *dehumanising*.

If the powers that affect children are largely dehumanising, then part of the Christian's participation in God's mission is to challenge such powers and to embody the hope that is the gospel of Jesus. As Illich subtly suggests, both Pandora's box and Noah's ark represent the presence of those who come bearing hope. Such narratives can be distorted, but there are still those who can imagine another world is possible. The recovery of 'hopeful trust' means that we can love people more than products. This recovery does not mean, however, that we counter the Promethean ethos with a simplistic anti-institutionalism or over-reactive technophobia. It means recovering the 'fittingness' of *limits* as the condition for – not a challenge or obstacle to – our flourishing. It means that we approach 'artefacts' not longer as 'lordless powers' but as available means 'to enhance [our] ability to tend and care and wait upon the other'.[22]

Recovering hope as a power that affects children is inherent to being Gospel people. It is knowing the 'creatureliness' of being created and recognising that human dignity is shaped and enhanced by conviviality. It is enabling children to grow into God's Kingdom as they are placed in the midst, in a community which claims Jesus as Lord, not the powers of institutions. As the testimony of the early church suggests, God's Spirit has enabled us to discern and to work for God's reign in novel and hopeful ways that not only display life in the Kingdom for ourselves but exist as a light, a beacon for the world to see that another world is not only possible, but is present here and now in Jesus.

---

[20] Illich, *Deschooling*, 114.

[21] Illich, *Deschooling*, 114.

[22] Illich, *Deschooling*, 116.

PART SIX

BROADER HORIZONS AND CONTINUING CHALLENGES

LEARNING TO BE NEIGHBOURS AND DISCOVERING INCARNATION IN THE 'VALLEY'

David Chronic

Children in the Valley

The 'Valley of the City', as those in Galati, Romania, call it, is a neighbourhood hidden behind the hill that leads up to the city centre and its university and local government buildings. It is hemmed in by the River Danube on one side and the local railway station on the other. Situated in a flood plain, the Valley holds communist-era industrial buildings, offices and hospitals connected with the railway and bus stations, some of which have been renovated, and others which have been left to crumble. Because of its risk of flooding, property values have been historically cheaper here, resulting in a poorer population. However, over the last ten years, some wealthier citizens have been willing to accept the risk of flooding to acquire less expensive land, upon which they have built villas. The contrast is stark: next to a large villa for a small family stands a one-room home, built of thatch and tar paper roofing in which eight people live. A large percentage of the neighbourhood population is Roma. In this neighbourhood the unemployment, illiteracy and school drop-out rates are high. There are squatters and deteriorating social housing. Alcoholism is rife, and drug use is growing. Theft is a frequent occurrence. Girls are at risk of violence and trafficking, and children are pushed out to the streets to beg.

We came to this neighbourhood when children who were living on the streets invited us to meet their families. A few years later, some of our community's members moved into the neighbourhood, and we established the Valley Community Centre, which supports about fifty children and their families on a daily basis. Our larger missional community, called Word Made Flesh,[1] serves in Asia, Latin America, Africa and Eastern Europe, among vulnerable children and exploited women. In Romania, we have worked among children who were abandoned due to HIV, children living on the streets, and children at risk of exploitation because of poverty. We have partnered with other organisations to establish homes for children, and we have set up drop-in centres, day centres and a community centre to support vulnerable children and their families.

---

[1] Word Made Flesh is identified with the 'New Friars' movement; see Scott Bessenecker, *New Friars: The Emerging Movement Serving the World's Poor* (Grand Rapids, MI: IVP, 2006); Scott Bessenecker (ed), *Living Mission: The Vision and Voices of New Friars* (Grand Rapids, MI: IVP, 2010).

One child, Nicu, participates in the community centre's activities. He lives with his four siblings, mother and stepfather in a room with a cement floor and thatch walls. Attached to the small courtyard are four more rooms, covered by a tin roof. By the gate, they have a water tap. They pay their neighbours to connect wires to their electric meter, and they heat their rooms with home-made terracotta stoves, which they fill with thrown-away scraps of combustibles. In these rooms live Nicu's uncles, aunts, cousins and grandparents – more than thirty-five in all, and none are employed. Although their heritage is Roma, only the grandparents speak Romani. Many of Nicu's cousins roam the streets scavenging for things they can burn, sell or eat.

Although he comes from an impoverished home, Nicu and other children from the Valley Community Centre told us, "You have to help Stefan." We met Stefan as he was begging at some kiosks along the River Danube. He was short and underweight, but with a sweet smile. We went with Stefan to his home. It was a dismal sight. Mouldy stucco was peeling off the old bricks. The roof was covered with tar paper patches. Where windows once stood were gaping holes covered in cellophane. There was no water in the home, but the family had dug a hole in the corner of the yard behind some makeshift sheds and built a toilet over it. The house consisted of two rooms; on one side lived Stefan's older sister and her family. Her three children, all under the age of five, played on the cold, corroding floorboards. The most recent flood had left watermarks and mould on the wall. On the other side lived Stefan, his two brothers and their mother. Just as Nicu had said, Stefan needed help.

Stefan had been spending much of his time on the streets, and rarely attended school. After developing a relationship with Stefan and involving him in the activities at the Centre, we saw him become more consistent with school, but he still struggled. Because Stefan is of Roma heritage, indicated by his darker skin, he was placed at the back of the classroom. Although many of the children we know face this problem, it was an even greater impediment to Stefan because of his difficulties with eyesight. When reading or writing, Stefan had to put the paper up to his face in order to see. We took Stefan to an eye doctor, who told us that Stefan has a degenerative eye disease. Since many of the doctors in Galati have been known to give incorrect diagnoses, we took Stefan to Bucharest for a second opinion. Sadly, the ophthalmologist confirmed the diagnosis. While we were not given hope for a cure for Stefan's disease, the doctor said we could slow its progress with proper spectacles. Although the spectacles were quite expensive, Stefan's vision began to improve, and his interest in learning has since grown.

Sadly, the racism Stefan experienced at school is prevalent in the church as well. Stefan wants to go to church with us, but he comes only sporadically: some of the children in the Sunday school programme have complained about the Roma kids coming. Often the church justifies these exclusionary attitudes and actions because 'they' are unhygienic, uneducated, unemployed and sometimes involved in shady business practices. The racism that Stefan feels at church impedes him from fully integrating.

Stefan's situation at home is also difficult. His mother has suffered from mental health issues. However, she often came to our monthly parent meetings after Stefan began coming to the Centre, and she was open about her struggles in raising children. All the same, we recognised that she lacked many resources in being a better mother. In years past, organisations with whom we partnered were taking children out of at-risk families like Stefan's and placing them in group homes. However, we found that in almost every instance, breaking the relationship between the child and the parent caused many more problems. So, except in cases of severe abuse, we work as much as possible to support the family in caring for the child.

On a cold January day, Stefan's mother sent him to the market to buy vegetables. Stefan had been doing more to help his mother round the house, including walking two kilometres to the market and back to buy vegetables. That day, however, Stefan went off to play with his friends. He returned after dark with groceries in hand. Because of his tardiness, his mother snapped. She hit Stefan. She took his glasses and broke them in half. Then she kicked him out and locked the door. In the dark, wounded and embarrassed, Stefan climbed into the shed, pulled a blanket over himself and tried to sleep. The temperature dropped to 25 degrees below. When Stefan woke up, he could not feel his legs.

For the next three days, Stefan stayed with neighbours, friends and relatives of friends. At one home, while sitting on the far end of the sofa watching the family's usual activities, Stefan was invited to eat dinner. The mother filled bowls of soup and passed them to each of her five children and then gave one to Stefan. As they fed themselves with bread and soup, a four-year-old daughter asked, "Mummy, aren't you going to eat?" She said that she would eat later, but Stefan realised that she was sacrificing her dinner for him. This affected Stefan profoundly. He realised this mother was giving him food from her own bowl, while his own mother would not let him come home.

Eventually, we went with Stefan to involve the police and child protection services. Although the situation is not ideal, Stefan is back at home, and things have improved.

Recently, on returning from our annual week-long camp with the children in the mountains, I talked with Stefan and other children about the week's events as we ate lunch at the community centre. I mentioned how sad I had been to drop off a group of children in a nearby village – especially to see that all were met by their mothers, except one. The boy that remained simply looked down, threw his bag over his shoulder and started his walk home. The children at the lunch table empathised with their neglected friend. Stefan muttered that no one came to welcome him from camp either. Knowing Stefan's pain and anger towards his mother, I asked, "Would you have wanted her to come and welcome you?" He thought for a second. Then pain and grief swept across his face. He gulped and nodded that he would.

As a community we do not have solutions for the profound needs and struggles of Stefan and the others in the Valley, but we are committed to being with them and to seeking the God who has come near to them.

Christ in the Valley

'The Word became flesh and blood, and moved into the neighbourhood.'[2] This incarnational impulse guided our community to engage with the complexities, tensions and struggles of the Valley neighbourhood.[3] For Protestants, incarnational ministry grew from a reaction to trans-cultural missionaries who lived in western-style compounds and who went into indigenous communities to transmit the gospel, and then returned to their isolated homes. John Perkins calls 'relocation' an essential aspect of incarnational mission.[4] By relocating to live among the poor, one shares in others' pain and begins to understand their problems.

Incarnational ministry means not only relocation but also identification. The Son 'became poor' for our sakes and 'emptied himself, taking the form of a slave, being born in human likeness'.[5] Viv Grigg, a Protestant missiologist, calls incarnational ministry 'becoming one of the poor', or 'depending on the poor'.[6] It entails identification, non-destitute poverty and inner simplicity.[7] By 'non-destitute poverty', Grigg limits identification with the poor, saying that 'Jesus' incarnation was not that of becoming a malnourished beggar, but becoming fully human in the context of inhumanity'.[8] A commitment to simplicity is the non-poor's rejection of

---

[2] John 1:14. Eugene Peterson, *The Message: The Bible in Contemporary Language* (Colorado Springs, CO: Alive Communications, 2002).

[3] 'Incarnational' is a word at risk of becoming too nebulous by over-use. Some use incarnational to mean 'authentic Christian' (Tony Jones, 'I am an incarnational Christian', www.patheos.com/blogs/tonyjones/). Some use it to refer to moving from thought to action, see Allen Yeh, *Routes and Radishes* (Grand Rapids, MI: Zondervan, 2010), 206. Others use 'incarnational' as the positive antithesis to technologies which disembody consciousness, presence, experience, identity and environment. See James Hunter, *To Change the World: The Irony, Tragedy & Possibility of Christianity in the Late Modern World* (New York: OUP, 2010), 239-41.

[4] John Perkins, 'What is Christian Community Development?', in John Perkins (ed), *Restoring At-Risk Communities* (Grand Rapids, MI: Baker Books, 1995), 21-22.

[5] 2 Corinthians 8:9; Philippians 2:7.

[6] Viv Grigg, *Cry of the Urban Poor* (Monrovia, CA: MARC, 1992), 136.

[7] Grigg, *Cry of the Urban Poor*, 116.

[8] Viv Grigg, *Companion to the Poor: Christ in the Urban Slums* (Monrovia, CA: MARC, 1992), 54.

privilege and wealth as a means of identifying with those to whom they transmit the gospel.[9] Another important aspect of incarnational ministry is inculturation, which seeks to communicate the gospel through indigenous modes of thinking and acting in order to create truly indigenous churches.[10]

The incarnational approach, as promoted by Grigg, Perkins and others, has inspired many to move into harsh environments to live out the gospel. The approach has provided a helpful critique of missional practices that have indiscriminately promoted western culture as part of their 'gospel', and that have isolated missionaries within their compounds so as to maintain comparatively luxurious lifestyles. However, there can be problems with certain aspects of incarnational theology, particularly where it teeters on the brink of heresy by ascribing to humans something that is only true of God. God, in the person of Jesus, becomes incarnate. The incarnation is God's identification with humanity, not humanity's identification with God. Viewing incarnational ministry as the latter can support an over-inflated sense of self in coming to help the poor, and may conceal a Messiah-complex.[11]

Another major problem occurs when 'incarnation' becomes a strategy, style and instrument of mission. As David Bosch points out, Protestant churches have had an under-developed theology of incarnation, whereas liberation theology explicitly frames Christian mission in terms of the incarnate Christ.[12] For example, the Jesuit liberation theologian, Jon Sobrino, says that Jesus became flesh 'as a person of the poor, surrounded by the poor, and serving the poor';[13] he continues, 'Jesus' incarnation in poverty is basic for a spirituality of today. Systematically, that incarnation means making an option for the poor'.[14] In contrast to Protestant approaches, the missionary is not seen as incarnating the gospel; rather, the poor are. Jesus' identification with the poor is an invitation to the church to encounter Jesus himself among the poor.

Sobrino's friend, Ignacio Ellacuria, goes further by calling the poor 'the crucified people'.[15] For Ellacuria, the poor are a collective Christ and, through this incarnation, bear salvific potential. While there is something to

---

[9] Grigg, *Companion,* 204.

[10] Rob O'Callaghan, 'What do we mean by incarnational methodology?' in *The Cry,* 10:3 (Fall 2004), 6-7, 21-22.

[11] Jude Tiersma [Watson] deals with this in: 'What does it mean to be incarnational when we are not the Messiah?', in Charles Van Engen and Jude Tiersma (eds), *God So Loves the City* (Monrovia: MARC, 1994), 7-26.

[12] David Bosch, *Transforming Mission: Paradigm Shifts in Theology of Mission* (Maryknoll, NY: Orbis, 1991), 512.

[13] Jon Sobrino, 'Spirituality and the Following of Jesus', in Ignacio Ellacuria and Jon Sobrino (eds), *Mysterium Liberationis: Fundamental Concepts of Liberation Theology* (Maryknoll: Orbis, NY: 1993), 688.

[14] Sobrino, 'Spirituality', 689.

[15] Ignacio Ellacuria, 'The Crucified People', in *Mysterium Liberationis,* 580-603.

be said for the historical salvation of oppressors through the salvation of the oppressed, as evident from the judgment in Matthew 25, Ellacuria's view overreaches itself when it identifies the poor with the incarnation of God. Jürgen Moltmann's poignant question points to the limits of the salvific potential of the poor: 'If the crucified people are to redeem the world, who then redeems the people?'[16] Moltmann corrects this view by pointing out that Jesus' identification with the poor is unilateral: the equation 'Just as you did it to the least of these ... you did it to me' is established by Christ and is therefore not reversible.[17]

Although it does not approach contextualisation in the same way as liberation theology,[18] 'child theology' is attentive to the voice and person of those without social status precisely in Jesus' unilateral identification with the child: 'Whoever welcomes one such child in my name, welcomes me.'[19] However, child theology does not emphasise Jesus' identification with the child, but rather Jesus' signifying of the Kingdom of God through the child.[20] As such, the child is more an invitation to emulate God's humility and God's welcome than representing a privileged locus of God's incarnational presence.

Hence liberation theologians focus on the poor as the incarnational presence; Protestant missiology sometimes describes the action of the missionary as incarnational; both may be criticised for relying on assumptions that are not grounded in the Christian tradition. Marxist notions of the emancipation of humanity through the proletariat influence the approaches of liberation theologians. Protestant approaches to incarnational ministry reveal an underlying individualism. Both exhibit a dichotomy between grace and nature, where the grace of the Incarnation is primarily manifested either through the poor or through the missionary.

This grace/nature dichotomy can be found in Scholastic theology, and is especially pronounced in Calvinist thought, which prioritises the sphere of grace (gospel) on one side, and nature (natural law) on the other.[21] The

---

[16] Jürgen Moltmann, *Experiences in Theology: Ways and Forms of Christian Theology* (Minneapolis, MN: Fortress, 2000), 295-97.

[17] Matthew 25:40; Jurgen Moltmann, *The Church in the Power of the Spirit* (Minneapolis, MN: Fortress, 1993), 123-30.

[18] See Haddon Wilmer and Keith J. White, *Entry Point: Towards Child Theology With Matthew 18* (London: WTL, 2013), Chapter 1.

[19] Matthew 18:5. See Wilmer and White, *Entry Point,* Chapter 6.

[20] Although there is an implicit identification in the phrase, 'Whoever welcomes the least of these little ones in my name welcomes me', Child Theology thus far has tended to stress the child as a 'sign' of the Kingdom of God.

[21] Using Aristotle's metaphysical principles of matter and form, Aquinas distinguishes, but does not separate, nature and supernatural grace. See Thomas Aquinas, *On the Principles of Nature*, in Ralph McInerny (ed), *Thomas Aquinas: Selected Writings* (London: Penguin, 1998), 18-29. On Calvinist thought, see James Torrance, 'The Incarnation and "Limited Atonement"', in *Evangelical Quarterly,* Vol. 55 (1983), 83-94.

dichotomy has continued in Enlightenment thought, especially through the scientific method that denounces anything unproven by experiment and which therefore cannot conceive of the supernatural. However, Church Fathers like Augustine asserted that because the cosmos is the creation of God, and because God came into creation through the Incarnation, all of nature is contingent upon, and being perfected by, grace.[22] Jesus' placing a child in the midst of his disciples also challenges the nature/grace dichotomy. The child is not totally deprived, separated from grace, or a lesser person awaiting adulthood; rather, the co-mingling of grace and nature is evident in the child, a creation in the image of God.[23] This is accentuated by Jesus inviting the child to himself, his affirmation of the child as a sign of the Kingdom of God, and Jesus' command to protect the child.[24]

Following Augustine, John Milbank says that 'there is no hierarchy of mediators' between grace and nature because God is equally present to all of creation.[25] God's Spirit is poured out upon all flesh,[26] thus God interacts with creation as Creator and restores creation through the Incarnation. In this way, humanity is called to participate in God's incarnational ministry rather than being or discovering the Incarnation in a particular locus. Moreover, the church is identified as 'the Body of Christ'.[27] By participating in God's action in the world, the church participates in the Incarnation.

Furthermore, the church throughout its history has not called humanity to identify so much with the Incarnation, as with the obverse of the Incarnation: deification (or *theosis*). The Church Father, Athanasius famously said, 'The Word of God, indeed, assumed humanity that we might become god'.[28] As Kallistos Ware explains, the doctrine of *theosis* is based on the creation of humanity in the image and likeness of the triune God; as each person of the Trinity indwells the others, so humanity is invited to mutual indwelling with God.[29] Through the incarnation of the Son, humanity 'may become participants in the divine nature'.[30] *Theosis* is also relational, caring for neighbours and the needy as well as for all of

---

[22] Augustine, *Confessions,* III.6 and IV.15 (London: Penguin, 1971), 60-62, 85-87.

[23] Genesis 1:27.

[24] Matthew 18:1-6.

[25] John Milbank, 'Stanton Lecture 5: Participated Transcendence Reconceived' – www.theologyphilosophycentre.co.uk/papers/Milbank_StantonLecture5.pdf, 3.

[26] Acts 2:17.

[27] Romans 12:5; 1 Corinthians 12:12-27; Ephesians 3:6, 5:23; Colossians 1:18, 1:24.

[28] Athanasius, *On the Incarnation*, 54 (New York: St Vladimir's Seminary Press, 1996), 93.

[29] Kallistos Ware, *The Orthodox Church* (New York: St Vladimir's Seminary Press, 1995), 231.

[30] 2 Peter 1:4.

creation.[31] Nikos Nissiotis says that 'the process of the humanization towards the *humanum* is the same process for recovering it in the *divinum*; by deification, therefore, is a process towards authentic humanization'.[32] The vision for *theosis* as a fully human life is portrayed in Jesus' words: 'I came that they may have life, and have it abundantly.'[33] *Theosis* means participating in God's intentions for human beings to live abundant lives. Through God's healing, salvation and the process of *theosis*, human beings are humanised. That is, they live fuller into God's purposes and potentiality for their lives.[34]

The implications of the incarnation of God and the humanisation of people do have particular significance for the poor. As Peter Brown points out, by worshipping the Son of God, who came to the lowest ranks of humanity in order to reconcile all humanity to God, the church made God accessible to the poor, giving them social status and investing them with theological value.[35] For the child, *theosis* may mean humanisation through development, but more importantly, *theosis* means that participation in God is accessible to the child as a child.

In addition, the poor offer the church the gift of an epistemological breach – an interruption in the narrative traditions, interpretative methods and theories of knowledge.[36] While some liberation theologians insist on an epistemological privilege of the poor for interpreting Scripture, Sobrino insists on an epistemology of the theologian with and for the poor, where knowing Christ means following Christ among the impoverished. The epistemological breach is a critique of the pervasive dominant culture by those who are dominated.[37] But because all theology is embedded in narrative and tradition,[38] Milbank considers the 'epistemological breach' a fiction because one cannot transcend previous narrative discourse.[39]

---

[31] Ware, *The Orthodox Church*, 234, 237; cf. 1 John 4:20; James 1:27; Revelation 21:1. While *theosis* is relational, we would not affirm the indwelling of humans in humans as Ware does. Rather, the mutuality of indwelling for humanity is through each person being in God, as reflected in Jesus' High Priestly prayer: 'As you, Father, are in me and I am in you, may they also be in us' (John 17:21).

[32] Nikos Nissiotis, 'Secular and Christian Images of Human Person', in *Theologia*, Vol. 34 (Athens, 1963), 90-122, 117.

[33] John 10:10.

[34] Archimandrite George, *Theosis: The True Purpose of Human Life* (Mount Athos: Holy Monastery of St Gregorios, 2006).

[35] Peter Brown, *Power and Persuasion in Late Antiquity: Towards a Christian Empire* (Madison, WI: University of Wisconsin Press, 1992), 153.

[36] Jon Sobrino, *Jesus the Liberator: A Historical-Theological View* (Maryknoll, NY: Orbis, 1993), 35.

[37] Julio Lois, 'Christology in the Theology of Liberation', in *Mysterium Liberationis*, 171-72.

[38] Alasdair MacIntyre, *After Virtue: A Study in Moral Theory* (Notre Dame, IN: University of Notre Dame, 1984), 216.

[39] John Milbank, *Theology and Social Theory: Beyond Secular Reason* (Oxford:

Following Milbank, Bell asserts that theology originates in social praxis, and praxis always occurs already rooted in a narrative.[40] However, although the narrative tradition cannot be breached, it can be interrupted and disrupted by the marginalised. This is the effect of Jesus' placing a child in the midst of the disciples' argument about power and the Kingdom of God. In this way, the marginalised child may critique, challenge and reform our theologies of incarnation.

Following Christ in the Valley

Considering Willmer's Triangle of theology-mission-child enables us to reflect more intentionally on our interactions with children. Although the concepts overlap, these two implications from incarnational theology – participation and humanisation – can guide us in our interaction with Stefan, Nicu and those in the Valley neighbourhood.

Participation

By resisting incarnational approaches that identifies either the missionary or the poor with Jesus, and by affirming God's positive interaction (grace) with creation (nature), mission can be structured for participation in God's incarnational action. This means that God's presence does not come to the neighbourhood primarily through the missionary or in the poor; rather, God is prevenient. That is, God is already present and active in the neighbourhood, though perhaps not yet recognised.

Upon entering the neighbourhood, we therefore ask, 'Where is Christ in the Valley?' A typical expectation would be to find God's action in the church. The incarnational activity of God moves people towards incorporation into the Body of Christ. We invite others to be members of the Body of Christ and to be filled with the Spirit.[41] However, not all of our neighbours in the Valley are Christians and only a few participate in church. There are a few Orthodox parish churches to which those in the Valley go for baptisms, funerals, holidays and sometimes weddings. Frequent participation in the life of the church is sparse, however, and these churches have no social programmes for those in the Valley beyond the distribution of memorial offerings. There is also a new church plant by a Baptist group; some have come to faith through this church, although it is somewhat narrowly focused on saving souls, Bible studies and prayer and has sometimes drawn people through hand-outs of clothing and food.

Wiley-Blackwell, 2006), 254. Milbank may be criticised for understanding narrative discourse as overly constraining and even deterministic.

[40] Daniel M. Bell Jr., *Liberation Theology After the End of History: The Refusal to Cease Suffering* (New York: Routledge, 2001), 75.

[41] 1 Corinthians 12:13.

Sadly, as their faith in Christ has begun to develop, our neighbours have often been marginalised by racism within the churches they encounter.

So, participation in the church does not necessarily mean participating in God's incarnational work. By rejecting a grace/nature dichotomy, the church stops seeing itself as a space of grace, and the world as a space into which the church takes grace. Rather, the church and its interaction with the world can be understood as a liminal space – an ambiguous space in which creation sometimes corresponds with and participates in God's action, and sometimes contradicts and works apart from God's action. John Yoder advises that instead of asking, 'What is God doing in the world?' we should ask, 'How can we distinguish, in the midst of all the things that are going on in the world, where and how God is at work?'[42] The key phrase in Matthew 18 is surely 'in my name'. Yoder is resisting the claim that all activity in the neighbourhood is God's activity, and presses for the community's involvement (to which we may add notions like Spirit, Scripture, tradition, etc) in discerning God's activities in the midst of all human activities. Upon discernment, Christians are invited to join in on what God is doing.

As liminal space, the church, too, is a place where discernment is needed to distinguish God's work from other happenings. For our community, this has meant affirming God's action in the churches, regardless of Christian tradition, and encouraging those in the Valley to regularly participate in the life of a particular church. We also have addressed problematic issues like racism with church leaders and congregations, through conversations, teaching and publications; our approach is to see children as a part of the community. To welcome a child in the name of Jesus is to find a myriad of interwoven challenges, institutional, ideological and personal. Through their attraction to the gospel and their desire to participate in church, the children, like Stefan, are also disrupting the church's narrative traditions that assume that salvation is more difficult and more unlikely for Roma than for Romanians, or that they are mere objects of charity.

If incarnational ministry is participatory, then the missionary and the poor are both subjects invited to participate in God's incarnation. This implies that the poor are not objectified by programmes to meet their needs or to convert them, neither are they objectified as a means of salvation for the non-poor, or reduced to a means through which we serve God. One way to test for objectification is to note whether or not the missionary remains in relationship with a vulnerable person even when they do not respond according to the missionary's desires. For example, when Stefan's mother treated him so badly, it was a difficult test for us to continue to invest in that relationship.

---

[42] John Howard Yoder, *Royal Priesthood: Essays Ecclesiological and Ecumenical* (Scottdale, PA: Herald Press, 1998), 203.

As subjects, the 'least of these' indicates the direction of the church. As Moltmann argues, the poor do not tell us what the church is or who the church is, but 'where the church belongs'.[43] The child, and especially the orphan, is understood as being among those most vulnerable, and Jesus specifically speaks of his identification with the child: 'Whoever welcomes this child in my name welcomes me.'[44] As such, the vulnerable direct the participation of the church in God's incarnational action.

In our community's experience, we received the invitation to participate in God's incarnational action in the Valley neighbourhood through the children. Whereas Jesus calls us to welcome the child, here it was the children who welcomed us. The children introduced us to their families and led us to relocate into the Valley neighbourhood. Their acts of hospitality were signs of God's prevenient grace. The vulnerable children, like Nicu, also acted as hosts by directing us to extremely needy children like Stefan. Others in the Valley continued to give us lessons in hospitality by receiving Stefan at their dinner table, and sacrificing their own food in order to feed another. For us, the children's participation directed us to those who were extremely vulnerable.

Understanding both the missionary and the poor as participatory subjects helps cultivate sensitivity to the power dynamics at work in relationships between poor and rich, child and adult, outsiders and insiders, socially disadvantaged and advantaged. This issue is particularly sensitive when interacting with vulnerable children in an impoverished neighbourhood. Sensitivity to power dynamics means recognising vulnerability and not imposing relationships, discipline or programmes with preconceived solutions onto the children. It means affirming the power of the children to invite and to host, even when the children and their families do not feel empowered or able to be welcoming. By developing intentional relationships with the parents, we express that we do not want to usurp their parenting responsibilities, that we do want to support them in caring for their children, and that we want to be accountable to them for our interactions with their children. By listening to their stories about life and the way they understand their needs and challenges, we posture ourselves as friends rather than Christian workers. O'Callaghan sums this up: 'What we mean by incarnational mission, then, is a commitment to be *with* people, to embody the good news we preach, and through the Spirit to mediate the presence of Christ.'[45]

Relationality between a missionary and vulnerable children also facilitates reciprocity. Our missional community also shares in the life of the neighbourhood. When someone marries, we celebrate with them. When there is flooding in the Valley, we suffer along with our neighbours. At one

---

[43] Moltmann, *The Church*, 129.

[44] Luke 9:48.

[45] O'Callaghan, 'Incarnational Methodology', 22.

point, when a married couple serving on staff with our community suffered a miscarriage, they struggled to make sense of it all. The event through which they truly sensed divine comfort was when Stefan, a boy familiar with suffering, said nothing, gave them a hug, and sat with them on the courtyard bench.

Cultivating sensitivity to power dynamics does not mean denying our own capabilities. We are able to facilitate relational connections with the city council, child protection services, the police and schools. We do not disempower those who are vulnerable by speaking for them, but rather we create access and accompany them in speaking for themselves.

For us, participation in God's incarnation includes commitment – commitment to relationship, commitment to neighbourhood, commitment to the long-term. Our rootedness has created stability. Some, like Stefan, have told us that we are their family.

Humanisation

Understanding incarnational ministry as humanisation allows for identification, presence and inculturation to be structured in terms of movement towards abundant life. As role models, we intentionally mentor the children and parents, modelling education and discipline methods as well as healthy values. For example, we promote hygiene, literacy, life skills and housing with basic utilities, and we inform about the risks of drug abuse, human trafficking, emigration and consumerism. While abundant life is a criterion, it is not based on an ideology of progress or of social advance. For some children, it means helping them experience a full life today. As Moltmann says:

> Life in abundance is not measured in terms of length, but in terms of the depth of life experience, a quality that will never be reached by a mere quantity of years lived and time spent. Life that is abundant in every present moment has to be affirmed and respected by others, by parents and educators, and should not be sacrificed on the altar of progress.[46]

The lives of the vulnerable are sometimes permanently damaged and their futures shortened. The bodies of the vulnerable are often under-developed, wounded and broken by hunger, addiction or abuse. In hunger and addiction, the spirit is dominated by the perceived need to survive.[47] In abuse, the spirit is separated from the body.[48] The incarnation of God, however, is a profound affirmation of the body – indeed, affirmation of negated bodies. Flesh touches flesh by helping the wracked bodies find

---

[46] Jürgen Moltmann, 'Child and Childhood as Metaphors of Hope', in *Theology Today*, 56:4 (2000), 592-603.

[47] See Monika Hellwig, *The Eucharist and the Hunger of the World* (New York: Paulist Press, 1976).

[48] See William Cavanaugh, *Torture and Eucharist* (Malden: Blackwell, 1998).

places for nourishment, care, protection and healing. Incarnational ministry brings humanising action to places where people have been dehumanised. The body is not seen as something that needs to be cared for so that we can get onto the really important work on the spirit. Helping the vulnerable access healthy meals, medical care, counselling, therapy and a safe and healthy home is ministry to the whole human person.

Because humanisation through *theosis* is not only for the vulnerable but for every human person, we most effectively humanise by modelling a life that seeks *theosis*. We want our following of Christ, our spiritual disciplines, our values and our relationships to be evident to the children and their families. We want our lifestyles, possessions and income to be accessible to those among whom we serve. In short, we want to live lives that are follow-able. We must ask ourselves hard questions, such as: Is how we are living worthy of humanity? Is it healthy? Does what I do or have impede being followed? If my lifestyle is inaccessible to the vulnerable, then should I move ahead in this direction?

Conclusion

The incarnation is the context for any Christian activity. When God's Word assumes humanity, humanity is permanently brought into participation in the triune God. God's incarnational action leads us in our neighbourhood. While our approach is incarnational, it is not about human beings incarnating an idea or an action, and neither is it about humanity identifying with God's incarnation; rather, humanity is invited to participate in God's incarnational action. We also do not assert that the poor are the sole locus of God's incarnation; rather, God's grace is interacting with all of creation. Still, the vulnerable, like Stefan and Nicu, indicate the orientation of God's people in their participation in God's incarnational action. Participating in God's incarnation happens, with discernment, within the church; but because God's presence is also beyond the church, the whole neighbourhood is invited to participate in God's incarnational action. This means that the church and the broader neighbourhood are liminal spaces in which God's action and all other action need to be discerned. Here we can ask questions of discernment about where God is at work and what kind of human activity befits our participation in God.

Because all – including the child – are invited to participate in God's incarnational action, all are subjects in their own right, and not objects of ministry. As participatory subjects, there is a basis for relationality and reciprocity.

God's incarnation makes possible humanity's deification (*theosis*). This means moving towards more abundant human life. Humanisation happens through better health, nutrition, care and education. But a better life does not necessarily translate to a longer life. Although the lives of the vulnerable may be permanently affected by hunger or abuse, we continue to minister to their bodies so that they can move towards God. Mostly, the humanising work of God is modelled in the lives of Jesus' followers. Therefore, the missional community must ask themselves not only if their lives are consistent with the Messiah and his church but also if their actions and lifestyles can be followed by those who are vulnerable.

Although we seldom have absolute solutions for the problems of our friends in the Valley, we are committed to the ongoing process of participation in God's incarnational activity and of learning to be neighbours. Through their love, respect, resilience, imagination for change and hope for a new future, the children are showing us how.

THE CHILD IN THE FAVELLA AND CHRIST OF LUKE 9:46-48

Stuart Christine

An argument started amongst the disciples as to which of them would be the greatest. Jesus, knowing their thoughts, took a little child and made him stand beside him. Then he said to them, 'Whoever welcomes this little child in my name welcomes me; and whoever welcomes me welcomes the one who sent me. For he who is least among you all – he is the greatest.' Luke 9:46-48 (NIV)

I stood with my wife Georgie in the middle of the *favela* of Jardim Olinda on the outskirts of the city of São Paulo, my physical, emotional and theological senses assailed by the landscape of social deprivation that surrounded us. 'What on earth does Church and Gospel look like here?' The journey to piece together a partial answer to those questions was to form the centre of our lives over the coming years, and was signposted in a most unexpected way by children of the *favela*.

Our call had been to facilitate the emergence of an authentic expression of the Body of Christ in that community. This was what might be called a 'generic missional goal'. The purpose of this chapter is to give readers the opportunity to share our reflections upon just three of the encounters with children which catalysed and critiqued our thinking and actions in pursuit of that goal.

'Here comes Jesus!'

It was just after 9 a.m., and the smell from the open sewer that ran along between the wooden shacks was increasing with the rising temperature. Sonia Costa had arrived over an hour earlier and, with the enthusiastic help of a swarm of young children, had already loaded and carried away two lorry-loads of the dank cardboard boxes and general detritus that had taken over the dark inside space of the wood and corrugated iron lean-to that Abel, and an indeterminate number of younger brothers, sisters and cousins, knew as their home. I had come to help. Suddenly a shrill cry went up, 'Here comes Jesus!' Unbidden, a thought sprang into my mind, 'Thank God! ... to bring an end to all this suffering!' But there was no apocalyptic trumpet blast or rush of archangelic wings: it was only Sonia, a portly lady in her forties, gingerly descending the narrow alleyway that led from the road above to the sewer-side hovel below. But a child had seen Jesus, and was ready to start loading his lorry again!

The voice crying in the alleyway, proclaiming the arrival of the Word-made-flesh, was that of a child, Abel, who like millions of children, live a life defined by the deprivation. The rubbish gleaned from the streets of the city had stolen his space, shut out the light, and brought rats and dampness into his world. With the rats came the urine, the leptospirosis, and the teeth that chewed his baby sister as she slept. With the dampness came the bronchitic diseases that threatened his life only a little less than the violence of the big people who fought over the rubbish during the day, and drank and drugged themselves at night. But why did Abel suddenly identify the Christ of God in the form of a forty-something female walking into his world? Had he not seen what Jesus was like? Sunday by Sunday, in the lean-to at the edge of the *favela* which served as the 'church-without-walls', there were puppets like latter-day prophets proclaiming a God getting involved, getting his hands dirty, changing lives. Not just words from a big person talking about a Jesus, but Jesus, in cloth and felt, his own size, at his level; something real. Then suddenly here is Sonia, talking like Jesus, caring like Jesus, doing the things that this Jesus did. How natural for Abel, used as every child is to understanding the world in 'real time' and 'real things', to perceive the Saviour in Sonia.

Karl Barth, speaking of the impact that singing simple songs about Gospel events and acting them out as a child had upon his spiritual development, said, 'Yes, it was very naïve, but perhaps in the very naïvety there lay the deepest wisdom and greatest power.'[1]

Luke was deeply concerned that Theophilus, to whom he addressed his account of the life of Jesus, should have no doubt as to the authenticity of Simeon's epiphany. This is why he affirms in the second chapter of his work, that three times it was the agency of the Holy Spirit that enabled the ageing saint to see the Lord's Christ in the infant Jesus in his arms.[2] Does Abel's identification of the Christ in the adult merit comparable credibility, or is it merely an outburst of childish imagination, a charming irrelevancy in the grown-up world? It is my contention that Luke has a positive and consistently demonstrated motif of the child as a hermeneutical key to gaining an assured understanding of the teaching about Jesus. So his Gospel offers us theological grounds for reflecting upon this question.

In 9:46-48, Luke presents his adult reader with a child, taken by Jesus and set at his side in response to his followers' discussion about 'grown-up greatness'. With the child standing beside him, Jesus asserts that, should the disciples' receive/welcome the child in his name, he would give himself to be received, side-by-side with the child, just as he stood before them. Furthermore, as a corollary of the 'Sent-One' being received would be the receiving of the 'Sending-One' also. Here we find the critique of the disciples' question as to what constitutes the grounds of true greatness:

---

[1] Karl Barth, *Church Dogmatics*, IV/2 (Edinburgh: T&T Clark, 1958), 113.
[2] Luke 2:25-35, especially 25-27.

Jesus speaks not of an *attitude* towards, or imitative of, children, but of the *act* of receiving the child in his name. The child, an embodiment of weakness, vulnerability and social inconsequentiality in the grown-up power-status-dominated world of his day (and ours), becomes a lens by which to investigate the transformative nature of Jesus' Messianic mission as affirmed by Luke.[3]

Sonia had indeed acted to receive the child in the name of this Messiah. She had opened her heart to receive the hopes and fears, pleasures and pains, of the children of the Jardim Olinda *favela*. She had opened her schedule to make time, as well as resources from her commercial wood-yard, available to remove the adult rubbish from Abel's world. Motivated and empowered by commitment to Jesus, and in his name, she had received the child suffering from the consequences of adult deprivation into her own adult world. In doing so, she had become a bridge across which Jesus might pass to bring Kingdom transformation into this 'real world'; Jesus had made himself present as promised, and had been witnessed at around 9.30 that Saturday morning! As I heard the words, 'Here comes Jesus,' I saw only Sonia, but this does not necessarily mean that Jesus was not present to be witnessed. The cry of the child alerted me to the present reality of the Kingdom, the glorious and real 'now' of the 'not yet', in anticipation of the final establishment of the Kingdom. In my mind, this eschatological hope had immediately leapt into view, and had become really present in the 'now'.

Two questions have provoked me to reflect further on the significance of the event: 'Why was it that the child made such an impact upon me?' and 'What if the child had not been present?'

Children tell it as they see it. What might, from an adult, be interpreted as a shout conditioned by religious convention, a pious or even irreverent outburst from a child's lips simply hangs in the air as an authentic exclamation of perceived reality and refuses to be dismissed. Despite the best efforts of my intellectual firewalls to avoid or diminish the implications of the words, I was impacted by the disingenuous challenge to let the Jesus of Luke 9:46-48 invade the reality of a 21st century Brazilian slum.

If the child and his startling acclamation had been absent that day, the sanitisation of the shack would no doubt still have been achieved, and there would have been some short-term improvement in the living conditions of Abel's family. But the event would, I suspect, have long passed unremembered into history amongst many other similar enterprises: it was part of my mission task, scheduled for a Saturday morning between breakfast and an afternoon outing with my own family. Its lasting – or dare

---

[3] See the prophetic utterances of Mary (Luke 1:46-55) and Simeon (Luke 2:34, 35), taken up by Jesus in Luke 4:17-21 as he embraces the Isaiah 61 vision of Messiahship.

I say 'everlasting' – value for me was that as Jesus made himself present to that child, I was drawn into the encounter in a way that informed and enriched my understanding and relationship with Jesus, also. It resonates with the experience of the disciples on the Emmaus road when they were joined by Jesus: 'Did not our hearts burn within us when he met with us …?'[4] For me, that place and that child, epitomes of worthlessness in worldly terms, became endowed with the gracious honour and status of the incomparably greater order of existence grounded in the good purposes of Jesus and the one who had sent him. Although the event circumscribed by the transience of the human condition has passed, the vision of the Son of God clearing away rubbish alongside children remains, offering the hope of joy and transformation in the harshest of circumstances.

Luke's commentary on the joy of the disciples as they reported their own mission experience of the in-breaking of the Kingdom of God,[5] presents Jesus filled with Spirit-inspired joy, praising his Heavenly Father for enabling 'little children' to see and hear such expressions of the long-awaited divine Kingdom.[6] The Seventy-Two are warned of the harsh and threatening environment of unbelief and opposition in which they are called to conduct their mission;[7] unbelief and opposition that would characterise the whole of their journey towards Jerusalem, and eventually culminate in Jesus' death. Yet even in that context, as in the midst of the Kingdom-denying reality of Abel's *favela* world, the 'little children' are enabled to witness the transformative power associated with the name and presence of Jesus: 'In your name even the demons submit to us.'[8]

For these, and perhaps for other reasons I have yet to discover, this experience became and continues to be an encouragement to stand alongside and identify with the 'little children', in the ongoing mission of Jesus. It is an encouragement to look in faith for Kingdom revelation and transformation, even in the most challenging contexts. At that moment there could have been no greater greatness than to be alongside the child with Jesus, embracing and embraced by the purposes of 'the one who sent' him.

'Now We Have Hope!'

I didn't recognise the young mother who had taken the microphone from me. She had been saying how thrilled she was that her six-year-old was attending the PEPE, a pre-school education programme that Georgie had begun three months earlier. This mum had never learnt to write her own name, but now her daughter could. For Mum, school was synonymous with the experience of

---

[4] Luke 24:30-32.
[5] Luke 10:1-20.
[6] Luke 10:21-24.
[7] Luke 10:3.
[8] Luke 10:17.

failure and exclusion, but her daughter was looking forward to starting big school in January. Then, with the promising aroma of the roasting Christmas turkey gradually pervading the hall where the parents of the first term of PEPE children had gathered, she turned and spoke the words ... 'Before you came to Jardim Olinda, we had no hope, but now we have hope.' Not, 'My daughter has hope,' or 'I have hope,' or even, 'Our family has hope,' but somehow – anonymously, for I never did find out her name – this mother articulated a community truth, that through the tiny windows of life that were the community's children, a light had shone that challenged their sense of community hopelessness.

After only three months of starting the PEPE, the hugely positive response of the community in the *favela* of Jardim Olinda had taken us by surprise. From informal observations and conversations with mums, we were pretty confident of the relevance of the initiative.[9] However, we had failed to take into account two key factors which would accelerate and amplify its impact across the community: children's natural propensity to chatter about things they enjoy, and the extended family networks that were characteristic of the *favela*. There was no doubt that the community, taken as a whole, had other priorities regarding social improvement, such as less aggressive policing, better water and electricity provision, a better-staffed and more accessible local health clinic. But children touched the heart of almost everyone who individually made up the community.

Unlike the older kids, who soon became seen as 'public enemies' and a social problem, the vulnerability and dependence of pre-schoolers made them everyone's concern, especially if they were counted among your grandchildren, cousins, nieces, etc. Children had a special place in the 'heart' and social dynamic of the community. To help them was to capture the positive attention of everyone. The PEPE, in preparing the children to enter school socially, spiritually and educationally equipped to do well, was also offering help that many families understood to be really important for the future well-being of their children. The effects of falling behind and falling out of school were all too well understood.[10] Mums in particular, the most stable elements in the community structure, saw in the PEPE a chance for change in the otherwise grim social prognosis that hung over their children's futures. The PEPE was perceived as offering hope for a way out from the toxic cycle of school drop-out, teenage criminality, early pregnancy, and further economic deprivation.

---

[9] With the help of students from the São Paulo Baptist seminary we later conducted a community survey of 100 families to discover that seven out of ten households had at least one child of pre-school age – at that time in São Paulo, that meant up to six years of age.

[10] Of the twenty or so young adolescents that became associated with the church one way or another, almost half had died a violent death before they reached twenty years of age, caught up into drug-related crime and gang violence.

For a handful of Christians, with very limited resources, wanting to find an authentic expression of the gospel that could impact the community as widely as possible, it became apparent that the PEPE represented not only a pathway for the development of each child individually, but a doorway into the heart of the community as a whole. As relationships were built from the children 'inwards' to the families, and 'outwards' into the community, the programme became the driver for what proved to be an effective church-based mission strategy in Jardim Olinda, and subsequently in many other socially deprived communities across Latin America and Africa.[11]

The resilience of affective relationships between adults and children, even in situations of significant social deprivation, is testimony to the 'natural order of creation', in which the well-being of children depends upon adults. In social or personal circumstances where adults are finding it difficult to fulfil this role, support offered by groups or individuals to help them is generally well received, and can readily form the basis for developing relationships that offer the potential of transformation for the adults themselves. This is perhaps particularly the case when adults are aware of deficiencies in their own childhood experience, which they wish to avoid becoming the experience of their children. The possibility that things can be different for their children can reawaken latent hope that a new beginning is possible both as individuals and as a community.

It is widely attested that children benefitted by socio-educational programmes can become the agents of community change, either as catalysts of fresh hope for the adult community, encouraged by the fact that someone is bothered for them enough to help, or through themselves as agents of change, modelling more positive or productive attitudes and activities. It is worth noting here that in the introduction to his Gospel, Luke appears to embrace a similar understanding of children having the metaphorical potential to represent attitudes and lifestyles appropriate to the true sons and daughters of God, to whom the leaders of the current community need look for renewal.[12]

From the earliest references in Scripture, God's commitment to share his life with the life of human beings has been expressed in trans-generational terms.[13] He promises that the current generation's adults can count upon his faithfulness towards their children and so on into his future. It is not just that, for a community, tomorrow offers the possibility of change for the better in its children's lives, but that God has already declared himself 'for' its children *now*, and in that tomorrow as well. It was often the case that when such confidence was called into question by difficult circumstances, the adult stewards of the covenant, though fear or faithlessness, went 'after

---

[11] See www.pepe-network.org for more information on the development of the PEPE network and its approach to holistic mission in deprived communities. It currently operates in more than twenty countries.

[12] Luke 1:16, 17.

[13] Genesis 9:12; 15:12, etc.

other gods' and lost touch with God's good purposes for themselves. The initial failure to enter the Promised Land is attributed by Moses to the people's fear that they would fail and their children would be taken into captivity.[14] Yet despite their disbelief, and the consequences this brings upon the adults, God's promise to the children was reaffirmed.

Children, then, can become powerful signs of both judgement and hope for the community. They have an unparalleled metaphorical potential to serve as signifiers of any societal disregard of the needs of all groups who, because of particular cultural, social or economic conditions, find themselves in need of support. In Isaiah – Luke's primary scriptural source for framing Jesus' ministry – this potential is recognised and set at the heart of the prophet's appeal to the nation's leaders for religious and social reform. The prophet hauls the nation's religious and political leaders before the court of the Torah,[15] where God's intended rule of justice for the Davidic kingdom is seen to be based on his own parent-child commitment to Israel,[16] and finds them guilty of neglecting this divinely decreed responsibility for the weak and dependent. His pronouncement of judgement, followed by a promise of gracious restoration,[17] is dramatically set before the current Davidic incumbent, Ahaz, in acts of prophetic symbolism. Isaiah is instructed by God to give names to his three children which make them living embodiments in the community of his message of hope, presence, and judgement.[18]

These divine responses to the nation's rebellious lifestyle are declared by the prophet in Isaiah 8:18: 'Here I am, and the children the Lord has given me. We are signs and symbols in Israel from the Lord Almighty.' Matthew explicitly links Jesus' birth to the prophecy in Isaiah 7:14 of Immanuel, and the virgin's child.[19] The dramatic fulfilment of Isaiah's pronouncement of future hope for Israel (and indeed for the world beyond Israel), comes with the birth of the promised Davidic Messiah. Simeon's inspired recognition of the light to the Gentiles and glory to Israel in the form of the baby Jesus,[20] gives unequivocal affirmation of the potential of the child to embody and become the vehicle of revelation *par excellence* of God's

---

[14] Deuteronomy 1:39.

[15] Isaiah 1:17, 23; 10:2.

[16] Isaiah 1:2. This expression of the parent-child metaphor to speak of God's relationship to his people is richly developed in the closing chapter of Isaiah, where the message of Israel's judgement and restoration is set in an explicitly eschatological framework, and described again using the same motif, but with the unusual adoption of the female parenting metaphor (Isaiah 66:7-11).

[17] Isaiah 1:24-26.

[18] The names are Shear-jashub, meaning 'A remnant shall return'; Immanuel, 'God is with us'; and Maher-shalal-hash-baz, 'Pillage hastens: looting speeds' (Isaiah 7:3, 14; 8:3).

[19] Matthew 1:23.

[20] Luke 2:32.

commitment to transform and restore communities to their true calling as his people. When the church acts to express this same commitment to a community's children, this 'gospel of hope' is reaffirmed and the adult community is encouraged to believe again, even in the face of their own hope-denying experience.

'You Pray After Me'

Joanna skipped homewards after another lively morning at the PEPE. Along the narrow passageway and beneath the overhanging upper rooms which protected her from the rain, there was hardly space for the water drops to find a way through to the shadowed alleyway below. Arriving home, she was met by a flood of anger and profanity from her mother's lips. No more PEPE for you ... out every day to find money on the street ... that **** father of yours has left and now it's up to you to help get food! Joanna sat down, waiting for the deluge to pass, then quietly took her mother's hand and, without daring to look up into the eyes of the storm, said, 'We mustn't speak like that. Let's ask God to help us. You pray after me.' After coming to know about the Friend Jesus in the PEPE down the alley, she led her mum, word by word to speak to him in the storm-centre of their home. The father told me later that he hadn't been able to sleep that night. Dozing off, he had woken hearing the voice of Joanna calling him to come home. The next morning with eyes still red from the previous day's drink, sleeplessness and tears, he went home.

'What on earth was going on?' Joanna's mother's world had come crashing down. From her perspective, the number of key players in her daily drama of life had suddenly been reduced from three to two, and so Joanna would have to give up being a child and take up a role as breadwinner.

'What in heaven was going on?' Joanna's world had grown bigger since she'd begun attending the PEPE. There was God in her world now, and somehow that meant there were more possibilities. And there was Jesus whom she had come to enjoy as her Friend, who was always there.

'On earth' Joanna had no voice; she had to stand and try to weather the storm. She was only a child, sometimes listened to, more often ignored or told to do as she was told. 'In heaven' she was embraced, made to understand that she was part of what God was doing in the world, that she was loved and valued as a person, and able to share her life with her special Friend who was always there. But suddenly the world had been turned upside-down, and Joanna realised that the vulnerable one, the weak and dependent one, was her mum. Inspired by the Spirit of the upside-down Kingdom of God, she reached out from her world to her mum. It was her mum who had taken her to the PEPE where she had discovered her 'heavenly' world, and been embraced by Jesus. And now it was her turn to take the lead, something that was possible in God's Kingdom. Not with an adult's sympathetic, 'I'll pray for you,' but with all the assurance of someone who had come straight from the arms of Jesus, she invited her mum to come into the Kingdom and talk to him herself, along with her; like an unwritten sequel to the adults bringing children to Jesus in Luke 18:15-17.

However one might imagine the thoughts and emotions behind that prayer, surely a dramatic expression of Kingdom status-reversal had taken place. With a child's readiness to emulate her own encounter with Jesus, Joanna simply invited her mum to follow and do what was 'natural' in her own Kingdom-infused world. The child had taken the lead. Any sense of fearfulness or resentment had been overcome by a 'childlike' Kingdom naïvety, reminiscent of the Israelite slave girl's concern for her master, the mighty Naaman, commander of the armies of Syria.[21] And God had honoured the encounter. As adults, and passport-carrying citizens of a world of many gods or none, we are assailed on every side by the faith-reducing, relativising reasonableness that gets in the way of our experience of God. During that naturally less complicated stage of being human that is childhood, 'the little ones of the Kingdom' give us an opportunity to see modelled realities of the Kingdom that will be all the more impactful when experienced by us in the context of all the complexities and chaos of adulthood.

Closing Reflections

We have encountered, in this chapter, three children:
- A child who expresses his experience of the real presence of Jesus in exuberant proclamation;
- A child whose enthusiasm for the PEPE inspires hope in his community; and,
- A child who invites her mother to follow her in calling upon the heavenly Father.

In these three incidents, children became the vehicles or catalysts of epiphany or encounter with God in a way that invited transformation. Yet their power to provoke thought and stimulate fresh understanding does not spring from any close personal relationship with or knowledge of the children involved.[22] Rather, they are made special because, in the same way that the child of Luke 9:46-48 appears with no particular personality or pedigree, they are surprisingly taken up by Jesus and held before us. Whilst remaining 'only' children, he made them special when he unexpectedly lifted each one onto centre-stage, into significance, and up to the place where true greatness is defined – at his right hand. Yet it is perhaps from this 'only-ness' as children, with no prior relational or personal claim upon us, as 'only' child players, sidelined and irrelevant in the power games of the adult world, that their potential as 'signs' draws its power to point to the

---

[21] 2 Kings 5:2-4.

[22] I never knew the name of the second child, and the names of the others I recall only with uncertainty as Abel and Joanna.

possibility of transformation enabled by the Lord of the upside-down Kingdom of God.

The child that Jesus sets before his disciples while their hearts and minds are preoccupied with becoming great[23] would be primarily a symbol of vulnerability and needy dependence, were it not for the fact that Jesus had taken hold of him and in doing so made him special: '*this* child'. The child of transformation, the 'this-child' of Luke 9:48, is the child he has taken and honoured, and the one we are invited to take and receive and honour in his name. And so the sign Jesus sets before us is not the child alone, but the rather his act of taking and holding the child in honour. Thus the disciple is not called to a particular 'attitude' in regard to children, or an emulation of children and their childlikeness, but rather to a faith-action of acceptance and affirmation of the child '*in Jesus' name*'. The adult's response to the child that promises empowerment and transformation must include a response to Jesus as he holds the child, and cannot be effective apart from Jesus' prior and gracious response to the child.

After the first ten years of *favela* experience with Christ and children, I coined a phrase, *the child stands as a doorway to God's Kingdom*. But the extent to which this is a valid perspective depends entirely upon Jesus' offer to meet us in the child. The renowned Brazilian Protestant social theologian, Carlos Queiroz, made a similar point in a critique of Latin American Liberation Theology, when he wrote that, to consider the child itself as a source of absolute revelation, 'would be to commit the same error as the Theology of Liberation. The child cannot be sacralised in the way liberation theology did with the poor'.[24]

Jesus' invitation to 'receive this child' (*touto to paidion*), is suggestive of his invitation at the last supper to 'receive this cup' (*touto to poterion*).[25] Both are calls to faith-action in his name. Yet without the self-giving of Jesus, both child and cup would remain only child and cup, full of symbolic potential but empty of transformative power.

The signal action that Jesus enacts, to challenge the disciples as to what constitutes greatness in God's world order, demands a reorientation of mind and heart which is as full of potential as it is radical. As Karl Rahner has reflected, it is a call for the would-be disciple to make a lifelong commitment to 'a wonderful adventure ... becoming a child to an ever-increasing extent, making his childhood of God real and effective ... [For] this is the task of his maturity'.[26]

---

[23] Luke 9:46.

[24] Carlos Queiroz, speaking at the Brazil Consultation on Child Theology held in Itu, in *The First Brazil Child Theology Consultation* (London: Child Theology Movement, September 2006), 21 (author's translation).

[25] Luke 21:20.

[26] See Karl Rahner, 'Ideas for a Theology of Childhood', in *Theological Investigations, Vol. 8: Further Theology of the Spiritual Life 2* (London: Darton, Longman & Todd, 1971), 33-50.

But as the disciples' subsequent failure to recognise the value of the children and receive them gladly into the gracious presence of Jesus shows,[27] progress in this inner adventure is not guaranteed apart from a commitment to follow Jesus through the antagonism of a world committed to greatness defined on its own terms. And so the transformation of outlook and experience offered by the three children (above) is under constant threat: not from any conditionality of Jesus' commitment to the children, but rather from our adult ambivalence in recognising and embracing the graceful self-giving of Jesus found in and through the child of the counter-cultural Kingdom whom he sets before us.

If the church can look to Abel's experience, and be encouraged to expect to encounter and proclaim Jesus with uninhibited exuberance, even in the harsh realities of a world that defies or denies the values of God's Kingdom, then it must receive Abel, and be there with him and for him, for only then will Jesus be known and experienced by them together with the missionary Father who sent his Son. If deprived communities are going to live out the hope inspired by one of their children enthused by a church-based programme, and not subsequently experience disillusionment like that expressed on the Emmaus road,[28] there must be a readiness to open up to the one who, having taken up and honoured the child, set his face towards Jerusalem,[29] where he would face the power-brokers and vested interests, to experience and unveil divine vindication as the one who would die but be raised again. If Joanna's mum continues to live out her life, knowing God as the heavenly Father that her daughter introduced her to, it will be because she has herself continued to follow the sign Jesus set before her.

The Scriptures throughout display an appreciation of the potential of children and childhood as signs of the purposes of God, the God of Abraham, Isaac and Jacob, and the Father of our Lord Jesus Christ, in his dealings with and purposes for humanity.[30] Since children and childhood represent a fundamental and universal dimension of human experience, this is perhaps to be expected, all the more so since God's commitment to humanity is consecrated in the ontological identification expressed through the Incarnation. Luke enthusiastically and with characteristic and thoroughgoing care embraces and develops this appreciation into a key motif, crystallised in the child action-sign of Luke 9:46-48, which provides his readers with a hermeneutical aid to our understanding of Jesus and the nature of his missionary call to his disciples.

---

[27] Luke 18:15-17.

[28] Luke 24:21.

[29] Luke 9:51.

[30] For a helpful collection of essays exploring the references to children and childhood throughout Scripture, see Marcia J. Bunge (ed), *The Child in the Bible* (Grand Rapids, MI: Eerdmans, 2008).

Reflecting, in the light of Scripture, on the children that God has placed in our own missionary journey has proven for Georgie and myself a stimulating and relevant aid to discerning the shape and dynamics of the Gospel in the deprived communities in which we have been called to serve. It is a gift, as we continue our own wonderful adventure as children of the Father. We thank God for all such children we have encountered, and for God's Son, their Saviour and ours, whom we have encountered in each one.

FAITH FORMATION IN AN INTERFAITH WORLD: PASSING ON THE FAITH TO CHILDREN AMIDST THE REALITIES OF RELIGIOUS PLURALISM

Marcia J. Bunge

Whether they like it or not, children and families around the world and from all faith traditions now live with religious pluralism. They are exposed to people of other faiths in their neighbourhoods, schools and places of work. Many also have friends or relatives in their extended family who identify with other faith traditions. Even if children live in countries or regions with a majority religion, they nevertheless see and hear about other faiths on television, in the news or on the Internet. Furthermore, in a complex global economy and given the realities of wars and civil strife, many communities around the world host foreign workers or sponsor refugees who come from diverse religious backgrounds.

Thus, whether children live on an isolated farm in rural Minnesota (USA) or in a crowded neighbourhood in metropolitan Manila (Philippines), religious pluralism is a fact and force. Even though Minnesota, for example, has a high percentage of confessing Christians, it also has the highest number of Hmong and Somali refugees and immigrants in the United States.[1] Many of these refugees were sponsored by Christian congregations and social service agencies. In addition, Minnesota immigrants in the nineteenth century included not only Christian Swedes, Germans and Norwegians, but also German Jews. Thus, even though today Jews, Muslims and Buddhists make up only one per cent each of the population, almost all Minnesotans, including children, meet in person or hear directly about people of many other faiths. Furthermore, although Minnesotans are primarily Lutherans and Roman Catholics, they hear about or are exposed to various Christian traditions through contact with native-American Christians, and with recent Christian immigrants from Mexico, Ethiopia, Korea, Kenya and the Philippines.[2]

---

[1] Currently, the number of Somalis in Minnesota is estimated to be about 50,000. www.worldreliefmn.org/about-refugees/refugee-populations-in-minnesota/somalis/. For more information about religions in the United States, see for example: Lehman, Jeffery (ed), *Gale Encyclopedia of Multicultural America* (Detroit, MI: Gale Group, 2000); Diana L. Eck, *A New Religious America: How a 'Christian Country' Has Become the World's Most Religiously Diverse Nation* (New York: Harper One, 2002); and the Pluralism Project at Harvard University.

[2] By country of origin, the largest groups of foreign-born residents in Minnesota

Since religious pluralism is a fact and a force in most communities around the world, it must inform Christian understandings of and approaches to faith-formation and religious education. Christian parents, church leaders, religious educators and child advocates cannot isolate children from other faiths, assuming they can grow up being only exposed to Christianity, and only later deal with people of other faiths. Religious pluralism and people of other faiths are all around them – directly in their neighbourhoods and indirectly through the mass media. At the same time, Christian pastors and parents cannot simply let children wander through a religiously pluralistic landscape without helping them to learn about Christianity, and showing them how to live out the faith and to follow Jesus Christ in their daily lives. Some Christians today mistakenly believe that being a tolerant citizen and loving the neighbour means they must 'tone down' or hide their Christian identity, even from their own children. Within some Christian communities here in the United States, for example, we sometimes hear parents even saying they are intentionally not bringing up their children in the Christian faith because they want them to be tolerant of others, and to 'choose' their own faith when they grow up.

As children grow and develop, they will certainly have to assimilate, publically confess, and 'own' their faith. Yet as they develop and grow, they are already exposed to values, beliefs and commitments around them. Thus, the burning question regarding faith-formation is not 'Will our children have faith?' but rather 'What kind of faith will they have?' We live in not only a religiously pluralistic world but also a highly consumer-oriented global economy. Companies spend billions of dollars marketing goods to rich and poor children around the world. If parents and church leaders do not help children understand and live out central Christian values, virtues and commitments, then they will certainly be shaped by other values, whether in the market-place of religions or the shopping mall.

How do we pass on the faith with integrity to children, then, in a religiously pluralistic world? This is a burning question for parents and church leaders not only today but also in the past. Religious pluralism is not 'new'. Christians in the early church lived in a wildly religiously pluralistic world. All early Christians were Jews. Yet the Jewish community itself at the time of Jesus was diverse, as the New Testament and other ancient documents testify. Furthermore, Christianity gradually spread to Gentiles who were devoted to a vast range of philosophical schools, mystery religions and deities. As scholars of the history of global Christianity remind us today, Christianity has never been monocultural or hermetically

---

come from Mexico, Laos, India, Somalia, Vietnam, Canada, Ethiopia, Korea, Liberia, China, Thailand, Germany, former USSR/Russia, Kenya and the Philippines. www.minneapolisfoundation.org/CommunityIssues/Immigrantsand Refugees.aspx. See also the Minnesota Department of Health, 'Demographic and Health Screening Data of Primary Refugees to Minnesota: New Arrivals – County and Ethnicity, 2005.' www.health.state.mn.us/divs/idepc/refugee/stats/index.html

sealed in a mono-Christian world, but rather has been multilingual and intercultural, and Christians in the past as today have been in contact with people of diverse religious traditions.

The aim of this chapter is to address Christian identity and faith-formation in a religiously pluralistic and complex world. The chapter finds that we can best help pass on the faith to children and young people in such a world by more intentionally immersing them in the beliefs and spiritual practices of the Christian faith. A rigorous and purposeful approach to faith-formation helps children live out and deepen their own faith as well as strengthen religious freedom, religious literacy, and religious co-operation, because living out the Christian faith in a vital and authentic way involves: 1) respecting and treating all people as human beings; 2) loving, serving, and seeking justice for the neighbour; 3) working with our neighbours to seek justice and to contribute to the common good; and 4) testifying to and openly sharing the story and foundations of one's Christian faith. This chapter supports this claim by showing how these four tenets are central to Christian faith and life, faith-formation, and the history of Christianity, and how all four paradoxically strengthen Christian identity as well as safeguarding religious freedom, foster religious literacy, and also build religious understanding and co-operation.

Treating All People as Human Beings Made in the Image of God, and Safeguarding Religious Freedom

One tenet of the Christian faith is that all human beings are made in the image of God. Like Judaism, Christianity affirms that all people are made in God's image and worthy of human dignity and respect. The basis of this claim is Genesis 1:27, which states that God made humankind, male and female, in God's image and likeness. Regardless of race, gender, age, class or religious affiliation, all human beings have intrinsic value. Human persons have different cultural, ethnic and religious identities, but according to the Christian tradition they are all made in the greater image of God. The sense of the integrity of each person is also grounded in a view of God who intimately knows the number of 'even the hairs of your head',[3] forms your 'inward parts', and 'knit' you together in the womb.[4] Although some Christians have certainly treated people of other religions, races, ethnicities or sexual orientations, as 'not quite human' and have abused and even murdered people of other faiths, Christianity radically affirms their full humanity.

Since all human beings are made in the image of God, Christians must at the simplest level respect other human beings and protect their basic human right and desire to flourish. Christians must live out this conviction and

---

[3] Matthew 10:30.
[4] Psalm 139:13.

teach it to their children. They can do so in many ways, such as ensuring that all people in their communities have enough food, adequate health care, and equal access to education. Since people in their communities and around the world are affiliated with diverse religious traditions, Christians must also help protect religious freedom along with other fundamental human rights.

Although Christians disagree about the value of religious tolerance – some viewing it negatively as having to put up with worldviews you do not appreciate, and others viewing it positively as promoting appreciation of diverse forms of religion and worldviews – Christians can agree that the Christian notion that all people are human beings mandates and indeed informs the protection of fundamental human rights, including religious freedom. As stated well in the Roman Catholic *Declaration on Religious Freedom*, 'This freedom means that all [human beings] are to be immune from coercion on the part of individuals or of social groups and of any human power, in such wise that no one is to be forced to act in a manner contrary to his own beliefs, whether privately or publicly, whether alone or in association with others, within due limits.'[5] Most Christians live in societies that are religiously diverse, and engage with fellow citizens of diverse backgrounds and faith commitments. Whether or not these faith commitments clash or might even be mutually offensive, people of all faiths must work together to ensure peaceful co-existence. Certainly, one way to help build a peaceful society is by honouring and protecting religious freedom. As Pope John Paul II eloquently stated in a speech to the President and religious leaders of the ethnically and religiously diverse country of Kazakhstan in 2001:

> Having learned from the experiences of your ancient and recent past, and especially from the sad events of the twentieth century, you must see to it that your commitment to your country is always based on *the safeguarding of freedom*, the inalienable right and profound aspiration of every person. In particular, recognize *the right to religious freedom*, which enables people to express their most deeply held beliefs. When in a society citizens accept one another in their respective religious beliefs, it is easier to foster among them the effective recognition of other human rights and an understanding of the values on which a peaceful and productive co-existence is based. In fact, they feel a common bond in the awareness that they are brothers and sisters, because they are children of the one God, who created the universe.[6]

---

[5] Declaration on Religious Freedom, *Dignitatis Humanae*. On the Right of the Person and of Communities to Social and Civil Freedom in Matters Religious Promulgated by His Holiness Pope Paul VI on 7 December 1965:
www.vatican.va/archive/hist_councils/ii_vatican_council/documents/vat-ii_decl_19651207_dignitatis-humanae_en.html (accessed 14 December 2013).
[6] 22 September 2001: www.ewtn.com/library/papaldoc/jp2arast.htm (accessed 14 December 2013).

Christians around the world have both neglected to safeguard basic human rights, including religious freedom, and have also been the victims of persecution when their own basic needs and rights have been violated. For example, many Christians in Germany during World War II failed to honour the humanity of their Jewish neighbours and their religious freedom when they allowed the government first to deny Jews their civil liberties, then to destroy their synagogues and to murder over six million Jews. Both Protestant and Catholic German Christians today regret and seek forgiveness for their failure to act on behalf of their fellow Jewish citizens and to treat them as human beings. At the same time, Christians themselves are often the target of persecution and injustice. This is especially true for Christian minorities today in several parts of the world, including the Middle East and North Africa – the very region in which Christianity first arose but is now threatened by Muslim majorities. Indeed, in the last one hundred years alone, the percentage of Christians in the Middle East has now fallen from twenty per cent of the population to about four per cent, and this region now has the lowest concentration of Christians of any major geographic region in the world.[7] In 2013 alone, over thirty Coptic churches were destroyed in Egypt.[8]

Loving and Serving Others in Our Various Vocations, and Learning about Their Religious Beliefs and Practices

Christian interactions with agnostics, atheists and people of other faiths is grounded not only in an understanding that all people are made in the image of God, but also in Jesus' command to 'love your neighbour as yourself', and in his own example of compassion towards children, the poor, the vulnerable and the marginalised. Jesus commands his followers to 'love the Lord your God with all your heart, and with all your soul, and with all your mind, and with all your strength' and to 'love your neighbour as yourself'.[9] Jesus extends love of neighbour even to enemies, commanding his followers to 'Love your enemies, do good to those who hate you'.[10] He himself also shows compassion to the most marginalised and rejected: tax-collectors, lepers, the sick, prostitutes, and the poor. He also shows compassion directly to children. He welcomes them, receives them, touches them and heals them. He takes them up in his arms and blesses them. Furthermore, Jesus, himself a Jew, reached out to Gentiles,

---

[7] See the Pew Forum's 'Global Christianity: A Report on the Size and Distribution of the World's Christian Population': www.pewforum.org/2011/12/19/global-christianity-exec/ (accessed 14 December 2013).

[8] See, for example: www.persecution.org/category/countries/africa/egypt/ (accessed 14 December 2013).

[9] Cf. Mark 12:28-24; Matthew 22:34-40; Luke 10:25-28.

[10] Luke 6:27.

healing the daughter of a Canaanite woman and the slave of a Roman centurion.[11]

In line with Jesus' own teaching and actions, all Christians are called to use their particular talents to love and serve their neighbour, to seek justice and to contribute to the common good. All Christians are called to love and serve others, and they carry out this general calling or vocation in 'particular vocations', depending on their particular gifts, contexts and spheres of responsibility, whether in the home, at work or in public life. Cultivating attention to those in need and living out a life of service begins early. Christian parents should not wait until their children 'grow up' to help their children both understand the importance of service and actually carrying out works of love and kindness. Like all Christians, children can attend to the needs of others in their own sphere and in accordance with their particular growing capacities and responsibilities, starting with simple chores or acts of loving-kindness. Parents must also provide their children with the education and opportunities they need to continue to develop their capacities and to become responsible and caring citizens.

Given this notion of calling or vocation, Christians understand that educating and guiding their own children involves two related tasks: on the one hand, nurturing their children in the faith and teaching them to love God and neighbour, and, on the other hand, providing them with the schooling and formal education they need to cultivate their particular gifts and contribute to the common good. Several biblical passages speak about the responsibilities of teaching children the commandments and helping them to live out 'the great commandment': to love God and to love their neighbours as themselves. For example, Christians, like Jews, refer to the famous lines from Deuteronomy 6:5-7: 'You shall love the Lord you God with all your heart, and with all your soul, and with all your might. Keep these words that I am commanding you today in your heart. Recite them to your children and talk about them when you are at home and when you are away, when you lie down and when you rise.' Adults are to 'train children in the right way' and to tell children about God's faithfulness and 'the glorious deeds of the Lord'.[12] They are to teach children the words of the law, and what is right, just and fair.[13]

There are also many examples in the Christian tradition of theologians who took seriously the faith-formation and schooling of children so that they could cultivate their capacities to love and serve their neighbour, especially those in need. Christians have encouraged adults to nurture the next generation in a number of ways: reading the Bible, praying, participating in worship, telling stories of faith, singing, serving others, and educating them. For example, John Chrysostom, the fourth-century

---

[11] Mark 7:24; Matthew 15:21; Luke 7:1-10; Matthew 8:5-13.
[12] Proverbs 22:6; Isaiah 38:19; Psalm 78:4b.
[13] Deuteronomy 11:18-19; 31:12-13; Genesis 18:19; Proverbs 2:9.

theologian who is still highly influential in Eastern Orthodox communities of faith today, wrote sermons on parenting and the duties of parents to nurture the faith of their children.[14] He often spoke about the family as a 'little church' or a 'sacred community'. For him, the family as a 'little church' means that parents should read the Bible to their children, pray with them, and be good examples. However, being a little church also means that the family reaches out to the poor and needy in the community. Chrysostom ranks the neglect of children among the greatest evils and injustices.[15] For him, neglect of children includes inordinate concern for your own needs and affairs above those of your children. He also believes that we neglect children when we focus on secular standards of success, which at that time, as today, means mainly financial success, or when we are preoccupied with accumulating possessions. In similar vein, the Roman Catholic Church today also stresses that helping to bring up children in the faith involves helping them identify with the poor and developing their capacities to serve others and seek justice. As families 'bring children to participate in the development of society', 'children should come to identify with the most needy in the community, especially poor and suffering children, and should develop a lifelong commitment to serving those in need in the name of justice and peace'.[16]

This notion that all Christians are called to love, serve, and seek justice for others, in whatever ways they can and at every age, certainly provides grounds for Christian concern for all people, compelling them to learn about the needs and the situation of others. Thus, loving, serving, and seeking justice for others requires also religious literacy: knowledge about the beliefs, practices and needs of the neighbour. Jesus taught his followers to love 'the neighbour', and the neighbour is not restricted to family members or fellow Christians. 'The neighbour' is all people, regardless of age, health status, race, ethnicity, country, socio-economic status, or religious or non-religious identity. 'The neighbour' even includes, according to Jesus, one's enemies and those who hate you. Thus, by helping their own children to live out their calling to love and serve others, both Christian parents and their children are reminded they are called to open their hearts and minds to all people. They must understand the situation and needs of the neighbour and 'see' them as they are. Seeing the 'other' requires understanding and learning about significant aspects of their lives, including their religious worldview.

---

[14] See, for example, John Chrysostom, *On Marriage and Family Life*, trans. Catherine P. Roth and David Anderson (New York: St Vladimir's Seminary Press, 1986); see also the chapter by D.J. Konz in this volume.

[15] Vigen Guroian, 'The Ecclesial Family: John Chrysostom on Parenthood and Children,' in *The Child in Christian Thought,* ed. Marcia J. Bunge (Grand Rapids, MI: Eerdmans, 2001), 64, 73.

[16] National Conference of Catholic Bishops, *Putting Children and Families First* (Washington, DC: United States Catholic Conference, 1991), 5.

Seeking Justice and Contributing to the Common Good, in Co-operation with People of Other Faiths

Given Jesus' command to love others and seek justice, and given their varied callings in life, Christians will and must often work with people of other faiths or no faith at all to serve others and contribute to the common good. It often 'takes a village' to address serious social injustices. Although Christians have led social movements and made positive changes in the world on their own, in the historical Christian tradition and among Christian communities today we see a long history of 'inter-religious co-operation'.

For example, in the 1960s, Martin Luther King, Jr., a Christian, fought for civil rights for African-Americans in the United States, walking alongside and in co-operation with Jewish leaders, such as Rabbi Abraham Joshua Heschel. Howard Thurman, the African-American preacher who influenced Martin Luther King, Jr. and other civil rights leaders, and Dietrich Bonhoeffer, a leading twentieth-century Lutheran theologian who was executed by the Nazis, were both inspired by Gandhi. And Gandhi's own non-violent approach to social change was informed by the teachings of Jesus.

A more recent example of inter-religious co-operation is the 2011 Nobel Peace Prize winner, Leymah Gbowee. She is a Lutheran Christian who worked closely with Muslim women to help end Liberia's civil war. During the war, Gbowee brought together Christian and Muslim women to form a non-violent movement that helped achieve peace and stability in 2003. Her story is told in her memoir, *Mighty Be Our Powers,* and in the documentary, *Pray the Devil Back to Hell.*

Such examples of 'inter-religious co-operation' are part of both the history and present reality of Christianity that should be introduced to children and young people. Indeed, focusing on addressing common concerns and social problems with people of diverse faith is the basis of several innovative approaches to building positive inter-religious relationships today. For example, several peace studies institutes and programmes, such as Emory University's programme for Religion, Conflict and Peacebuilding, focus on common concerns among diverse faith communities. The Interfaith Youth Core (IFYC), founded and directed by Eboo Patel and based in Chicago, promotes inter-religious understanding and co-operation by bringing together young people from various faith communities to carry out service projects. The aim of the movement is to help create a world characterised by 'respect for people's diverse religious and non-religious identities; mutually inspiring relationships between people of different backgrounds; and common action for the common good'.[17] Another movement gaining popularity is 'Scriptural Reasoning',

---

[17] See www.ifyc.org/about (accessed 14 December 2013). See also *Building the Interfaith Youth Movement,* eds. Eboo Patel and Patrice Brodeur (New York:

which fosters inter-religious co-operation and understanding by bringing together small groups of religious leaders and scholars to read together passages from Jewish, Christian, and Muslim scriptures that highlight a particular theme, story or image.[18] This movement started within the academy but is quickly spreading to the wider public.

Being Able to Share One's Faith Story and Distinctive Religious Identity while also Exploring Truths and Common Values in Other Religions

Even as Christians respect, seek justice for, and work in co-operation with, people of other faiths, they must be ready to speak about their own distinctive religious identity and grounds for their faith. Safeguarding religious freedom, becoming more religiously literate, and engaging in inter-religious projects does not mean Christians should hide their own religious identity in pluralistic contexts in which free speech is protected. The situation is more complex, of course, in contexts in which religious freedom and freedom of speech are not allowed, and where Christians are being persecuted or murdered. In such life-threatening situations, Christians must weigh many obligations to themselves and others, making the best judgments they can. However, wherever Christians are able to speak freely in pluralistic contexts, they must be ready to share openly the story and foundations of their faith, and they must help their children do the same. As the New Testament states: 'But in your hearts sanctify Christ as Lord. Always be ready to make your defence to anyone who demands from you an accounting for the hope that is in you; yet do it with gentleness and reverence. Keep your conscience clear, so that, when you are maligned, those who abuse you for your good conduct in Christ may be put to shame.'[19]

Although most Christians around the world would agree on the value of speaking about one's faith, they certainly hotly debate and disagree about approaches to spreading the gospel and proper conceptions of persuasion, proselytisation, evangelisation, proclamation and mission. Of course, Christians today across the political and theological spectrum universally denounce forced conversions and deeply regret chapters in the history of Christianity in which 'Christian mission' was simply a form of violence and oppression. They also agree that Christians – wherever in the world they find themselves – are to care for and seek justice for their neighbours.

Rowman &Littlefield, 2006); and Eboo Patel, *Acts of Faith: The Story of an American Muslim in the Struggle for the Soul of a Generation* (Boston, MA: Beacon, 2010).

[18] David F. Ford and C.C. Pecknall (eds), *The Promise Of Scriptural Reasoning* (Oxford: Blackwells, 2007). See: www.scripturalreasoning.org; and http://etext. lib.virginia.edu/journals/jsrforum/gateways.html (accessed 14 December 2013).

[19] 1 Peter 3:15-16.

Yet Christians today disagree about and are searching for appropriate ways to spread the gospel with compassion, and to follow Christ's command to 'Go therefore and make disciples of all nations'.[20] For example, some understand 'mission' more as 'accompaniment': being present with and accompanying those in various situations of oppression or suffering. While also honouring this notion of 'accompaniment', others want to include in their view of mission intentionally 'teaching' about Jesus and 'preaching' the word. Others include language of 'conversion' in their understanding of mission, yet define the nature of 'conversion' in vastly different ways. Still others want to recapture a positive notion of 'proselytism', recognising, as Paul Griffiths argues in a detailed discussion about the term, that if proselytism basically involves moral judgments of error (in assent) or impropriety (in action), then proselytism is virtually unavoidable since 'almost everyone is a proselytiser on behalf of something'.[21] Anyone with political, ethical or theoretical (not just religious) commitments is engaged in proselytising.

Even if Christians do not agree about the proper form of mission today, they can agree that they should be ready to share their religious identity and stories of their faith with others, and they should more intentionally help prepare their children to do the same. Indeed, the more Christians of all ages learn about and engage with people of other faiths, the more they are challenged to learn more about their own faith and to articulate more clearly their own beliefs. Just as when we learn much about our own language or country by learning another language or visiting another country, we learn much about our own faith by learning about and working with people of other faiths. Religious literacy and inter-religious co-operation do not aim to erase religious identity; rather they challenge people of all faiths to articulate more clearly their own faith and religious commitments.

Although most Christians would agree they and their children should be able and willing to speak about their own religious identity and the teachings and message of Jesus, parents and church leaders need to be more intentional in helping children and young people talk about their faith. I teach at a church-related college where people of all faiths or no faith at all are welcome. Since we do live in a region of the country with a strong majority of Christians, over ninety per cent of our students identify themselves as Christians. However, they know little about their own faith and have little experience speaking about their religious identity or commitments. The experience of our students is mirrored in a major study of teenagers across the United States entitled *Soul Searching: The Religious and Spiritual Lives of American Teenagers*; this study shows that although

---

[20] Matthew 28:19.
[21] See, for example, Paul J. Griffiths and Jean B. Elshtain, 'Proselytizing for Tolerance,' in *First Things*, No. 127
(November 2002).

most teens do identify with a religious tradition, they know little about it and have difficulty expressing anything substantive about their faith.[22]

Being able to speak about one's own distinctive religious identity and aspects of Christian faith and life is also crucial for meaningful participation in inter-religious dialogue and co-operation. If participants are unable to speak substantively about their religious tradition, then how can they participate in meaningful dialogue? Genuine inter-religious dialogue and co-operation does not force participants to stoop to some imagined lowest common denominator or to spout irenic platitudes. The false understanding of 'inter-faith dialogue' that assumes all religions are basically 'one' is so widespread that, as a way to signal some genuine differences among religions, one scholar entitled his recent book on world religions, *God is Not One*.[23]

When participants in inter-faith dialogue know about their own traditions, they can more easily enter a process of exploring real differences as well as common truths and values among the world's religions. Understanding differences helps participants see their own traditions with new eyes, to discover lost or neglected elements of their tradition, and to gain new insight into the structure and inner workings of their tradition. Christian dialogue with Buddhists, for example, has helped Christians rediscover and reaffirm their own environmental commitments and responsibilities based on a biblical view of creation.

At the same time, Christians can learn from and are free to explore truths and values expressed in other religious traditions. This freedom is based on a variety of biblical and theological convictions, as a number of theologians have argued. For example, the influential twentieth-century Catholic theologian, Karl Rahner, claims that even though non-Christian religions might contain errors, they also possibly contain truths and 'supernatural, grace-filled elements'. He bases his claim on a particular understanding of a God who wills the salvation of all people and whose grace is 'given to all [human beings] as a gratuitous gift on account of Christ'.[24] Karl Rahner, like many other theologians, views Christianity as the clearest expression of God's revelation to human beings, yet recognises that other religions contain genuine truths, basing his claim not on political correctness or a thin notion of tolerance but on his view of God. His views have shaped many Roman Catholic understandings of inter-religious dialogue still today.

A Lutheran view of God and freedom in Christ also compels Christians to keep their hearts and minds open to pursuing truth, wherever they find it,

---

[22] Christian Smith, *Soul Searching: The Religious and Spiritual Lives of American Teenagers* (Oxford: OUP, 2005).

[23] Stephen Prothero, *God is Not One: The Eight Rival Religions that Run the World – and Why Their Differences Matter* (New York: Harper One, 2011).

[24] Karl Rahner, 'Christianity and the Non-Christian Religions,' trans. Karl H. Kruger, in *Theological Investigations*, Vol. 5 (New York: Seabury, 1966), 121.

including in other religions. The American novelist John Updike, raised as a Lutheran in Shillington, Pennsylvania, expresses this freedom to pursue truth in this way:

> God is the God of the living, though His priests and executors, to keep order and to force the world into a convenient mold, will always want to make Him the God of the dead, the God who chastises life and forbids and says No. What I felt, in that basement Sunday school of Grace Lutheran Church in Shillington, was a clumsy attempt to extend a Yes, a blessing, and I accepted that blessing ... Having accepted that old Shillington blessing, I have felt free to describe life as accurately as I could, with especial attention to human erosions and betrayals. What small faith I have has given me what artistic courage I have. My theory was that God already knows everything and cannot be shocked. And only truth is useful. Only truth can be built upon.[25]

These are just two of many example of how Christians today and over the course of centuries commonly affirm that genuine truths and common values can be found outside Christianity, even if they offer diverse answers to the question of whether or not non-Christians can be saved. Regardless of Christian (what are commonly called) 'exclusivist, inclusivist or universalist' views on salvation, the Bible and Christian theology provide many grounds for discovering truths and common values outside Christianity. Christians can disagree wildly about the notion of salvation or eternal life, but they generally do and must affirm that Christians can discover truths outside Christianity, whether through the observation of God's creation, in the work of scholars in disciplines outside theology, or in other religions.

Conclusion

Certainly, faith-formation and living out the Christian faith in any context are complex tasks. Intentionally passing on the faith to children involves teaching about and living out the Christian faith through daily spiritual practices and acts of love and kindness. As many religious educators and children's ministry programmes rightly advocate, and as I myself have emphasised here and elsewhere more fully, faith-formation involves teaching children about the faith and also introducing them to a host of spiritual practices, such as reading the Bible, worshipping, praying, singing, and serving others. Passing on the faith also involves introducing children and young people to contemporary and ancient stories of faith, providing them with mentors, helping them discern their particular talents and vocations, educating them for service in the world, and helping them find a partner.[26]

---

[25] John Updike, *Self-Consciousness: Memoirs* (New York: Fawcett Crest, 1989), 243.
[26] 'Practices for Nurturing the Best Love of and by Children: A Protestant Theological Perspective', in *The Best Love of the Child: Being Loved and Being*

Passing on the faith in these and many other ways in pluralistic contexts also involves, as this essay has aimed to show, learning not only about Christian doctrine and practices, but also protecting, understanding, serving, co-operating with, and learning from, people of other faiths. Precisely because Christians are to treat their neighbours as human beings, to love and serve them, to seek justice and the common good, and to pursue the truth as they live out their vocations and callings in life, Christian identity and faith-formation will always be bound up with the tasks of safeguarding religious freedom, fostering religious literacy, and building religious understanding and co-operation. Since followers of Christ are to love the neighbour as themselves, nurturing our children's faith and helping them cultivate a strong sense of their Christian identity involves advocacy for religious freedom, religious literacy, and the many layers of what Eboo Patel and Cassie Meyer have called 'interfaith literacy':

> First, interfaith literacy involves what we might call a 'theology of interfaith co-operation': knowledge of how one's own faith or philosophical tradition offers an imperative for engaging with others. Second, it involves knowledge of the important historical moments in history that speak of interfaith co-operation: the peaceful co-existence of Jews, Christians, and Muslims in medieval Spain; the way [Martin Luther] King [Jr.] worked with Abraham Joshua Heschel during the civil rights movement. Third, it necessitates a basic appreciative knowledge of other traditions; and last, it includes knowledge of the shared values – such as mercy, compassion, and hospitality – that exist between different religious traditions.[27]

Of course, the four examples of inter-faith relationships and interactions outlined in this short essay are not exhaustive, and the Bible and the diverse forms of Christianity flourishing around the world today offer many other principles and mandates that prompt Christians to respect, protect, understand, work with, and learn from, people of other faith traditions.

Taught to Love as the First Human Right, ed. Timothy P. Jackson (Grand Rapids, MI: Eerdmans, 2011), 226-50; 'The Vocation of Children and Parents: Sacred Vision and Spiritual Practices,' in *Children's Voices. Children's Perspectives in Ethics, Theology and Religious Education*, ed. Annemie Dillen and Didier Pollefyt (Leuven, Belgium: BETL, Peeters-Publishing, 2010), 329-56; 'Biblical and Theological Perspectives on Children, Parents, and "Best Practices" for Faith Formation: Resources for Child, Youth, and Family Ministry Today', in *Dialog* 47 (Winter 2008), 348-60; 'The Vocation of the Child: Theological Perspectives on the Particular and Paradoxical Roles and Responsibilities of Children', in *The Vocation of the Child*, ed. Patrick McKinley Brennan (Grand Rapids, MI: Eerdmans, 2008), 31-52; and 'The Vocation of Parenting: A Biblically and Theologically Informed Perspective', in *Understanding God's Heart for Children: Toward a Biblical Framework*, eds. Douglas McConnell, Jennifer Orona, and Paul Stockley (World Vision: 2007), 53-65.

[27] Eboo Patel and Cassie Meyer, 'The Civic Relevance of Interfaith Cooperation for Colleges and Universities', in *Journal of College and Character*, 12:1 (February 2011), 5.

Nevertheless, even these few selected perspectives and examples from the past and present help illustrate the deep grounds for inter-faith relationships and interactions that reside deep within the Bible, and the central beliefs and practices of Christianity.

Christians themselves have certainly not always acted according to their beliefs, and Christianity's long history includes chapters of the abuse and murder of people of other faith traditions and even other Christian traditions.[28] Yet the Christian tradition also recognises that all have fallen short; all have failed to love their neighbour as themselves. In biblical terms, all have sinned, and 'there is no one who is righteous, not even one'.[29] Recognising their own failings and sins, many Christians around the world today are confessing the wrongs and atrocities they have committed against their neighbours. Jesus called for repentance, and Christians have an obligation to confess their sins both in the ways they have directly harmed people of other faiths or stood by silently, failing to act on their behalf. The Christian message also includes a message of forgiveness and renewal, and this message provides hope that Christians can acknowledge their wrongs, receive God's grace, and with God's help act in the future in ways that build on their deepest commitments and that honour the dignity and contributions of people of other faith traditions.

Such actions of confession, forgiveness and renewal are also central to the story of Christianity and the faith-formation of children and young people. As we all seek to bring up our children in pluralistic contexts, perhaps these actions of repentance and renewal can encourage our children as well as people of other faith traditions or no faith tradition at all to reflect more deeply both on the ways they have neglected to serve their neighbours, and on their own moral and spiritual resources for understanding and working with people of other faiths in their midst and around the world.

---

[28] In the sixteenth century, Roman Catholics, Lutherans and Reformed all called for the execution of Anabaptists. In the twentieth century, not only Christians in Germany but Christians around the world played a role in the murder of millions of Jews, whether by killing them directly, silently standing by as they were oppressed, or openly refusing to accept them as refugees.

[29] Romans 3:9-10; cf. 5:12.

THE CALL OF CHRIST – THE CALL OF THE CHILD

Elizabeth Waldron Barnett

He called a child ... Matthew 18:3

The language of 'call' is commonplace in theology and in missiology. We hear of men and women who testify to a sense of 'call' from God to ministry and mission. This I do not question.

'Call' is a thoroughly biblical word. It has a rich heritage, woven from many texts and textures. Call is a wide-open word, a word of possibility and risk. Call is a dynamic word – a declarative word. It makes things happen by its very use. And it is a flexible word – a noun and a verb. It may summon or name or attend or announce – or all of these at the same time.

But in Christian circles to the present day 'call' ('vocation') has often been used in a narrow ecclesiastical sense for something that triggers a person to enter training for ordained full-time ministry of word and sacrament, within an institutional denomination. Or missiologically, for something that arouses a person to serve in transnational/cross-cultural service. In some ways it has been reduced to a code word for determining a hierarchy of spiritual roles. Some are 'called' specifically to ministry or mission, and others (so it is implied) are not.

Alongside other texts, this volume has drawn deeply from the theological resources of Matthew 18. Attending to this passage once again, we encounter the call of Christ. Among his disciples, who are grasping for greatness, Jesus issues a call. He calls a child.

In the simplicity of this mundane moment, the 'call' is in danger of being lost. This is a transition, a bridge between the problem of the disciples and the resolution Jesus gives. We are prone to magnifying these binary oppositions, especially in mission – the problem and solution, the question and the answer, the sin and the salvation, the atheist and the apologist, the oppression and the freedom, the need and the donation – as if life can be divided so simply.

But Jesus makes other moves. Jesus calls a child – not just in passing, but in deliberate action – as part of the entire sequence of events. Like so many passages in a symphony, the modulation itself also contains the theme. So focused on identities and things as we are, it is easy to miss that what Jesus *does* is as important and declarative, as the people in the drama, or what he says about it.

Few commentaries, if any, have recognised the significance of Jesus' primary response to the disciples as a call. This is his opener, calling a child, but it is often eclipsed by attention to other issues that have preoccupied readers, such as 'what is it about the nature of a child that Jesus wishes to make exemplary?'

So let us pay attention to Jesus' actions, to his ways.

Jesus Calls a Child

The significance of 'call' in biblical tradition cannot be underestimated. It is a signature word that underwrites the initiatives of relationship between God and humans. While much is made of the language of 'salvation', and even 'conversion' in evangelical missiology, the language of 'call' is arguably more consistent with biblical vernacular. 'Call' indicates deep and transformative interventions, interactions, and invitations by God in a non-categorisable collection of narratives. So many different types and means and objects and outcomes of calls can be named, and commend investigation. Further reduction of these to summaries of 'type', however, is not helpful. The personal and plentiful history of call testifies to the creative relational freedom, which befits God to apprehend and address us in any way God chooses.

In this chapter, I will explore some missiological, theological and anthropological directions that arise from considering the Call of Christ as modelled through the call of the child in Matthew 18. I suggest ways in which this model can inform, enrich and energise our vision of the theological responses, anthropological relationships and missiological roles that arise from the call of Christ in our midst.

Call and Response: Theological Directions

In this volume we have spoken about the conversation between the voices of Theology, Mission and the Child placed by Jesus in our midst. If this has been a work of 'child' theology, or a work of missiology, we hope it has been clear that neither 'child' nor 'mission' has been the subject. This is not somehow to assert a premium of 'theology' over other disciplines, content or methods. Whether child theology or missiology, theology is always *theology*: about God. More than this, God is the 'subject' of theology – not the object; God is the one speaking, acting, moving, purposing, creating, revealing – and theology comes in response to the prior initiative of God.

Call is familiar in both the Old and the New Testaments. God calls things into fruitful being.[1] God calls to the deceived humans who are retreating in shame.[2] The call of God to Abraham comes, not (overtly at least) in instigating his departure from Ur, nor in establishing the promise of a child, nor even in the suggestion that he sacrifice Isaac, but uniquely arrives at the cataclysmic, reality-redefining moment to prevent the

---

[1] Genesis 1.
[2] Genesis 3.

slaughter of the child. God's call to Moses in the barren anonymity of the wilderness is self-revelatory; it is in the mystery of call that God's identity is made known. God calls Samuel in the night to a prophetic task, which cannot be entrusted to adults.[3]

More typically though, in both Old and New Testament texts, God calls communities. Hosea describes an intimate call between God and his community of people, though they are personified as one, in the guise of child, and later, lover. Jesus calls disciples, always in community – originally in working pairs, then adding to this cohort. He calls sick and suffering men, women, children, Jews and Gentiles embedded in crowds, to him for healing and teaching. Jesus calls when he is hosted by others.

Paul speaks of his own experience not as conversion from Judaism, but a call to the Gospel.[4] And this becomes the way he speaks of all his brothers and sisters scattered in communities around the empire.[5] For Paul, entry into right relationship with God begins and continues with the call of God. It is the reminders of call that sustain communities under persecution in the pastoral epistles.[6] Finally, various calls unfold the vivid imagery in the great apocalyptic drama of Revelation.

God's call is creative, redemptive, restorative, prophetic, re-orienting, advocative, declarative, affective, adjudicative – all of these attributes are possible in manifestations of call, but their variety in no way weakens the utmost specificity of call. The theological essence of call is that it is of God.

The Call of the Child – Any Qualifiers?

Is this at all unsettling? Does it seem that I am stretching the 'call' of the child of Matthew's Gospel to hold equivalence with other 'calls' of a different order or quality? Is there an assumption that somehow there is a simple direct 'ordinary' meaning to the call of the child, whereas the calls of Moses or Samuel or Israel are rather more serious, or (as we are so fond of saying) more 'spiritual'?[7]

---

[3] 1 Samuel 3.

[4] Galatians 1:13-16.

[5] Romans 1:1; 1 Corinthians 1:2; Galatians 1:6; Ephesians 1:18; 2 Timothy 1:9.

[6] 1 Peter 1:15, 2:9, 21, 5:10; 1 John 3:1; Jude 1.

[7] Given the expansive history and diversity of conditions of biblical call, I think the danger is not that the call of the child might represent an over-extension of the boundaries of 'call', but that to exclude the call of the child betrays an overstretching of 'spiritualisation', which is of greater concern. The category of 'spiritual' is absent from the Old Testament and not particularly native to New Testament writings either. The more concrete action and motivation of the Spirit qualifies events frequently enough, but the nebulous adjective 'spiritual' does not occur so often. Further, 'spiritual', where it does appear, cannot be taken automatically as a positive indicator of association with God. 'Spiritual' is as likely

Three aspects of call in the Old and New Testament texts can be noted.

First, the important qualitative factor in biblical calls, from Genesis 1 to Matthew 18 and beyond, is the calling subject. It is God who calls, always calls and who imbues the call with God's own self. In this way there can be no more or less 'spiritual' call – for all 'calls of God' are 'calls' 'of God'. God as the initiator of call gives it legitimacy, making other qualities – age, gender, ethnicity, purity, faith, sanity or capacity of the one who is called – absolutely secondary. There can be no ranking of those who are recipients of God's call.

Secondly, to place calls to children on a lesser footing than calls to adults also ignores the difficulty in assessing definitions of children and adults in the ancient texts. Sometimes the age of the person is clear, but sometimes it is not. Is the paralytic in Mark 2 a child or an adult? There is no particular evidence either way. Jesus does address the paralytic as 'child', perhaps worth reading plainly, rather than as an affective mannerism, as so often suggested by commentators who assume the paralytic to be an adult. Further to this, adults who are called, often protest unworthiness on the basis of lack of knowledge or speech, the very criteria by which children are often thought to be disqualified from full participation in faith. The Psalmist, Jeremiah, and John the Baptist all bear witness to calls that precede birth and consciousness, discrediting links between cognition, competency and call. The lines between child and adult, although sociologically distinct in the ancient societies of the biblical texts, are blurred theologically and textually in the received documents of the canon.

Thirdly, we ought to exercise extreme caution in proclaiming limits of 'reasonableness' on the acts of God in scripture. The very incongruity, unreasonableness and subversion of a call of a child carries at least as great a weight of veracity as any other of God's incongruous, unreasonable and subversive acts, often going by the name of miracles and wonders. The unreasonableness of the incarnation, death and resurrection, and the Spirit-breathed gospel project, give us confidence in the lack of so-called reason, or a foundation of alternative systems of prophetic reasoning in the scriptures.

Response

Much is made in various theologies of salvation and faith of the place and role of reason in the development of faith. Much hinges on the perceived limits of cognition in children. Psycho-social models of prediction and

---

evil as it is holy and may be displeasing to God. (See, for example, the curious juxtaposition of 'spiritual' nourishment and the displeasure of God in 1 Corinthians 10:1-5.) As we move forward in considering the Call of Christ and the Call of the Child in our text, we leave behind the seduction to 'spiritual' meritocracy. The concrete presence of the Spirit is with us.

description of early childhood are thorny fields that are constantly being revised, as new consideration is given to the interactions of deep and surface learning, and outcomes in episodic social science methods of research. This is not to say this data is of questionable value. But it is of questionable scope. Researchers are beginning to acknowledge that we are only able to assess the 'tip of the iceberg' of the actual perception and cognition operating in a much more complex way in the youngest infants than previously thought.

Putting measures of rationality and cognition aside, however, even in the youngest children – and for the sake of argument here, let's consider the embryo *in utero* as our sample: even in these, the act of being called is possible, relational and significant. An embryo may be lovingly or fearfully called – and relationship initiated. It is obvious that the called embryo performs sometimes-powerful functions in the world: in community, industry, politics and most importantly in love. Call precedes understanding, but delivers content and awareness in a declarative act. Call creates relationship from one side – and so holds theological carriage with affirmations that God is reconciler, that Jesus is the one who saves, that we are 'put right' with God by his grace – in fact, it insures against claims that our effort is required at all.

'Call', then, is the determinative framework for relationship with God, from the human perspective. Whatever it is about God that makes relationship possible (grace, justice, mercy, holiness) and whatever God does that makes this possible (covenant, salvation history, justification, propitiation – or all of these), our interface with God begins with God's call. We have briefly pointed to a variety of samples by which we can be assured this is both biblically sound and, even with the youngest of children, developmentally appropriate and authentically observable. 'Call' rightly reminds us that children and adults are the recipients of grace, not the attainers of righteousness. God comes to us, God calls to us, and thereby makes us his own. Even adults are 'called' to be born from above, and called to be children of God. Thus the 'call of Christ' requires that we hear it as the call of the child.

As thoroughly biblical as this notion of call may be, it has suffered tough competition from the alternative term 'conversion'. After the fashion of industrialisation and consumerism, the criterion of 'conversion' has colonised not only old worlds and new, established and developing, economic and cultural, but has also taken over our theology.

While the language of 'conversion' (or even 'change') is scant in the Bible, as the *lingua franca* of the global economic expansions, in which materials and trade and humans and land must be 'converted' into currency, it has grown familiar and made lexicographical invasions into the literature and language of the church and mission, evangelism and service. With the introduction of the term 'conversion', not only has the focus and nature of the way we imagine humans coming into relationship with God been corrupted, but 'call' has been divorced from this primary process and made a secondary step. We hear the heresy of being 'converted', and then later 'called'. I name this as heretical and dangerous, and the evidence across the church in the West at least is self-explanatory: sadly, many Christians have been taught that it is possible to be 'saved' without being 'called'. Consumption of religion can be attained as an end in itself. This is foreign in every sense to the New Testament, in which to be 'saved' was indeed to be called. The unity of ideas here lies in the sense of call, not to a task, but to Christ himself. The posture appropriate to call is response. We respond to the call of Christ in relationship. Affirming the dynamics of 'call and response' in faith indicates the need to re-think our approach to apologetics, epistemology, education and ecclesiology – some of which I address below, and some of which remain exciting explorations for another time.

In responding to the call of Christ, we find ourselves necessarily caught up in the *missio Dei* or the mission of God. To be in Christ is to be called to mission, for as Paul says, 'It is no longer I who live, but Christ who lives in me.'[8] The call of Christ, the call to Christ, is a call to participate in the self-giving life to others.

Consonant with this general observation of the nature of call through its ubiquity in scripture, 'call' and 'child' are particularly linked in prophetic significance and as Kingdom signs in the ministry of Jesus. Jesus calls children to himself, not for their own sake but with the vocation of embodying something of how the Kingdom works, for the sake of others. The very truest embodiment of this is seen as Jesus is placed as an incarnate embryo in the womb of Mary 'out' or 'from' the Holy Spirit, a sign and an inauguration for the Kingdom of God, the giving of God's very self for the world.

Call and Role: Missiological Directions

The literature on 'call' is full of stories of people who find themselves serving God in the midst of a discipleship community. A sense of call then, strangely, leads them away from integration into the missional community of disciples, to seminary or theological education, and the assumption of a role of office, leadership and power. A 'Christian' call has come to mean 'distinction from', not 'placed in the midst of' disciples.

Consistently, 'call' has become a catalyst for institutionalisation, for re-education, and for re-identification. Each of these factors signals an important investigation to be made, especially in relation to the demise of Christendom in minority western cultures and the new tasks of mission in post-Christian communities. Moreover, these are also important investigations for considering the enmeshment of protagonists, agendas and identities that are the result of a century of the ill-fitting, superimpositions

---

[8] Galatians 2:20.

of Christendom (including colonial, managerial, and aid and development missiological models) on the 'target' nations of mission in the majority world. How can the call of Christ, which can be seen in the call of the child, placed with silent eloquence in powerful weakness in the midst of disciples, be disentangled from impulsive institutionalism?

Role and identification with Christ

The call of the child offers a Jesus-initiated and Christological pattern for renewing our understanding of call to mission, to the world. It does this through several distinctions that challenge some of the conventional ways we speak and think of call:

- The call of Christ is not a call to a task or role, but a call to himself. The call *of* Christ is the call *to* Christ.
- The call of Christ mirrors the christological dramatic shape of *kenosis* or self-emptying.
- The call of Christ seen in the call of the child demonstrates the call to a ministry of reconciliation in the identity of Christ.

The nature of this call, as is characteristic of calls in the Gospel narratives, is that Jesus calls to himself: προσκαλεσαμενος is a call to, a summons. This is not a general 'shout out' but the personal call of invitation. And yet the narrative further informs the nature of the 'personal' in this call. Beyond introspective *therapeusis*, the personal call of Christ, revealed in the call of the child, is the call to embody Kingdom humility and the reconciling revelation of God. Thus the call of Christ in connection with the call of the child is not a call to ministry or to mission, but a call to Jesus – who then reveals the Kingdom of God in relation to that call, the effect of which is a witness to reconciliation. It is not clear just how this action of Jesus silences the dissension of the disciples, but the argument is clearly terminated.

The action of Jesus, standing the child amid a power squabble, directly parallels the narrative shape of the Gospel passions and the christological shape of the hymn of *kenosis* in Philippians 2:5-11. Seen across these three contexts, the pattern is affirmed in local, historical, and cosmological spheres.[9] The alignment of these biblical spheres is an important antidote to human compulsions to reduce the acts of God to merely an isolated situational problem, an unfolding historical schemata, or a cosmic spiritual drama of which we are only shadows or pawns. Reading these passages in canonical conversation, and in conversation with other passages, disinhibits our captivity to over-realisation, over-spiritualisation and over-historicisation.

Generous attention is given to the Matthew 18 episode, the local concrete form of this pattern, throughout this volume and in other writings

---

[9] See Matthew 18, the passion narratives, and Philippians 2:5-11 respectively.

of the Child Theology movement. I will not rehearse this separately here, but rather explore the resonances between the Matthew 18 episode, the passion narratives and the Christ Hymn in Philippians 2:5-11.

Jesus, the blameless child of God, is placed in the midst of the warring powers of the cosmos – concretely seen in Imperial Rome, and in the resistance and accommodation movements of Second Temple Judaism. Each of the gospel narratives notes Jesus' silence as he stands trial. The dynamics of conflict oddly circle around Jesus, and yet are evidently between other parties. The conflict of power is as much between the imperial Roman governor who desires one kind of peace (political and economic strategic fluency), and the Jewish elite who seek another kind of peace (cultic and cultural coherence and purity).

Philippians 2 intones a cosmic poem in the same christological and missiological shape. Christ becomes a slave (δουλος), a status symmetrically aligned in the power relations of the ancient world with children. Masters to slaves were also fathers to children, making these relationships coterminous.

The Christ is placed in the midst by obedience to death, θανατου δε σταυρου, even death on a cross. It is in the act as the 'crucified' that Jesus occupies the place of the eloquent silent critic of the powers of the cosmos; both the concrete assault of Roman oppression over the conquered Jew, and the contentions of all forms of evil in every sphere of existence in their (futile) resistance to the reconciling reign of God.

The exaltation of Christ, in the Christ-hymn, the passion narratives and in Matthew 18, is an exaltation not to power, but to the reconciled and reconciling identity in Christ. Jesus draws a strange parallel between becoming like a child, and the identity of child having equivalence with the identity of God. It is not that children usurp God, but rather union with God in Christ means assuming the God-designated status of a child, with which God in God's self identifies too. Here we see the strength of the child as a sign of the Kingdom *of God*. In Philippians 2 it is *in the name of Jesus* (εν τω ονοματι Ιησου) that the unity of creation will celebrate the uncontested Lordship of Christ in God.

Thus a tight identity is formed. Jesus the Lord is known as the crucified slave. Our union with him is incorporation into that scandalous salvific identity. The profile of 'child', so close in status to that of a slave, is a congruent sign of this same Kingdom. The Kingdom of God is demonstrated in the God of life who is slain for others. The closest to imperial power Jesus ever gets is in the courtroom scenes before the Roman Pilate, in which he remains in the demeanour of a slave, and silent as a child might be.

Both of these dramas contribute to our eschatological missiology, elaborating in pure and brilliant colours the vision of the Kingdom of God that we seek. The reign of God stands among us, in reconciling *kenosis*. Like the child, who reconciles the disciples without word or action, but by being so called and placed by Jesus. Like Jesus, who reconciles human brokenness and a disordered nature without word or action, but by being placed in the midst of terror, oppression and abuse, immobile and silenced except for misheard cries of anguish, crucified in the midst.

The call of the child here cannot be misapplied to argue for elevating children to shallow mimicry of adult tasks and roles. Many of our ministry and mission 'roles' are ecclesial echoes and expressions of education, management, political and other professional roles. This does not discount them – all such roles have the capacity to serve human community in life-giving and redemptive ways. What must be distinguished is the structure of such roles, which are essentially task-oriented, linear and transient, and the substance of God's Kingdom, which is revelatory, multi-dimensional and ever-being.

When we assess the suitability of children for leadership or ministry 'tasks', we ask linear and transient questions, such as 'are they ready for this? Have they developed sufficient skill/awareness/maturity/experience? Will they complete the task?' These are valid questions for completing tasks, but the revelation of God's Kingdom is not a task set before us, but a reality that accosts us, convicts us, transforms us. The questions that can be asked about children as participants in the revelation of God's Kingdom are of quite a different order. Jesus invites children to take their place, as they are, among the disciples. The question of 'fitness for leadership' is replaced by demonstration of revelation. The very question of 'role' is, in fact, set aside.

As we consider all of our systems and machinery for what we consider missional Gospel endeavour, with training and accreditation, sponsorship, strategy and organisation, the call of the child reminds us that helpful and functional as they may be, these orders are not aspects of God's Kingdom. In our zeal for the Gospel and our love for God, Christians are easily prone to the compulsion of spiritualisation. Cognisant of the immanence of the Kingdom, the incarnational revelation of Jesus and the presence of God at work in the world, it is tempting to undertake a process of divinisation or ordination of our structures and strategies. It is a misplaced enthusiasm for sanctification that deploys the language of 'call' on positions of power, positions which command rhetorical strength.

In Matthew's telling of the encounter, Jesus' call addresses entering God's Kingdom – that is, new beginnings in the Kingdom; not greatness, nor identity drawn from position. If there is any 'greatness' in the Kingdom of God, it is simply in entering it. As Jesus addresses the disciple's question of greatness, he redirects the discussion to terms of 'entering', 'becoming' and 'receiving' or 'welcoming'. These are terms, not of greatness, but of response, in which the roles of initiator and responder, giver and receiver, are blurred. What is Jesus saying about mission here? What vision of mission is held in these understandings of a disciple's role in the Kingdom?

Luke weaves his stories in such an order as to thread this strand in alongside explicit instructions for mission methodology.[10] There is no conflict between Jesus' grammar for mission and the evocation of the child as a demonstration of God's Kingdom. Jesus prescribes the same weakness, vulnerability, resourcelessness, dependence on hospitality and the essential action; the central verb in the missiological syntax is δεχεται, to welcome or receive. Jesus makes apostles from disciples by making them paedomorphic. Jesus' sent ones are instructed to carry nothing, to accept hospitality from those to whom they go. They are to take the place of dependants, like children in the households in which they are received, and to which they bear peace and good news of the nearness of the Kingdom of God.

> Go on your way. See, I am sending you out like lambs into the midst of wolves.
>
> Carry no purse, no bag, no sandals; and greet no one on the road.
>
> Whatever house you enter, first say, 'Peace to this house!'
>
> And if anyone is there who shares in peace, your peace will rest on that person; but if not, it will return to you.
>
> Remain in the same house, eating and drinking whatever they provide, for the laborer deserves to be paid. Do not move about from house to house.
>
> Whenever you enter a town and its people welcome you, eat what is set before you; cure the sick who are there, and say to them, 'The kingdom of God has come near to you' (Luke 10:3-9).

Call and Relationship: Anthropological Directions

Finally, the call of Christ as the call of the child to Christ requires a reassessment of our anthropology of child. We have seen the close identification of God's Kingdom with the sign of the child in our midst, and the close identification of Christ with the child, questioning definitions of sources and targets, and redirecting our missional and theological paths; so also, our sense of who children are may be liberated from various anthropological distortions. Foundationally, we affirm that the child is not 'another' kind of human – but first and foremost fully human. It is not by adults that children may be defined, but rather adults together with children in terms that theologically agree. Jesus defines disciples (of mixed ages – usually assumed to be adult, though nowhere exclusively claimed to be so by the Gospel texts), by a child. If we are to know what humans are, we best look first to children (whatever we might imagine such a category to include). This presents practical problems – the most immediate of which is the diversity of developmental stages, and the accompanying skills, reflexes, tensions and limitations of each. Which are we to take for a

---

[10] Luke 9:1-6; 10:1-12.

constructive anthropology? The category of 'child' as it comes to us mediated via the biblical witness releases us from question of skill, cognition or agency. It is not that children lack these – the cognitive activity of a newborn displays breathtaking power – but simply that these are not the basis on which children stand in our midst.

Call to Mission: How Deep a Pattern?

In Matthew 18, Jesus calls a child, and stands (εστησεν) them in the midst of the competing disciples. The child stands as a sign of God's Kingdom – a sampler by which disciples might see the ways of the Kingdom of God. In a similar passage in Luke 9, Jesus calls the child and stands her / him by his side – the place for which James and John vie in Mark's Gospel. The child is called into the midst of the disciples in order that the disciples be set right.

We wonder how deep a pattern Jesus might have intended here? Might this be seen as the inauguration (or perhaps restoration if we have paid attention to Jewish traditions) of ecclesial (church) or liturgical (worship) or reflective theological practice for those who would follow Jesus?

What might it mean to call and stand a child in our midst? (And not, as I have written elsewhere, on the stage).[11]

Do our children still exercise the vocation of Jesus in our midst, or have we reworked or perhaps reduced their role?

What might it mean for those of any age who belong to Jesus, to be called and to be placed, standing in the midst of conflict, and the contention for power, like a child?

For those of us who understand mission as 'rescue', Jesus' action of placing the child in the midst of the conflicts of power is confronting. Why doesn't Jesus protect the child from the power plays of the adults? Why wouldn't Jesus remove the child, who is obviously in proximity, though until this point remains unseen and unacknowledged? Where adults are in competition for power and 'greatness' children are indeed vulnerable. Can this mean that God's Kingdom is only present with the vulnerable? The presence of the Kingdom isn't predicated on oppression or abuse of the vulnerable, but on the tenderness of the child. Where there is a claim of self-sufficient strength, confidence and invincibility, the affront to the ways of God is clear. The impulse to offer the Kingdom in power negates the authenticity of the Kingdom of God itself.

I write as an Australian, conscious of the great shame that we bear over the removal of children in our history. Our 'Stolen Generations' of indigenous children were taken from their communities as an act of

---

[11]Barnett, 'Jesus placed a child in their midst, not on the stage: Reflections on the 4-14 Window Conference, Singapore 2011' http://ctm.uca.edu.au/childrenfamilies/files/2013/05/BB-Jesus-placed-a-child-in-their-midst-not-on-the-stage1.pdf

disempowerment of those communities by the Australian government of the time. Often in cohorts with 'mission' agencies, the government planned a stealthy victory over the traditional custodians of the land, in which adults were defeated because their children were not present. This is paradoxically counter-intuitive, for we easily imagine that adults might be better able to fight a fair fight and defend themselves without their children nearby. How little we understand of how peace and victory might be made. The connection between the possibility of co-operation and reconciliation, and the presence of children in our midst, is important for all those entrusted with power to comprehend. Where we remove children, somehow we remove the means of justice, hope and the very presence of the Gospel. Mission as 'rescue' is not enough.

For those who understand mission as 'colonisation', Jesus' act radically upsets the direction of power. There is plenty of regret in both secular political culture and the church for the role Christian mission played in the expansion of both old and new world European empires on both sides of the Atlantic. The direct corruption of mission through systemic 'civilising' and 'colonising' has been widely decried, and significant repentance and fresh Gospel thinking has emerged. However, much of the old colonial language that was once social, political, cultural and systemic, has now gone 'underground' and is found still infiltrating our theologies of 'conversion'. The language of 'reaching' people groups, descriptions of people being 'won' for the Lord and Gospel 'penetration' still occurs.

But this is neither the pattern we see in Jesus' explicit statements of greatness, nor a possible extrapolation from the crucifixion and resurrection event. Jesus gives up his power and allows others to dominate, colonise and abuse his body. Even in the resurrection there is no triumph of vindication over the alternative false powers. In this sense, Jesus' resurrection is entirely authentic and aligned with his words and actions. The humble 'in the midst' Jesus of the resurrection is consistent and congruent with the Jesus who appeared in the midst of the disciples, on the margins of the lake, breathing, coming alongside, incognito, wounded, and in need of hospitality.

Where we still think of mission as 'education', Jesus' action of calling the child into the midst of the disciples inverts the ratios and power dynamics in impossible ways. The conventional classroom has one adult (teacher) and many children (learners). Jesus sets, or rather upsets, a scenario in which there are many learners together (people of different and indeterminate ages). The child is called to join the disciples, and so is a learner in the lesson in which s/he is also didactic. If mission in the ways of Jesus is to include education, these unusual ratios must be somehow reconciled. Those who teach, those called to teach, like the child are to also be learners. Those who seek the Kingdom, those who would be great in the Kingdom, must learn with the least in their midst.

How then are we led by the call of Christ and the call of the child to re-envision mission? Jesus' call in Matthew 18 is characterised by presence. The call of the child is to stand in the midst: εν μεσω αυτων. This is just what the resurrected Jesus does.[12] At the moment where we might look to see the triumph over death, and the roll-out of God's saving purposes in mission for the world, Jesus quietly appears and stands 'in the midst' of his disciples. He breathes upon them, speaks of the purposes of God, invites them to keep living in the ways they have encountered in life with Jesus, and as we listen to Matthew,[13] promises them his ongoing presence.

The call of Christ in the call of the child is the call to a missional theology of presence. This call is confirmed in the character of the death and resurrection of Jesus. It came in the early epistolary witnesses and appropriations of the Jesus story in communities forming throughout the Roman Empire. The call of Christ to presence calls to us in the midst of our complex global contexts today. Jesus' call of the child wraps together a theology of response to God, the role of missiology in God's global Gospel project and a renewed anthropology of relationality. Because of this responsive relationality, just as the child in the midst is vulnerable, the Gospel is vulnerable too. The good news of Christ is no triumphant army or invincible force, flattening opponents, riding roughshod over history. The Gospel does not conquer, but redeems. Even as we bow and confess, in the name of Jesus, the cruciform lordship of Christ does not dominate us, but incorporates us – placing us in the midst with Jesus in the company of those who would know and follow Christ as Lord. The cruciform Christ and the child-shaped disciple/apostle are symmetrical signs of the Kingdom of God.

---

[12] Luke 24:36, John 20:19.
[13] Matthew 28:20.

BIBLIOGRAPHY

Andersen, William, David Cohen, Peter Morphew, Lynette Scott and Wendy Strachan, 'Theology of Childhood: A Theological Resource Framed to Guide the Practice of Evangelising and Nurturing Children', in *Journal of Christian Education* 46 (2003).

Aquinas, Thomas, *Summa Theologica*. (three parts in 60 vols) (ET) (London: Blackfriars, 1964-81).

———, 'On the Principles of Nature', in Ralph McInerny (ed), *Thomas Aquinas: Selected Writings* (London: Penguin, 1998).

Ariès, Philippe, *Centuries of Childhood: A Social History of Family Life,* trans. Robert Baldick (London: Jonathan Cape, 1962).

Arterbury, Andrew E., Entertaining Angels: Early Christian Hospitality in its Mediterranean Setting (Sheffield: Sheffield Phoenix Press, 2005).

Athanasius, *On the Incarnation* (New York: St Vladimir's Seminary Press, 1996).

Augustine, *Confessions and Enchiridion*, trans. Albert Cook Outler (Louisville, KY: Westminster John Knox Press, 1955).

Barth, Karl, *Church Dogmatics* (four vols) ed. G.W. Bromiley and T.F. Torrance (Edinburgh: T&T Clark, 1936-77).

———, *The Humanity of God* (Atlanta, GA: John Knox Press, 1960).

———, *The Epistle to the Romans,* trans. E.C. Hoskyns (6th edn) (Oxford: OUP, 1968).

———, *The Theology of Schleiermacher: Lectures at Göttingen, Winter Semester 1923-24,* ed. Dietrich Ritschl, trans. G.W. Bromiley (Edinburgh: T&T Clark, 1982).

Bell, Daniel M., Liberation Theology After the End of History: The Refusal to Cease Suffering (New York: Routledge, 2001).

Berryman, Jerome W., 'Children and Christian Theology: A New/Old Genre', in *Religious Studies Review*, 33:2 (April 2007).

———, *Children and the Theologians: Clearing the Way for Grace* (Harrisburg, PA: Church Publishing, 2009).

Bessenecker, Scott A., The New Friars: The Emerging Movement Serving the World's Poor (Grand Rapids, MI: IVP, 2006).

——— (ed), Living Mission: The Vision and Voices of New Friars (Grand Rapids, MI: IVP, 2010).

Bevans, S.B. and R.P. Schroeder, *Constants in Context: A Theology of Mission for Today* (New York: Orbis Books, 2004).

Bhakiaraj, Paul Joshua, 'From Invisibility to Indispensability: Sketches for a Child Theology', in *Dharma Deepika: A South Asian Journal of Missiological Research* (July 2008).

Bonhoeffer, Dietrich, *The Cost of Discipleship* (New York: Touchstone, 1995).

Bonhoeffer, Deitrich. 'Outline for a Book', *Letters and Papers from Prison*. New edition (New York: Touchstone, 1997).

Bosch, David J., Transforming Mission: Paradigm Shifts in Theology of Mission (Maryknoll, NY: Orbis, 1991).

Bottigheimer, Ruth B., 'The Bible for Children: The Emergence and Development of the Genre, 1550-1990', in Diana Wood (ed), *The Church and Childhood,* Studies in Church History, Vol 31 (Oxford: Blackwells, 1994).

Brewster, Dan, *Future Impact: Connecting Child, Church and Mission* (Colorado Springs, CO: Compassion International, 2010).

Brown, Peter, *Power and Persuasion in Late Antiquity: Towards a Christian Empire* (Madison, WI: University of Wisconsin Press, 1992).

Brown, Robert McAfee, *Spirituality and Liberation: Overcoming the Great Fallacy* (Louisville, KY: Westminster John Knox Press, 1988).

Browning, Don S. and Marcia J. Bunge (eds), *Children and Childhood in World Religions: Primary Sources and Texts* (New Brunswick, NJ: Rutgers University Press, 2009).

Brueggemann, Walter, S. Parks and T.H. Groome, *To Act Justly, Walk Humbly, Love Tenderly: An Agenda for Ministers* (New York: Paulist Press, 1986).

Brueggemann, Walter, *The Prophetic Imagination* (2nd edn) (Minneapolis, MN: Fortress Press, 2001).

————, Nineteen Theses: Overcoming the Dominant Script of our Age. Paper presented at the Emergent Church and Theology conference (Minneapolis, MN: 2005).

Budijanto, Bambang (ed), *Emerging Missions Movements: Voices of Asia* (Colorado Springs, CO: Compassion, 2010).

Bunge, Marcia J (ed), *The Child in Christian Thought* (Grand Rapids, MI: Eerdmans, 2001).

————, 'The Child, Religion and the Academy: Developing Robust Theological and Religious Understandings of Children and Childhood', in *Journal of Religion*, 86 (2006).

————, Terence E. Fretheim and Beverley Roberts Gaventa (eds), *The Child in the Bible* (Grand Rapids, MI: Eerdmans, 2008).

———— (ed), Children, Adults, and Shared Responsibilities: Jewish, Christian, and Muslim Perspectives (Cambridge: CUP, 2012).

———— (ed), *Child Theologies: Perspectives from World Christianity* (Grand Rapids, MI: Eerdmans, 2014).

Bush, Luis, *The 4/14 Window: Raising Up a New Generation to Transform the World* (Colorado Springs, CO: Compassion International, 2009).

Bushnell, Horace, *Christian Nurture* (New York: Scribner, Armstrong, 1876).

Byworth, J., 'World Vision's Approach to Transformational Development: Frame, Policy and Indicators', in *Transformation* 20:2 (2003).

Calvin, John, *Institutes of the Christian Religion* (two vols) (London: James Clarke, 1949).

Carroll, John T., '"What Then Will This Child Become?": Perspectives on Children in the Gospel of Luke', in Marcia J. Bunge (ed), *The Child in the Bible* (Grand Rapids: Eerdmans, 2008).

Carroll, Matthew, 'A Biblical Approach to Hospitality', in *Review and Expositor* 108 (Fall 2011).

Cavanaugh, William T., Torture and Eucharist: Theology, Politics, and the Body of Christ (Malden, MA: Blackwell, 1998).

Cho, P.H-S., Eschatology and Ecology: Experiences of the Korean Church (Oxford: Regnum, 2010).

Christian, Jayakumar, God of the Empty-Handed: Poverty, Power and the Kingdom of God (Monrovia, CA: MARC, 1999).

Cogswell, J.A., 'Relief and Development: Challenges to Mission Today', in *IMBR* 11:2 (April 1987).

Collier, John (ed), *Toddling to the Kingdom* (London: Child Theology Movement, 2009).

Cone, James, *God of the Oppressed* (San Francisco, CA: Harper San Francisco, 1975).

Constantineanu, Corneliu, The Social Significance of Reconciliation in Paul's Theology: Narrative Readings in Romans (London: T&T Clark Continuum, 2010).

——, 'Welcoming Children: Biblical Perspectives on Children's Welfare', in Patricia Runcan (ed), *Applied Social Sciences* (Cambridge: Cambridge Scholars Publishing, 2014).

——, '"Whoever Welcomes a Little Child, Welcomes Me": Re-Visiting the Doctrine of Reconciliation', in Marcia J. Bunge (ed), *Child Theologies: Perspectives from World Christianity* (Grand Rapids, MI: Eerdmans, 2014).

Couture, Pamela, Seeing Children, Seeing God: A Practical Theology of Children and Poverty (Nashville, TN: Abingdon Press, 2000).

Cunningham, Hugh, *Children and Childhood in Western Society since 1500* (2nd edn) (New York: Pearson Longman, 2005).

Daniel, M., 'Listening to Orphan Voices', in E. Biakolo, J. Mathangwane and D. Odallo (eds), *The Discourse of HIV in Africa* (Pretoria, RSA: ICT, 2003).

De Beer, Stephan, *The Gospel, Children and the City* (Pretoria, RSA: Imagine, 2005).

DeVries, Dawn, '"Be Converted and Become as Little Children": Friedrich Schleiermacher on the Religious Significance of Childhood', in Marcia J. Bunge (ed), *The Child in Christian Thought* (Grand Rapids, MI: Eerdmans, 2001).

Donovan, Vincent J., *Christianity Rediscovered: An Epistle from the Masai* (2nd edn) (London: SCM Press, 1982).

——, *The Church in the Midst of Creation* (London: SCM Press, 1991).

Dorr, Donal, *Spirituality and Justice* (Dublin: Gill & Macmillan, 1984).

Drane, John W., 'Sonship, Child, Children', in Ralph P. Martin and Peter H. Davids (eds), *Dictionary of the Later New Testament and Its Developments* (Downers Grove, IL: IVP, 1997).

Dulles, Avery, *Models of the Church* (New York: Doubleday, 1974).

Edwards, Jonathan, *Original Sin,* in Clyde A. Holbrook (ed), *The Works of Jonathan Edwards,* Vol 3 (London: Yale University Press, 1970).

Ellacuria, Ignacio, 'The Crucified People', in Ignacio Ellacuria and Jon Sobrino (eds), *Mysterium Liberationis: Fundamental Concepts of Liberation Theology* (Maryknoll, NY: Orbis, 1993).

Ferguson, Everett, Baptism in the Early Church: History, Theology, and Liturgy in the First Five Centuries (Grand Rapids, MI: Eerdmans, 2009).

Fernando, Ajith, 'To Serve is to Suffer', *The Global Conversation,* at www.christianitytoday.com/globalconversation/august2010/index.html

France, R.T., *The Gospel of Matthew* (Grand Rapids, MI: Eerdmans, 2007).

George, Archimandrite, *Theosis: The True Purpose of Human Life* (Mount Athos: Holy Monastery of St Gregorios, 2006).

Goodall, Norman (ed), *Missions Under the Cross* (Edinburgh: Edinburgh House Press, 1953).

Green, Joel, *The Theology of the Gospel of Luke* (Cambridge: CUP, 1997).

Grigg, Viv, Companion to the Poor: Christ in the Urban Slums (Monrovia, CA: MARC, 1992).

————, *Cry of the Urban Poor* (Monrovia, CA: MARC, 1992).

Gundry-Volf, Judith, 'The Least and the Greatest: Children in the New Testament,' in Marcia J. Bunge (ed), *The Child in Christian Thought* (Grand Rapids, MI: Eerdmans, 2001).

Gutierrez, Gustavo, 'The Irruption of the Poor in Latin America and the Christian Communities of the Common People', in Sergio Torres and John Eagleson (eds), *The Challenge of Basic Christian Communities: Papers from the International Ecumenical Congress of Theology, February 20-March 2, 1980, São Paulo, Brazil* (Maryknoll, NY: Orbis, 1981).

————, *On Job: God-Talk and the Suffering of the Innocent,* trans. Matthew J. O'Connell (Maryknoll, NY: Orbis, 1987).

————, *Theology of Liberation: History, Politics, Salvation* (15th anniversary edn), trans. Caridad Inda and John Eagleson (Maryknoll, NY: Orbis, 1988).

Hagner, Donald A., *Matthew 14-28,* in Word Biblical Commentary (Nashville, TN: Thomas Nelson, 1995).

Harnack, Adolf von, Die Mission und Ausbreitung des Christentums in den ersten drei Jahrhunderten: die Mission in Wort und Tat (University of Michigan, 1906).

Hellwig, Monika, *The Eucharist and the Hunger of the World* (New York: Paulist Press, 1976).

Henson, David R., 'Into the Wild: A Lenten Homily Not about Temptation', in *Patheos Progressively Christian Blog*, at www.patheos.com/blogs/davidhenson/2014/03/into-the-wild-a-lenten-homily-not-about-temptation/

Herzog, Kristin, Children and Our Global Future: Theological and Social Challenges (Cleveland, OH: Pilgrim Press, 2005).

Hesselgrave, David J., 'Will We Correct the Edinburgh Error? Future Mission in Historical Perspective', in *South-Western Journal of Theology* 49 (2007).

Hoinacki, Lee and Carl Mitcham (eds), *The Challenge of Ivan Illich: A Collective Reflection* (Albany, NY: State University of New York Press, 2002).

Holman, Bob, *Faith in the Poor* (London: Lion, 1998).

Horn, Cornelia B., 'The Lives and Literary Roles of Children in Advancing Conversion to Christianity: Hagiography from the Caucasus in Late Antiquity and the Middle Ages', in *Church History* 76 (2007).

Hunter, James, To Change the World: The Irony, Tragedy & Possibility of Christianity in the Late Modern World (New York: OUP, 2010).

Illich, Ivan, *Deschooling Society* (London: Marion Boyars, 1971).

Jamieson, R., Commentary: Practical and Explanatory on the Whole Bible (Grand Rapids, MI: Zondervan, 1974).

Janzen, Waldemar, 'Biblical theology of hospitality', in *Vision* (Spring 2002).

Jensen, David H., *Graced Vulnerability: A Theology of Childhood* (Cleveland, OH: Pilgrim Press, 2005).

Johnson, E., She Who Is: The Mystery of God in Feminist Theological Discourse (New York: Crossroads, 1993).

Johnson, Todd M. and Peter F. Crossing, 'Christianity 2013: Renewalists and Faith and Migration', in *IBMR* 37:1 (January 2013).

Jones, S. Feminist Theory and Christian Theology: Cartographies of Grace. Guides to Theological Inquiry (Minneapolis, MN: Fortress Press, 2001).

Jones, Tony, 'I am an incarnational Christian', at www.patheos.com/blogs/tonyjones/

Kalabamu, F.T., 'Towards Egalitarian Inheritance Rights in Botswana: The Case of Tlokweng', in *Development Southern Africa* 26:2 (2009).

Kennedy, David, 'Images of the Young Child in History: Enlightenment and Romance', in *Early Childhood Research Quarterly* 3 (1988).

Kilbourn, P. (ed), *Children in Crisis: A New Commitment* (Monrovia, CA: MARC, 1996).

——— (ed), Street Children: A Guide to Effective Ministry (Monrovia, CA: MARC, 1997).

——— and M. McDermid (eds), *Sexually Exploited Children: Working to Protect and Heal* (Monrovia, CA: MARC, 1998).

Kirk, J. Andrew, *What is Mission? Theological Explorations* (Minneapolis, MN: Fortress Press, 2000).

Klatzow, David and Sylvia Walker, *Steeped in Blood: The Life and Times of a Forensic Scientist* (Cape Town, RSA: Zebra Press, 2010).

Klaus, Byron, 'Historical and Theological Reflection on Ministry to Children at Risk', in *Transformation: An International Journal of Holistic Mission Studies*, 14 (1997).

Kligman, G., *The Politics of Duplicity: Controlling Reproduction in Ceauşescu's Romania* (Berkeley, CA: University of California Press, 1998).

Koyama, Kosuke, *Three Mile an Hour God* (Maryknoll, NY: Orbis Books, 1980).

———, 'A Holy Mystery: Welcoming a Little Child', in *The Living Pulpit* (October-December 2003).

Kritzinger, J.N.J., *Black Theology: Challenge to Mission,* DTh thesis (Department of Missiology, University of South Africa, 1988).

Ladd, G.E., The Presence of the Future: The Eschatology of Biblical Realism (London: SPCK, 1974).

Lapsley, Jaqueline E., '"Look! The Children and I Are as Signs and Portents in Israel": Children in Isaiah', in Marcia J. Bunge (ed), *The Child in the Bible* (Grand Rapids, MI: Eerdmans, 2008).

Lewis, J., Working Your Way to the Nations: A Guide to Effective Tentmaking (Grand Rapids, MI: IVP, 1996).

Locke, John, *Some Thoughts Concerning Education* (Oxford: Clarendon Press, 1989).

———, *An Essay Concerning Human Understanding* (Kitchener, Ontario: Batoche Books, 2001).

Loder, James E., The Logic of the Spirit: Human Development in Theological Perspective (San Francisco, CA: Jossey-Bass Publishers, 1998).

Lois, Julio, 'Christology in the Theology of Liberation', in Ignacio Ellacuria and Jon Sobrino (eds), *Mysterium Liberationis: Fundamental Concepts of Liberation Theology* (Maryknoll, NY: Orbis, 1993).

Luther, Martin, *Luther's Works* (55 vols), Jaroslav Pelikan and Helmut T. Lehmann (eds) (Philadelphia, PA: Fortress Press, 1955-86).

MacIntyre, Alasdair, *After Virtue: A Study in Moral Theory* (Notre Dame, IN: University of Notre Dame, 1984).

Maluleke, T.S., 'The Africanization of Theological Education: Does Theological Education Equip You to Help Your Sister?', in E. Antonio (ed), *Inculturation and Postcolonial Discourse in African Theology* (New York: Peter Lang, 2006).

Marie-Pierre, Sofia, 'Quinze mille enfants abandonnés chaque année dans les pays post-communistes', in *Le Monde* (online edn, 21 November 2012).

Maundeni, T., 'Cultural factors in the spread of HIV/AIDS among children and Young People in Botswana', in E. Biakolo, J. Mathangwane and D. Odallo (eds), *The Discourse of HIV in Africa* (Pretoria, RSA: ICT, 2003).

McAlpine, T.H., By Word, Work and Wonder: Cases in Holistic Mission (Monrovia, CA: MARC, 1995).

McDonagh, Sean, *To Care for the Earth: A Call to a New Theology* (London: Geoffrey Chapman, 1986).

McKnight, John, The Careless Society: Community and Its Counterfeits (New York: Basic Books, 1995).

———— and Peter Block, *The Abundant Community: Awakening the Power of Families and Neighborhoods* (San Francisco, CA: Berrett-Koehler Publishers, 2010).

McMaken, W. Travis, The Sign of the Gospel: Toward an Evangelical Doctrine of Infant Baptism After Karl Barth (Minneapolis, MN: Fortress Press, 2013).

Meens, Rob, 'Children and Confession in the Early Middle Ages', in Diana Wood (ed), *The Church and Childhood*, Studies in Church History, Vol 31 (Oxford: Blackwells, 1994).

Mercer, Joyce Ann, *Welcoming Children: A Practical Theology of Childhood* (St Louis, MS: Chalice Press, 2005).

Merleau-Ponty, Maurice, *The Primacy of Perception and Other Essays on Phenomenological Psychology, the Philosophy of Art, History, and Politics*, James M. Edie (ed), Northwestern University Studies in Phenomenology and Existential Philosophy (Evanston, IL: Northwestern University Press, 1964).

————, *Child Psychology and Pedagogy: The Sorbonne Lectures 1949-1952*, trans. Talia Welsh (Evanston, IL: Northwestern University Press, 2010).

Milbank, John, Theology and Social Theory: Beyond Secular Reason (Oxford: Wiley-Blackwell, 2006).

————, 'Stanton Lecture 5: Participated Transcendence Reconceived', at www.theologyphilosophycentre.co.uk/papers/Milbank_StantonLecture5.pdf).

Miles, G. and J.J. Wright (eds), Celebrating Children: Equipping People Working with Children and Young People Living in Difficult Circumstances Around the World (Carlisle: Paternoster, 2003).

Miller-McLemore, Bonnie J., *Let the Children Come: Reimagining Childhood from a Christian Perspective* (San Francisco, CA: Jossey-Bass, 2003).

Moltmann, Jürgen, *The Church in the Power of the Spirit* (Minneapolis, MN: Fortress Press, 1993).

————, *Experiences in Theology: Ways and Forms of Christian Theology* (Minneapolis, MN: Fortress Press, 2000).

————, 'Child and Childhood as Metaphors of Hope', in *Theology Today* 56:4 (2000).

Montgomery, Heather, *An Introduction to Childhood: Anthropological Perspectives on Children's Lives* (Chichester, UK: Wiley-Blackwell, 2009).

Myers, Bryant L., *Walking with the Poor: Principles and Practices of Transformational Development* (Maryknoll, NY: Orbis Books, 1999.

Nakah, Victor and Johannes Malherbe, 'Child Theology – A Challenge to Seminaries', in Keith J. White et al (eds), *Now and Next: A Compendium of Papers presented at the Now & Next Theological Conference on Children*, Nairobi, Kenya, March 9-12, 2011 (Penang: Compassion International, 2011).

Newbigin, Lesslie, *The Household of God* (London: SCM Press, 1953).

Newey, Edmund, *Children of God: The Child as Source of Theological Anthropology* (Burlington, VT: Ashgate, 2013).

Nissiotis, Nikos A., 'Secular and Christian Images of Human Person', in *Theologia* 34 (1963).

Nouwen, Henri J.M., D.P. McNeill and D.A. Morrison, *Compassion: Reflections on the Christian Life* (New York: Image Books, 1983).

O'Brien, Peter, 'Church' in Gerald Hawthorne et al (eds), *Dictionary of Paul and His Letters* (Downers Grove, IL: IVP, 1993).

O'Callaghan, Rob, 'What do we mean by incarnational methodology?', in *The Cry*, 10:3 (Fall 2004).

Oduyoye, M.A., 'Trinity and Community', in *Hearing and Knowing: Theological Reflections on Christianity in Africa* (Maryknoll, NY: Orbis, 1996).

Ozment, Steven E., *When Fathers Ruled: Family Life in Reformation Europe* (Cambridge, MA: Harvard University Press, 1983).

Padilla, Rene C., 'Holistic Mission', in John Corrie (ed), *Dictionary of Mission Theology* (Downers Grove, IL: IVP, 2007).

_____, *Mission Between the Times* (Carlisle: Langham Monographs, 2010).

Palmer, Parker, *To Know As We Are Known: Education as a Spiritual Journey* (San Francisco, CA: HarperOne, 1993).

Perkins, John, 'What is Christian Community Development?', in John Perkins (ed), *Restoring At-Risk Communities* (Grand Rapids, MI: Baker Books, 1995).

Peterson, Eugene, *The Message: The Bible in Contemporary Language* (Colorado Springs, CO: Alive Communications, 2002).

Plant, S., *Freedom as Development: Christian Mission and the Definition of Human Well-being* – available from Henry Martyn Centre online archives, at www.martynmission.cam.ac.uk (first presented 2002).

Prevette, Bill, *Child, Church and Compassion: Towards Child Theology in Romania* (Oxford: Regnum, 2012).

Rahner, Karl, 'Ideas for a Theology of Childhood', in *Theological Investigations, Vol 8: Further Theology of the Spiritual Life 2* (London: Darton, Longman & Todd, 1971).

———, *Theological Investigations,* trans. Edward Quinn (London: Darton, Longman & Todd, 1984).

Richards, Anne, *Children in the Bible: A Fresh Approach* (London: SPCK, 2013).

Riessman, Catherine Kohler, *Analysis of Personal Narratives* (Boston, MA: Boston University, 2000).

Rohr, Richard, *Everything Belongs: The Gift of Contemplative Prayer* (New York: Crossroad Publishing Company, 2003).

Rosenbaum, Alan and S. Hoge, 'Head Injury and Marital Aggression', in *American Journal of Psychiatry* 146 (1989).

Rousseau, Jean-Jacques, *Émile: Or, On Education*, trans. Allan Bloom (New York: Basic Books, 1979).

Ruether, Rosemary Radford, *Christianity and the Making of the Modern Family* (London: SCM Press, 2001).

Russell, Letty M., *Just Hospitality: God's Welcome in a World of Difference* (Louisville, KY: Westminster John Knox Press, 2009).

Samuel, Vinay and Chris Sugden, 'God's Intention for the World', in Vinay Samuel and Chris Sugden (eds), *The Church in Response to Human Need* (Oxford: Regnum, 2003).

Schleiermacher, Friedrich, *Christmas Eve: Dialogue on the Incarnation,* trans. Terrence N. Tice (Lampeter, UK: EM Texts, 1990).

Schwartz, Hillel, 'Early Anabaptist Ideas about the Nature of Children', in *Mennonite Quarterly Review,* 47 (1973).

Shahar, Shulamith, *Childhood in the Middle Ages* (London: Routledge, 1992).

Shoemaker, H., Stephen, *Godstories: New Narratives from Sacred Texts* (Valley Forge, PA: Judson Press, 1998).

Sider, Ronald J., *Evangelism and Social Action* (London: Hodder & Stoughton, 1993).

———, *Rich Christians in an Age of Hunger* (London: Hodder & Stoughton, 1997).

Simon, U., *A Theology of Auschwitz: The Christian Faith and the Problem of Evil* (Atlanta, GA: John Knox Press, 1979).

Simons, Menno, *The Complete Writings of Menno Simons c.1496-1561,* ed. John C. Wenger, trans. Leonard Verduin (Scottdale, PA: Herald Press, 1966).

Spitaler, Peter, 'Welcoming a Child as a Metaphor for Welcoming God's Kingdom: A Close Reading of Mark 10:13-16', in *JSNT* 31:4 (2009).

Sobrino, Jon, *The True Church and the Poor* (Maryknoll, NY: Orbis, 1984).

———, 'Spirituality and the Following of Jesus', in Ignacio Ellacuria and Jon Sobrino (eds), *Mysterium Liberationis: Fundamental Concepts of Liberation Theology* (Maryknoll, NY: Orbis, 1993).

———, *Jesus the Liberator: A Historical-Theological View* (Maryknoll, NY: Orbis, 1993).

Sölle, Dorothee, *Christ the Representative* (London: SCM Press, 1967).

———, *Suffering* (Philadelphia, PA: Fortress Press, 1975).

Song, C.S., *Jesus, the Crucified People* (Minneapolis, MN: Fortress Press, 1996).

Stark, Rodney, *The Rise of Christianity: How the Obscure, Marginal Jesus Movement Became the Dominant Religious Force in the Western World in a Few Centuries* (San Francisco, CA: HarperCollins, 1997).

Stott, John, 'Ten Years Later: the Lausanne Covenant', in E.R. Dayton and S. Wilson (eds), *The Future of World Evangelisation: Unreached Peoples '84* (Monrovia, CA: MARC, 1984).

Strange, W.A., *Children in the Early Church* (Carlisle: Paternoster Digital Library, 1996).

Tan, Sunny, *Child Theology for the Churches in Asia: An Invitation* (London: Child Theology Movement, 2007).

Taylor, John V., *The Go-Between God: The Holy Spirit and the Christian Mission* (London: SCM Press, 1972).

Tennent, Timothy C., *Invitation to World Missions: A Trinitarian Missiology for the Twenty-First Century* (Grand Rapids, MI: Kregel Academic, 2010).

Thiessen, Elmer J., *The Ethics of Evangelism: A Philosophical Defence of Ethical Proselytising and Persuasion* (Milton Keynes: Paternoster, 2011).

Thomas, R.S., 'In a Country Church', in *Selected Poems* (London: Granada, 1973).

Tiersma [Watson], Jude, 'What does it mean to be incarnational when we are not the Messiah?', in Charles E. Van Engen and Jude Tiersma [Watson] (eds), *God So Loves the City* (Monrovia, CA: MARC, 1994).

Todd, Margo, 'The Problem of Scotland's Puritans', in John Coffey and Paul C.H. Lim (eds), *The Cambridge Companion to Puritanism* (Cambridge: Cambridge University Press, 2008).

Torrance, James, 'The Incarnation and "Limited Atonement"' in *Evangelical Quarterly* 55 (1983).

Towner, Philip H., 'Households and Household Codes', in Gerald Hawthorne et al (eds), *Dictionary of Paul and His Letters* (Downers Grove, IL: IVP, 1993).

Villfane, E., *Seek the Peace of the City: Reflections on Urban Ministry* (Grand Rapids, MI: Eerdmans, 1995).

Volf, Miroslav, *Exclusion and Embrace: A Theological Exploration of Identity, Otherness and Reconciliation* (Nashville, TN: Abingdon, 1996).

Walker, Theodore, *Empower the People: Social Ethics for the African-American Church* (Maryknoll, NY: Orbis, 1991).

Ware, Timothy (Kallistos), *The Orthodox Church* (New York: Penguin, 1993).

Watson, Natalie K., 'Expecting or On Being Open to Children', in Angela Shier-Jones (ed), *Children of God: Towards a Theology of Childhood* (Peterborough, UK: Epworth, 2007).

Weber, Hans-Rüdi, *Jesus and the Children: Biblical Resources for Study and Preaching* (Geneva: WCC, 1979).

Wells, D.E., *God in the Wasteland: The Reality of Truth in a Land of Fading Dreams* (Grand Rapids, MI: Eerdmans, 1994).

Westerhoff, John H., *Will Our Children Have Faith?* (revd edn) (Harrisburg, PA: Morehouse, 2000).

White, Keith J., 'He Placed a Little Child in the Midst: Jesus, the Kingdom and Children', in Marcia J. Bunge (ed), *The Child in the Bible* (Grand Rapids, MI: Eerdmans, 2008).

——— and Haddon Willmer, *An Introduction to Child Theology* (London: Child Theology Movement, 2006).

——— et al (eds), *Now and Next: A Compendium of Papers Presented at the Now & Next Theological Conference on Children*, Nairobi, Kenya, March 9-12, 2011 (Penang: Compassion International, 2011).

Willard, Dallas, *The Divine Conspiracy: Rediscovering our Hidden Life in God* (San Francisco, CA: Harper Collins, 1998).

Williams, Rowan, *The Wound of Knowledge: Christian Spirituality from the New Testament to St John of the Cross* (London: Darton, Longman & Todd, 1990).

Willmer, Haddon, 'Transforming Society – or Merely Making It: A Theological Discussion with the Bible in One Hand and a Very Particular Newspaper in the Other', in *Society for the Study of Theology Conference Proceedings* (Leeds, UK: SST, 1995).

———, 'Review: Mission as Transformation', in *Transformation* 18 (July 2001).

———, 'Child Theology is Theology'. Paper presented at the *Global Child Theology Consultation*, Penang, Malaysia, at www.childtheology.org

———, *Experimenting Together: One Way of Doing Child Theology* (London: Child Theology Movement, 2007).

———, 'Child Theology and Christology', in John Collier (ed), *Toddling to the Kingdom* (London: Child Theology Movement, 2009).

———, 'Ant and Sparrow in Child Theology', in *Faith and Thought* 54 (April 2013).

——— and Keith White, *Entry Point: Towards Child Theology with Matthew 18* (London: WTL Publications, 2013).

Wink, Walter, *The Powers That Be: Theology for a New Millennium* (New York: Doubleday, 1998).

Wolff, P., *Discernment: The Art of Choosing Well: Based on Ignatian Spirituality* (Liguori, MS: Triumph, 2003).
Woolnough, Brian and Wonsuk Ma (eds), *Holistic Mission: God's Plan for God's People,* Regnum Edinburgh 2010 Series (Oxford: Regnum, 2010).
Wordsworth, William, *Poems, Volume One,* John O. Hayden (ed) (London: Penguin, 1977).
Wren, B., *What Language Shall We Borrow? God-talk in Worship: A Male Response to Feminist Theology* (London: SCM Press, 1989).
Wright, Christopher J.H., *The Mission of God: Unlocking the Bible's Grand Narrative* (Grand Rapids, MI: IVP Academic, 2006).
Yamamori, T. and Rene Padilla, *The Local Church, Agent of Transformation: An Ecclesiology for Integral Mission* (Buenos Aires: Kairos, 2004).
Yannoulatos, A., 'The Purpose and Motive of Mission from an Orthodox Theological Point of View', in *Porefthendos* 9 (1967).
Yancey, P. and Paul Brand, *Pain: The Gift Nobody Wants* (New York: Harper Collins Publishing, 1999).
Yeh, Allen, Mark Russell, Michelle Sanchez, Chelle Stearns and Dwight Friesen, *Routes and Radishes* (Grand Rapids, MI: Zondervan, 2010).
Yoder, John Howard, *Royal Priesthood: Essays Ecclesiological and Ecumenical* (Scottdale, PA: Herald Press, 1998).

Reports and Other Sources

Annual Report 2008/2009, Childline Botswana, Gaborone, 2009.
'Botswana: AIDS Orphans Exploited', in *IRIN News* (October 2002).
Botswana Child Monitor: A Bulletin of Recent Events, Statistics, Acquisitions about Children (UNICEF, 2005).
Botswana Children: Leading the Battle Against HIV/AIDS (UNICEF: Gaborone, 2001).
Care of Orphan and Vulnerable Children (Ministry of Local Government, Department of Social Services, Gaborone, 2010).
First Brazil Child Theology Consultation /1a Consulta Teologia da Criança – Brasil. Report from consultation held in Itu, São Paulo, 25-29 September 2006 (London: Child Theology Movement, 2006).
Report on the Global AIDS Epidemic (UNAIDS, Gaborone, 2001).
Report on the Global Epidemic (UNAIDS, Gaborone, 2010).
Report on the Study of the Socio Economic Factors Contributing to Girl Child Abuse in Botswana (UNICEF, Gaborone, 2007).
The Cape Town Commitment: A Confession of Faith and a Call to Action (Cape Town, RSA: The Lausanne Movement/The Didasko Files, 2011).
The Child Sexual Abuse Communication Strategy 2010-2014 (Department of Social Services and UNICEF, Gaborone, Botswana 2009).
The Impact of AIDS, UNAIDS Report (Gaborone, 2002).
The Rapid Assessment of Orphans in Botswana (AIDS/STD Unit, Gaborone, 1998).
User-Friendly Guide to the Care of Orphan and Vulnerable Children (Ministry of Local Government, Department of Social Services, Gaborone, 2010).
Women's NGO Coalition and SARDC (WIDSAA, 2005).

LIST OF CONTRIBUTORS

Elizabeth Waldron Barnett is a post-colonial, post-Christendom, post-modern, Australian practitioner, teacher, artist and resource writer. Thinking about, theologising, facilitating and advocating for children and families, as both vulnerable and vibrant participators in the community of the cosmos, of which Jesus is the resurrected and revealed Lord, has been at the heart of Beth's service in pastoral, local mission and denominational consulting roles. She is currently completing a doctorate in New Testament studies, reconsidering the hermeneutical marginalisation of 'images of the child' in Pauline literature, and discourses of maturity, development and power.

John Baxter-Brown is a consultant specialising in evangelism, mission, Christian unity and youth and children's ministry. Throughout his twenty-seven years of ministry, his passion has been seeing people join their lives with the story of Jesus. He has worked most recently with Compassion International, the 4/14 Movement, World Vision International, the World Evangelical Alliance (WEA), and the World Council of Churches (WCC), and has spoken in a number of seminaries and conferences around the world. His primary research interests are stories of evangelism from around the world, and 'evangelism through the eyes of Jesus' – a fresh look at the gospel narratives exploring Jesus' understanding and practice of evangelism. He works part-time as Advisor for Evangelism and Ecumenical Affairs of the Theological Commission of WEA. John was born in India, has lived in Scotland and Switzerland, but has spent most of his life in England, where he now lives with his wife and two teenage daughters.

Stephan de Beer, PhD, is the Director of the Centre for Contextual Ministry at the University of Pretoria. For twenty years he directed the work of the Tshwane Leadership Foundation, an ecumenical inner-city organisation committed to healthy communities reflecting the *shalom* of God. He is convenor of Leadership Foundations Africa, a peer-mentoring network of Christian community foundations committed to the socio-spiritual transformation of African cities. His first urban experience was children living and working on the streets of the inner city, and children and cities are still his greatest passions.

Paul Joshua Bhakiaraj, PhD, is a Commended Worker and Elder in the Tamil Brethren Church, and serves as a Professor at the South Asia Institute of Advanced Christian Studies (SAIACS) in Bangalore, India. Among other affiliations, he is an Associate of the Missions Commission of the World Evangelical Alliance; a member of the Lausanne Theology Working Group; and a member of the International Networking Team of the International Fellowship of Mission as Transformation (INFEMIT). He has published widely in books and journals, and exercises an itinerant preaching ministry.

Marcia J. Bunge, PhD, is a Professor and the Bernhardson Distinguished Chair of Lutheran Studies at Gustavus Adolphus College in Saint Peter, Minnesota. As the Director of the Child in Religion and Ethics Project, she has edited or co-edited four seminal volumes on religious views on children: *Children, Adults, and Shared Responsibilities: Jewish, Christian, and Muslim Perspectives* (Cambridge University Press); *Children and Childhood in World Religions: Primary Sources and Texts* (Rutgers University Press); *The Child in the Bible,* and *The Child in Christian Thought* (both Eerdmans). A fifth on Child Theologies in global perspective was forthcoming at the time of publication. Portions of her chapter here appeared previously in 'Biblical and Theological Perspectives: Resources for Raising Children in Faith', in *Lutheran Partners,* July/August, 2009.

Stuart Christine and his wife Georgie grew up in Nottingham, UK. Stuart studied physics at Oxford and worked in R&D while Georgie qualified as a teacher. After completing theological studies at Spurgeon's College, London, they spent ten years church-planting in Mato Grosso State, Brazil, with BMS World Mission. In 1988 Stuart accepted the position of New Testament Tutor at Spurgeon's. Four years later the family returned to Brazil with BMS, at the invitation of the São Paulo Baptist Seminary, where their work also included holistic mission in the city's *favela* slums. It was here that Georgie developed a church-based Pre-School Mission Program for deprived communities – PEPE – now in some twenty other countries, and attended by more than 10,000 children, and for which she received the OBE in 2006. In 2012 they moved to Manchester where they currently work with Brownley Green Baptist Church, and where Stuart is pursuing PhD studies in Child Theology and mission in deprived urban communities. They have four children and have recently become grandparents.

David Chronic has been living and serving in Romania since 1996. During his senior year of high school, David became a Christian and began struggling with what it means to follow Christ in a world of pain and poverty. He studied International Relations at the University of Nebraska, Omaha, receiving a scholarship to study in Romania and Moldova. While living in these countries, David developed relationships with children living on the streets or abandoned in state institutions. Passionate about having a theological basis for missional community, David completed a master's programme at the London School of Theology, and currently serves as Word Made Flesh's Regional Co-ordinator for Europe and Africa. Together with his wife Lenuṭa, he lives in Galati, Romania, and develops friendships among vulnerable youth and poor families, providing education, counselling and mentoring through Day Centres, Community Centres and community development initiatives. David has contributed articles and chapters on cross-cultural mission among the poor to qideas.org and Living Mission: the vision and voices of New Friars.

Corneliu Constantineanu, PhD, is Professor of New Testament Studies and Rector of Theological Pentecostal Institute in Bucharest, Romania. After an engineering degree with a specialisation in bio-technologies, Corneliu pursued theological studies obtaining his bachelor and masters in theology (*summa cum laude*) at Evanđeoski teološki fakultet in Osijek, Croatia. Corneliu then completed doctoral studies in theology at the Oxford Centre for Mission Studies, and the University of Leeds, UK, with interdisciplinary research in Pauline and contextual theology, examining the social dimension of reconciliation. He is the former Academic Dean of Evanđeoski teološki fakultet in Osijek, Croatia, where he taught for more than 16 years, and was also the former Executive Director of the Areopagus Centre for Christian Studies and Contemporary Culture in Timisoara, Romania. In addition to his specialisation and publications in the areas of Pauline theology and reconciliation, Corneliu has a special interest in pursuing a holistic understanding of the gospel as public truth, thus trying to integrate Christian faith with cultural, social and political realities of everyday life.

C. Rosalee Velloso Ewell is a Brazilian theologian from São Paulo. She serves as Executive Director of the Theological Commission for the World Evangelical Alliance and has contributed to panels and conferences on Children at Risk and Child Theology. She is also very busy in inter-faith discussions and in her local church. Rosalee lives with her husband Sam and their three children in Birmingham, UK, where they are part of an extended community of prayer, shared meals and chores. She hopes that soon their community will also have a goat.

Samuel E. Ewell is an urban farmer and community organiser. He holds degrees in Biology and Theology and is an ordained Baptist minister. Sam is originally from North Carolina, USA, but has spent much of his life in the Czech Republic and Brazil. Sam currently lives in Birmingham, UK, where he is completing a PhD on the theme of conviviality. Sam, Rosalee and their family together tend to a community garden, 17 chickens and four rabbits (and soon perhaps a goat).

Rosinah Gabaitse, PhD, is a lecturer in Biblical Studies at the University of Botswana, in the Faculty of Theology and Religion. She completed her PhD in 2013 at the University of KwaZulu-Natal in Pietermaritzburg, South Africa. Her academic interests include Luke-Acts, and hermeneutics. She is researching and writing about the role of gender in the church of Botswana, the spread of HIV/AIDs, women's issues, children's rights and masculinity. She is married to Gobonaone and has three children. She and her family live in Gaborone, Botswana. Beyond her academic interests, she also enjoys music.

Genevieve James, PhD, is the Director of the Chance 2 Advance programme, a development-through-education initiative of the University of South Africa (Unisa) that seeks to link relevant teaching and research to grassroots communities. She also serves as the Executive Assistant to the Pro Vice-Chancellor of Unisa. Previously, Genevieve served as senior lecturer in Missiology at the Department of Christian Spirituality, Church History and Missiology, Unisa.

D.J. Konz has served with the international Christian child development organisation Compassion for ten years, largely in the area of child advocacy in church, media and government policy arenas. DJ is currently a director of the international Child Theology Movement, and before moving abroad sat on the governance committee of the Micah Challenge, Australia, a campaign alliance of Christian aid and development organisations. DJ has a degree in Ministry, MA in Theology and Religious Studies, and postgraduate diplomas in Ministry, and Mission Studies. At the time of publication, he is writing a PhD dissertation in systematic theology, on the child in the mission of God with reference to the theology of Karl Barth, at the University of Aberdeen. DJ, his wife Louise, and two daughters Bethany and Emelyn, are Australian by birth but enjoy an idyllic life together in a rural Scottish village.

Mark Oxbrow has pastored local churches in the UK and ministered in the field of mental health. Mark served as a Director, and then Assistant General Secretary, of the Church Mission Society (CMS). In 2008 he left this Anglican mission to establish *Faith2Share*, an international network of mission agencies focusing on discipleship, collaboration and emerging mission movements. Mark also serves the Lausanne Movement as facilitator for Orthodox-Evangelical relations, is a board member of several mission agencies, works closely with the mission desk of the worldwide Anglican Communion, and undertakes consultancy in mission. His research and writing interests are in the contemporary practice of holistic mission, Orthodox missiology and the Christian theology of faiths. He ministers in his local church in Oxford, UK.

Bill Prevette, PhD, is the Admissions and Practitioner Research Tutor at the Oxford Centre for Mission Studies. His research focuses on youth and children at risk in the developing world. He also conducts studies on human trafficking and interventions, urban research, community development, and Pentecostalism in global mission. Bill is currently a board member for the Child Theology Movement in the UK and an appointed missionary to Europe with the Assemblies of God World Mission, USA. He serves as a member of several other boards and as a technical advisor to faith-based organisations in Romania, Moldova, Cambodia, and Africa. He conducts semi-annual academic seminars and lectureships, and is a member of the adjunct faculty in the School of Behavioral Sciences at Northwest University, Seattle. He is married to Ky and together they live in Oxford, UK.

Keith J. White, PhD, lives at Mill Grove, a Christian residential community that has been caring for children and young people in the East End of London, UK, since 1899. He is married to Ruth and they have four children and six grandchildren. He is the founder and Chair of the Child Theology Movement, a trustee of the UK Christian Child Care Forum, Frontier Youth Trust, Children England, and member of the UK government's Care Standards Tribunal. Among the books he has written or edited are *A Place for Us*; *In His Image*; *Caring for Deprived Children*; *Why Care?*; *Re-Framing Children's Services*; *Children and Social Exclusion*; *The Changing Face of Child Care*; *The Art of Faith*; *The Growth of Love, Reflections of Living with Children*; *In the Meantime*; *Now and Next*; and, most recently, *Entry Point: Towards Child Theology with Matthew 18* (co-written with Haddon Willmer). He also led the team that produced *The Bible [Narrative and Illustrated]* designed for ordinary Christians as well as those of other faiths. He has written widely on Child Theology, and since 2000 has |contributed monthly columns in www.childrenwebmag.com. Keith teaches the theological foundations module of Holistic Child Development (HCD) at Malaysia Baptist Theological Seminary in Penang, Malaysia. He has also taught and contributed to conferences and symposia on most continents. He has been an Associate Lecturer at Spurgeon's College since 1978, and is a member of the faculty of the Asian Graduate School Theology Alliance.

Haddon Willmer, PhD, retired as Professor from the University of Leeds in 1998, where he taught theology for thirty-two years, with special interests in forgiveness and politics, Barth and Bonhoeffer, and the future of Christian faith at the mercy of today's church and world. From 2000 to 2012, he enjoyed being a research tutor at the Oxford Centre for Mission Studies, accompanying at least thirteen interesting students on their way to PhDs. He has been a trustee of the Child Theology Movement from its inception, and of PACE (Parents against Child Sexual Exploitation) since it was founded in 1996. He is married to Hilary, a partner beyond price and a creative Christian social activist in Leeds. They have three children and eight grandchildren. Author of numerous books and scholarly articles, with Keith White he has recently published *Entry Point: Towards Child Theology with Matthew 18*. Writing the book over ten years, his eyes were opened afresh to Jesus.

REGNUM EDINBURGH CENTENARY SERIES

David A. Kerr, Kenneth R. Ross (Eds)
Mission Then and Now
2009 / 978-1-870345-73-6 / 343pp (paperback)
2009 / 978-1-870345-76-7 / 343pp (hardback)

Daryl M. Balia, Kirsteen Kim (Eds)
Witnessing to Christ Today
2010 / 978-1-870345-77-4 / 301pp (hardback)

Claudia Währisch-Oblau, Fidon Mwombeki (Eds)
Mission Continues
Global Impulses for the 21ˢᵗ Century
2010 / 978-1-870345-82-8 / 271pp (hardback)

Brian Woolnough and Wonsuk Ma (Eds)
Holistic Mission
God's Plan for God's People
2010 / 978-1-870345-85-9 / 268pp (hardback)

Kirsteen Kim and Andrew Anderson (Eds)
Mission Today and Tomorrow
2010 / 978-1-870345-91-0 / 450pp (hardback)

Tormod Engelsviken, Erling Lundeby and Dagfinn Solheim (Eds)
The Church Going Glocal
Mission and Globalisation
2011 / 978-1-870345-93-4 / 262pp (hardback)

Marina Ngurusangzeli Behera (Ed)
Interfaith Relations after One Hundred Years
Christian Mission among Other Faiths
2011 / 978-1-870345-96-5 / 338pp (hardback)

Lalsangkima Pachuau and Knud Jørgensen (Eds)
Witnessing to Christ in a Pluralistic Age
Christian Mission among Other Faiths
2011 / 978-1-870345-95-8 / 277pp (hardback)

Beth Snodderly and A Scott Moreau (Eds)
Evangelical Frontier Mission
Perspectives on the Global Progress of the Gospel
2011 / 978-1-870345-98-9 / 312pp (hardback)

Rolv Olsen (Ed)
Mission and Postmodernities
2011 / 978-1-870345-97-2 / 279pp (hardback)

Cathy Ross (Ed)
Life-Widening Mission
2012 / 978-1-908355-00-3 / 163pp (hardback)

Beate Fagerli, Knud Jørgensen, Rolv Olsen, Kari Storstein Haug and
Knut Tveitereid (Eds)
A Learning Missional Church
Reflections from Young Missiologists
2012 / 978-1-908355-01-0 / 218pp (hardback)

Emma Wild-Wood & Peniel Rajkumar (Eds)
Foundations for Mission
2012 / 978-1-908355-12-6 / 309pp (hardback)

Wonsuk Ma & Kenneth R Ross (Eds)
Mission Spirituality and Authentic Discipleship
2013 / 978-1-908355-24-9 / 248pp (hardback)

Stephen B Bevans (Ed)
A Century of Catholic Mission
2013 / 978-1-908355-14-0 / 337pp (hardback)

Robert Schreiter & Knud Jørgensen (Eds)
Mission as Ministry of Reconcilation
2013 / 978-1-908355-26-3 / 382pp (hardback)

Petros Vassiliadis, Editor
Orthodox Perspectives on Mission
2013 / 978-1908355-25-6 / 262pp (hardback)

Orthodox Perspectives on Mission is both a humble tribute to some great Orthodox theologians, who in the past have provided substantial contribution to contemporary missiological and ecumenical discussions, and an Orthodox input to the upcoming 2013 Busan WCC General Assembly. The collected volume is divided into two parts: Part I: The Orthodox Heritage consists of Orthodox missiological contributions of the past, whereas Part II includes all the papers presented in the Plenary of the recent Edinburgh 2010 conference, as well as the short studies and contributions prepared, during the Edinburgh 2010 on going study process.

Pauline Hoggarth, Fergus MacDonald,
Bill Mitchell & Knud Jørgensen, Editors
Bible in Mission
2013 / 978-1908355-42-3 / 317pp (hardback)

To the authors of Bible in Mission, the Bible is the book of life, and mission is life in the Word. This core reality cuts across the diversity of contexts and hermeneutical strategies represented in these essays. The authors are committed to the boundary-crossings that characterize contemporary mission – and each sees the Bible as foundational to the missio Dei, to God's work in the world.

Wonsuk Ma, Veli-Matti Kärkkäinen
& J Kwabena Asamoah
Pentecostal Mission and Global Christianity
*2014 / 978-1908355-43-0 / 397pp (*hardback)

Although Pentecostalism worldwide represent the most rapidly growing missionary movement in Christian history, only recently scholars from within and outside the movement have begun academic reflection on the mission. This volume represents the coming of age of emerging scholarship of various aspects of the Pentecostal mission, including theological, historical, strategic, and practical aspects.

Afe Adogame, Janice McLean & Anderson Jeremiah, Editors
Engaging the World
Christian Communities in Contemporary Global Societies
2014 / 978-1908355-21-8 / 235pp (hardback)

Engaging the World deals with the lived experiences and expressions of Christians in diverse communities across the globe. Christian communities do not live in a vacuum but in complex, diverse social-cultural contexts; within wider communities of different faith and social realities. Power, identity and community are key issues in considering Christian communities in contemporary contexts.

Peniel Jesudason Rufus Rajkumar, Joseph Prabhakar Dayam
& IP Asheervadham, Editors
Mission At and From the Margins
Patterns, Protagonists and Perspectives
*2014 / 978-1908355-13-3 / 283pp (*hardback)

Mission At and From the Margins: Patterns, Protagonists and Perspectives revisits the 'hi-stories' of Mission from the 'bottom up' paying critical attention to people, perspectives and patterns that have often been elided in the construction of mission history. Focusing on the mission story of Christian churches in the South Indian state of Abdhra Pradesh this collection of essays ushers its readers to re-shape their understanding of the landscape of mission history by drawing their attention to the silences and absences within pre-dominant historical accounts.

REGNUM STUDIES IN GLOBAL CHRISTIANITY

David Emmanuel Singh (Ed)
Jesus and the Cross
Reflections of Christians from Islamic Contexts
2008 / 978-1-870345-65-1 / 226pp

Sung-wook Hong
Naming God in Korea
The Case of Protestant Christianity
2008 / 978-1-870345-66-8 / 170pp (hardback)

Hubert van Beek (Ed)
Revisioning Christian Unity
The Global Christian Forum
2009 / 978-1-870345-74-3 / 288pp (hardback)

Young-hoon Lee
The Holy Spirit Movement in Korea
Its Historical and Theological Development
2009 / 978-1-870345-67-5 / 174pp (hardback)

Paul Hang-Sik Cho
Eschatology and Ecology
Experiences of the Korean Church
2010 / 978-1-870345-75-0 / 260pp (hardback)

Dietrich Werner, David Esterline, Namsoon Kang, Joshva Raja (Eds)
The Handbook of Theological Education in World Christianity
Theological Perspectives, Ecumenical Trends, Regional Surveys
2010 / 978-1-870345-80-0 / 759pp

David Emmanuel Singh & Bernard C Farr (Eds)
Christianity and Education
Shaping of Christian Context in Thinking
2010 / 978-1-870345-81-1 / 374pp

J.Andrew Kirk
Civilisations in Conflict?
Islam, the West and Christian Faith
2011 / 978-1-870345-87-3 / 205pp

David Emmanuel Singh (Ed)
Jesus and the Incarnation
Reflections of Christians from Islamic Contexts
2011 / 978-1-870345-90-3 / 245pp

Ivan M Satyavrata
God Has Not left Himself Without Witness
2011 / 978-1-870345-79-8 / 264pp

Bal Krishna Sharma
From this World to the Next
Christian Identity and Funerary Rites in Nepal
2013 / 978-1-908355-08-9 / 238pp

J Kwabena Asamoah-Gyada
Contemporary Pentecostal Christianity
Interpretations from an African Context
2013 / 978-1-908355-07-2 / 194pp

David Emmanuel Singh and Bernard C Farr (Eds)
The Bible and Christian Ethics
2013 / 978-1-908355-20-1 / 217pp

Martin Allaby
Inequality, Corruption and the Church
Challenges & Opportunities in the Global Church
2013 / 978-1-908355-16-4 / 228pp

Paul Alexander and Al Tizon (Eds)
Following Jesus
Journeys in Radical Discipleship – Essays in Honor of Ronald J Sider
2013 / 978-1-908355-27-0 / 228pp

Cawley Bolt
Reluctant or Radical Revolutionaries?
Evangelical Missionaries and Afro-Jamaican Character, 1834-1870
2013 / 978-1-908355-18-8 / 287pp
This study is based on extensive research that challenges traditional ways of understanding some evangelical missionaries of nineteenth century Jamaica and calls for revision of those views. It highlights the strength and character of persons facing various challenges of life in their effort to be faithful to the guiding principles of their existence.

Isabel Apawo Phiri & Dietrich Werner (Eds)
Handbook of Theological Education in Africa
2013 / 978-1-908355-45-4 / 1110pp
The *Handbook of Theological Education in Africa* is a wake-up call for African churches to give proper prominence to theological education institutions and their programmes which serve them. It is unique, comprehensive and ambitious in its aim and scope.

Hope Antone, Wati Longchar, Hyunju Bae, Huang Po Ho, Dietrich Werner (Eds)
Asian Handbook for Theological Education and Ecumenism
2013 / 978-1-908355-30-0 / 675pp (hardback)
This impressive and comprehensive book focuses on key resources for teaching Christian unity and common witness in Asian contexts. It is a collection of articles that reflects the ongoing 'double wrestle' with the texts of biblical tradition as well as with contemporary contexts. It signals an investment towards the future of the ecumenical movement in Asia.

Bernhard Reitsma
The God of My Enemy
The Middle East and the Nature of God
2014 / 978-1-908355-50-8 / 206pp
The establishment of the State of Israel in 1948 for the Church in the West has been the starting point of a rediscovery of its own roots. In the Middle East the effect has been exactly the opposite: Christians have become estranged from their Old Testament roots, because they have been expelled from their land exactly because of an appeal to the Old Testament. The concept of Israel changed from a nation in the Bible, with which they could associate, to an economic, political and military power that was against them

Pantelis Kalaitzidis, Thomas Fitzgerald, Cyril Hovorun, Aikaterini Pekridou,
Nikolaos Asproulis, Dietrich Werner & Guy Liagre (Eds)
Orthodox Handbook on Ecumenism
Resources for Theological Education
2014 / 978-1-908355-44-7 / 962pp (hardback)
We highly recommend the publication of this new *Orthodox Handbook* for Teaching Ecumenism edited by a group of orthodox theologians in collaboration with WCC/ETE Program, the Conference of European Churches, Volos Academy for Theological Studies in Greece, and Holy Cross Greek Orthodox School of Theology in Brookline, Massachusetts.

REGNUM STUDIES IN MISSION

Kwame Bediako
Theology and Identity
The Impact of Culture upon Christian Thought in the Second Century and in Modern Africa
1992 / 978-1870345-10-1 / 507pp

Christopher Sugden
Seeking the Asian Face of Jesus
The Practice and Theology of Christian Social Witness
in Indonesia and India 1974–1996
1997 / 1-870345-26-6 / 496pp

Keith E. Eitel
Paradigm Wars
The Southern Baptist International Mission Board Faces the Third Millennium
1999 / 1-870345-12-6 / 140pp

Samuel Jayakumar
Dalit Consciousness and Christian Conversion
Historical Resources for a Contemporary Debate
1999 / 81-7214-497-0 / 434pp
(Published jointly with ISPCK)

Vinay Samuel and Christopher Sugden (Eds)
Mission as Transformation
A Theology of the Whole Gospel
1999 / 978-18703455-13-2 / 522pp

Christopher Sugden
Gospel, Culture and Transformation
2000 / 1-870345-32-3 / 152pp
A Reprint, with a New Introduction,
of Part Two of Seeking the Asian Face of Jesus

Bernhard Ott
Beyond Fragmentation: Integrating Mission and Theological Education
A Critical Assessment of some Recent Developments
in Evangelical Theological Education
2001 / 1-870345-14-9 / 382pp

Gideon Githiga
The Church as the Bulwark against Authoritarianism
Development of Church and State Relations in Kenya, with Particular Reference to the Years
after Political Independence 1963-1992
2002 / 1-870345-38-x / 218pp

Myung Sung-Hoon, Hong Young-Gi (Eds)
Charis and Charisma
David Yonggi Cho and the Growth of Yoido Full Gospel Church
2003 / 978-1870345-45-3 / 218pp

Samuel Jayakumar
Mission Reader
Historical Models for Wholistic Mission in the Indian Context
2003 / 1-870345-42-8 / 250pp
(Published jointly with ISPCK)

Bob Robinson
Christians Meeting Hindus
An Analysis and Theological Critique of the Hindu-Christian Encounter in India
2004 / 987-1870345-39-2 / 392pp

Gene Early
Leadership Expectations
How Executive Expectations are Created and Used in a Non-Profit Setting
2005 / 1-870345-30-9 / 276pp

Tharcisse Gatwa
The Churches and Ethnic Ideology in the Rwandan Crises 1900-1994
2005 / 978-1870345-24-8 / 300pp
(Reprinted 2011)

Julie Ma
Mission Possible
Biblical Strategies for Reaching the Lost
2005 / 978-1870345-37-8 / 142pp

I. Mark Beaumont
Christology in Dialogue with Muslims
A Critical Analysis of Christian Presentations of Christ for Muslims
from the Ninth and Twentieth Centuries
2005 / 978-1870345-46-0 / 227pp

Thomas Czövek,
Three Seasons of Charismatic Leadership
A Literary-Critical and Theological Interpretation of the Narrative of
Saul, David and Solomon
2006 / 978-1870345-48-4 / 272pp

Richard Burgess
Nigeria's Christian Revolution
The Civil War Revival and Its Pentecostal Progeny (1967-2006)
2008 / 978-1-870345-63-7 / 347pp

David Emmanuel Singh & Bernard C Farr (Eds)
Christianity and Cultures
Shaping Christian Thinking in Context
2008 / 978-1-870345-69-9 / 271pp

Tormod Engelsviken, Ernst Harbakk, Rolv Olsen, Thor Strandenæs (Eds)
Mission to the World
Communicating the Gospel in the 21st Century:
Essays in Honour of Knud Jørgensen
2008 / 978-1-870345-64-4 / 472pp (hardback)

Al Tizon
Transformation after Lausanne
Radical Evangelical Mission in Global-Local Perspective
2008 / 978-1-870345-68-2 / 281pp

Bambang Budijanto
Values and Participation
Development in Rural Indonesia
2009 / 978-1-870345-70-4 / 237pp

Alan R. Johnson
Leadership in a Slum
A Bangkok Case Study
2009 / 978-1-870345-71-2 / 238pp

Titre Ande
Leadership and Authority
Bula Matari and Life - Community Ecclesiology in Congo
2010 / 978-1-870345-72-9 / 189pp

Frank Kwesi Adams
Odwira and the Gospel
A Study of the Asante Odwira Festival and its Significance for Christianity in Ghana
2010 /978-1-870345-59-0 / 232pp

Bruce Carlton
Strategy Coordinator
Changing the Course of Southern Baptist Missions
2010 / 978-1-870345-78-1 / 273pp

Julie Ma & Wonsuk Ma
Mission in the Spirit:
Towards a Pentecostal/Charismatic Missiology
2010 / 978-1-870345-84-2 / 312pp

Allan Anderson, Edmond Tang (Eds)
Asian and Pentecostal
The Charismatic Face of Christianity in Asia
2011 / 978-1870345-94-1 / 500pp
(Revised Edition)

S. Hun Kim & Wonsuk Ma (Eds)
Korean Diaspora and Christian Mission
2011 / 978-1-870345-89-7 / 301pp (hardback)

Jin Huat Tan
Planting an Indigenous Church
The Case of the Borneo Evangelical Mission
2011 / 978-1-870345-99-6 / 343pp

Bill Prevette
Child, Church and Compassion
Towards Child Theology in Romania
2012 / 978-1-908355-03-4 / 382pp

Samuel Cyuma
Picking up the Pieces
The Church and Conflict Resolution in South Africa and Rwanda
2012 / 978-1-908355-02-7 / 373pp

Peter Rowan
Proclaiming the Peacemaker
The Malaysian Church as an Agent of Reconciliation in a Multicultural Society
2012 / 978-1-908355-05-8 / 268pp

Edward Ontita
Resources and Opportunity
The Architecture of Livelihoods in Rural Kenya
2012 / 978-1-908355-04-1 / 328pp

Kathryn Kraft
Searching for Heaven in the Real World
A Sociological Discussion of Conversion in the Arab World
2012 / 978-1-908355-15-7 / 142pp

Wessley Lukose
Contextual Missiology of the Spirit
Pentecostalism in Rajasthan, India
2013 / 978-1-908355-09-6 / 256pp

Paul M Miller
Evangelical Mission in Co-operation with Catholics
A Study of Evangelical Tensions
2013 / 978-1-908355-17-1 / 291pp

Alemayehu Mekonnen
Culture Change in Ethiopia
An Evangelical Perspective
2013 / 978-1-908355-39-3 / 199pp

This book addresses the causes and consequences of culture change in Ethiopia, from Haile Selassie to the present, based on thorough academic research. Although written from an evangelical perspective, this book invites Ethiopians from all religions, ideological, and ethnic backgrounds to reflect on their past, to analyse their present and to engage in unity with diversity to face the future.

Godwin Lekundayo
The Cosmic Christ
Towards Effective Mission Among the Maasai
2013 / 978-1-908355-28- 7 / 259 pp

This book reveals a complex interaction between the Christian gospel brought by western missionaries and the nomadic Massai culture of Tanzania ... an important insider's voice courageously questioning the approach to condemn some critical Maasai practices, particularly polygamy, and its missionary consequences. This is a rare study from a Maasai Christian leader.

Philippe Ouedraogo
Female Education and Mission
A Burkina Faso Experience
2014 / 978-1-908355-11-9 / 263pp

This volume is the result of six years research in 'Overcoming Obstacles to Female Education in Burkina Faso'. It narrates how Christians and religious groups can speed up female education and contribute to the socio-economic growth of Burkina Faso. Religious culture and traditions were seen as a problem to female education. However, the evidence from this research shows that Christianity is also part of the solution to a quality female education, thus a key factor of socio economic growth
of the country.

Haw Yung
Mangoes or Bananas?
The Quest for an Authentic Asian Christian Theology
(Second Edition)
2014 / 978-1-908355-47-8 / 232pp

Over the past few decades there has been a growing awareness of the need for contextual theologies throughout Asia. But how genuinely contextual are these? Based on the premise that theology and mission are inseparable, the author applies four missiological criteria to representative examples of Protestant Asian writings to assess their adequacy or otherwise as contextual theologies.

Daniel Taichoul Yang
Called Out for Witness
The Missionary Journey of Grace Korean Church
2014 / 978-1-908355-49-2 / 167pp

This book investigates the theological motivation for GKC's missions: Reformed theology, Presbyterian theology, and mission theology. The book also shows the extent of the church's mission engagement by continents. Finally, the book turns its attention to the future with an evaluation of the church's missionary journey.

REGNUM RESOURCES FOR MISSION

Knud Jørgensen
Equipping for Service
Christian Leadership in Church and Society
2012 / 978-1-908355-06-5 / 150pp

Mary Miller
What does Love have to do with Leadership?
2013 / 978-1-908355-10-2 / 100pp

Mary Miller (Ed)
Faces of Holistic Mission
Stories of the OCMS Family
2013 / 978-1-908355-32-4 / 104pp

David Cranston and Ruth Padilla DeBorst (Eds)
Mission as Transformation
Learning from Catalysts
2013 / 978-1-908355-34-8 / 77pp

This book is the product of the first Stott-Bediako Forum, held in 2012 with the title *Portraits of Catalysts*. Its aim was to learn from the stories of Christian leaders whose lives and work have served as catalysts for transformation as each, in his or her particular way, facilitated the intersection between the Good News of Jesus Christ and the context in which they lived, in particular amongst people who are suffering.

Brian Woolnough (Ed)
Good News from Africa
Community Transformation Through the Church
2013 / 978-1-908355-33-1 / 123pp

This book discusses how sustainable, holistic, community development can be, and is being, achieved through the work of the local church. Leading African development practitioners describe different aspects of development through their own experience.

Makonen Getu (Ed)
Transforming Microfinance
A Christian Approach
2013 / 978-1-908355-31-7 / 264pp

"This book highlights the important role that Christian-based organisations bring to the delivery of financial services for the poor. It is times, significant and important and deserves a wide circulation".

Lord Carey of Clifton, former Archbishop of Canterbury

Jonathan Ingleby, Tan Kand San, Tan Loun Ling, (Eds)
Contextualisation & Mission Training
Engaging Asia's Religious Worlds
2013 / 978-1-908355-40-9 / 109pp

Contextualisation & Mission Training, offers "contextual frameworks" and "explorations" in order to enhance deeper engagement with the complexity of Asian social, cultural and religious systems.

On Eagle's Wings
Models in Mentoring
2013 / 978-1-908355-46-1 / 105pp

David Cranston writes unashamedly as a Christian for whom no account of mentoring would be complete without placing it in the biggest context of all – that of the relationship between humans and God.

John Lennox, Professor of Mathematics, University of Oxford
Fellow in Mathematics and Philosophy of Science

GENERAL REGNUM TITLES

Vinay Samuel, Chris Sugden (Eds)
The Church in Response to Human Need
1987 / 1870345045 / xii+268pp

Philip Sampson, Vinay Samuel, Chris Sugden (Eds)
Faith and Modernity
Essays in modernity and post-modernity
1994 / 1870345177 / 352pp

Klaus Fiedler
The Story of Faith Missions
1994 / 0745926878 / 428pp

Douglas Peterson
Not by Might nor by Power
A Pentecostal Theology of Social Concern in Latin America
1996 / 1870345207 / xvi+260pp

David Gitari
In Season and Out of Season
Sermons to a Nation
1996 / 1870345118 / 155pp

David. W. Virtue
A Vision of Hope
The Story of Samuel Habib
1996 / 1870345169 / xiv+137pp

Everett A Wilson
Strategy of the Spirit
J.Philip Hogan and the Growth of the Assemblies of God Worldwide, 1960 - 1990
1997 /1870345231/214

Murray Dempster, Byron Klaus, Douglas Petersen (Eds)
The Globalization of Pentecostalism
A Religion Made to Travel
1999 / 1870345290 / xvii+406pp

Peter Johnson, Chris Sugden (Eds)
Markets, Fair Trade and the Kingdom of God
Essays to Celebrate Traidcraft's 21st Birthday
2001 / 1870345193 / xii+155pp

Robert Hillman, Coral Chamberlain, Linda Harding
Healing & Wholeness
Reflections on the Healing Ministry
2002 / 978-1- 870345-35- 4 / xvii+283pp

David Bussau, Russell Mask
Christian Microenterprise Development
An Introduction
2003 / 1870345282 / xiii+142pp

David Singh
Sainthood and Revelatory Discourse
An Examination of the Basis for the Authority of Bayan in Mahdawi Islam
2003 / 8172147285 / xxiv+485pp

REGNUM AFRICA TITLES

Kwame Bediako
Jesus in Africa, The Christian Gospel in African History and Experience
(2000) (Theological Reflections from the South series)
SECOND EDITION FORTHCOMING 2013

Mercy Amba Oduyoye
Beads and Strands, Reflections of an African Woman on Christianity in Africa
(Theological Reflections from the South series)
2002 / 1-870345-41-X / 114pp

Kä Mana
Christians and Churches of Africa Envisioning the Future, Salvation in Christ and the Building of a new African Society
(Theological Reflections from the South series)
2002 / 1-870345-27-4 / 119pp

Ype Schaaf
On Their Way Rejoicing, The History and Role of the Bible in Africa
2002 / 1-870345-35-9 / 252pp

E.A.W. Engmann
Kpawo-Kpawo Toi Kpawo – Vol. 1, Adesai, Oboade, Lalai, Ajenui ke Shwemoi (Folklore of the Ga People)
(Gbotsui Series - Indigenous Sources of Knowledge in Ghanaian Languages)
2009 / 978-9988-1-2296-6 / 70pp

Philip Tetteh Laryea
Yesu Homowo Nuntso (Jesus, Lord of Homowo)
(Nyamedua series in Mother-tongue Theology)
(reprinted 2011) / 1-870345-54-1 / 176pp

E.A.W. Engmann
Kpawo-Kpawo Toi Kpawo – Vol. 2, Kusumii (Folklore of the Ga People)
(Gbotsui Series - Indigenous Sources of Knowledge in Ghanaian Languages)
2012 / 978-9988-1-2294-2, 186pp

Philip T. Laryea
Ephraim Amu: Nationalist, Poet and Theologian (1899–1995)
2012 / 978-9988-1-2293-5, 425pp

Jon P. Kirby
The Power and the Glory, Popular Christianity in Northern Ghana
(Trends in African Christianity Series)
2012 / 978-9988-1-2295-9, 350pp

For the up-to-date listing of the Regnum books visit www.ocms.ac.uk/regnum

Regnum Books International
Regnum is an Imprint of The Oxford Centre for Mission Studies
St. Philip and St. James Church
Woodstock Road
Oxford, OX2 6HR